First World War
and Army of Occupation
War Diary
France, Belgium and Germany

16 DIVISION
Divisional Troops
Royal Army Medical Corps
112 Field Ambulance
19 December 1915 - 27 April 1919

WO95/1967/2

The Naval & Military Press Ltd
www.nmarchive.com
Published in association with The National Archives

Published by

The Naval & Military Press Ltd

Unit 10 Ridgewood Industrial Park,

Uckfield, East Sussex,

TN22 5QE England

Tel: +44 (0) 1825 749494

www.naval-military-press.com

www.nmarchive.com

This diary has been reprinted in facsimile from the original. Any imperfections are inevitably reproduced and the quality may fall short of modern type and cartographic standards.

Contents

Document type	Place/Title	Date From	Date To
Heading	WO95/1916. 16 Divisional Troops Dec 1915-June 1919 112 Field Ambulance		
Heading	16th Division 112th Fld Ambulance Jan 1916-1919 Jun		
Heading	16th Div F/149/1 Dec 1915		
War Diary	Havre	19/12/1915	20/12/1915
War Diary	Houchin	21/12/1915	21/12/1915
War Diary	Map-France 36b.k.15.g.	21/12/1915	24/12/1915
War Diary	Houchin	25/12/1915	28/12/1915
War Diary	Auchy Aux Bois Map 36a T.14	29/12/1915	29/12/1915
War Diary	Auchy Aux Bois	30/12/1915	31/12/1915
Heading	16th Division F/149/2 Jan 1916 Dec 18		
Heading	War Diary No. 112 Field Ambulance 1st To 31st January 1916.		
War Diary	Auchy Aux Bois Dept Pas De Calais	01/01/1916	05/01/1916
War Diary	Auchy Aux Bois	06/01/1916	31/01/1916
Heading	112th 7a Vol 3		
Heading	112th Field Ambulance Feb 1916		
Miscellaneous	M.H 125. A.G At The Base.	02/03/1916	02/03/1916
War Diary	Auchy Aux Bois Dept Pas De Calais.	01/02/1916	06/02/1916
War Diary	Auchy Aux Bois	07/02/1916	26/02/1916
War Diary	Busnes 36.A.1-40000 P.26.C.2.4	24/02/1916	29/02/1916
Miscellaneous	March April 1916		
Heading	War Diary Of No. 112 Field Ambulance March 1st-31st. Vol 4		
War Diary	Busnes 36.A. P.26.C.2.4	01/03/1916	07/03/1916
War Diary	Busnes	08/03/1916	08/03/1916
War Diary	Lillers 36.A. U.11.F.3.4	09/03/1916	12/03/1916
War Diary	Lillers	13/03/1916	26/03/1916
War Diary	Nueux Les Mines 36 B. K.18.d.9.8	27/03/1916	27/03/1916
War Diary	Noeux Les Mines	27/03/1916	31/03/1916
Heading	War Diary From April 1st 1916 To April 30th 1916. No 112. Feb Ambce Vol 5		
War Diary	Noeux Les Mines 36.B12.18.D.98	01/04/1916	03/04/1916
War Diary	Noeux Les Mines.	04/04/1916	30/04/1916
Heading	War Diary From 1st May To 31st 1916 Of No. 112. Field Ambulance. Vol 6		
War Diary	Noeux Les Mines 36.B.K.18.D 98	01/05/1916	05/05/1916
War Diary	Noeux Les Mines	06/05/1916	31/05/1916
Heading	War Diary Of No. 112. Field Ambulance From. 1.6.1916. To 30.6.1916 Vol 7		
Miscellaneous	M.H.313 A.G.at The Base	06/06/1916	06/06/1916
War Diary	Noeux Les Mines 36.B.K.18.d.98	01/06/1916	04/06/1916
War Diary	Noeux Les Mines	05/06/1916	30/06/1916
Heading	112th Field Ambulance July 1916		
Heading	War Diary 112th Field Amb. RAMC 1st. July 1916 To 31st. July 1916. Volume No. 8.		
War Diary	Noeux Les Mines 36.B K.18.d.9.8	01/07/1916	06/07/1916
War Diary	Noeux Les Mines.	07/07/1916	31/07/1916
Heading	War Diary. 112th Field Ambulance. Month Of August. 1916. Volume 9		

War Diary	Noeux Les Mines 36.B. K.18.D.9.8.	01/08/1916	06/08/1916
War Diary	Noeux Les Mines	07/08/1916	24/08/1916
War Diary	Allouagne 36 B. C.7.A.4.7	25/08/1916	25/08/1916
War Diary	Allouagne	26/08/1916	29/08/1916
War Diary	Corbie Amiens. 17.	30/08/1916	30/08/1916
War Diary	Dive Copse 62.D.S.24.	31/08/1916	31/08/1916
War Diary	Dive Copse	31/08/1916	31/08/1916
Heading	War Diary 112th Field Ambulance RAMC For Month Of September, 1916 Volume 10		
War Diary	Dive Copse XIV Corps Main Dressing Station Somme 62 D.N.E. J.24. b.	01/09/1916	03/09/1916
War Diary	Dive Copse	04/09/1916	07/09/1916
War Diary	Dive Copse & Carnoy A.D.S.62. C.N.W. A.B.4.9	08/09/1916	08/09/1916
War Diary	Carnoy	09/09/1916	09/09/1916
War Diary	Carnoy & Bronfay Farm 62.D.N.E F.30.A	10/09/1916	10/09/1916
War Diary	Bronfay Farm	11/09/1916	11/09/1916
War Diary	Villa Des Etangs Nr Corbie. 62. D.N.W. I.30.	12/09/1916	17/09/1916
War Diary	Allery (Abbeville Map) No Proper Reference Obtainable	18/09/1916	20/09/1916
War Diary	Westoutre Trench Map 28.SW. M.9.E3.7.	21/09/1916	25/09/1916
War Diary	Westoutre	26/09/1916	30/09/1916
Heading	War Diary Month Of October, 1916. 112th Field Ambulance RAMC Volume 11		
War Diary	Westoutre Trench Map 28.S.W. M.9.C.3.7.	01/10/1916	06/10/1916
War Diary	Westoutre	07/10/1916	31/10/1916
Heading	War Diary For Month Of November, 1916. 112th Field Ambulance Volume 12		
War Diary	Westoutre Trench Map 28 S.W.M.9.C.3.4	01/11/1916	07/11/1916
War Diary	Westoutre	08/11/1916	30/11/1916
Heading	War Diary For Month Of December, 1916. Volume 13		
War Diary	Westoutre 28. S.W M.9.C 3.7	01/12/1916	07/12/1916
War Diary	Westoutre	08/12/1916	31/12/1916
Heading	War Diary For Month Of January, 1917. RAMC 12th Field Ambulance Vol 14		
War Diary	Westoutre 28. S.W. M.9.C.3.7.	01/01/1917	06/01/1917
War Diary	Westoutre	07/01/1917	31/01/1917
Heading	War Diary For Month Of February, 1917. 112th Field Ambulance Volume 15		
War Diary	Westoutre 28 S.W. M.9.C.3.7	01/02/1917	06/02/1917
War Diary	Westoutre	07/02/1917	28/02/1917
Heading	War Diary For Month Of March, 1917 112th Field Ambulance RAMC Volume 16		
War Diary	Westoutre 28.S.W.M.9.C.3.7.	01/03/1917	05/03/1917
War Diary	Westoutre	06/03/1917	30/03/1917
War Diary	Hazebrouck Sheet 27. (1.20000) V.16 A6	31/03/1917	31/03/1917
Heading	War Diary For Month Of April, 1917. 112th Fd Ambce RAMC Vol 14		
War Diary	Arques. Hazebrouck. 5A D-4. 6.8	01/04/1917	01/04/1917
War Diary	Nordausques Hazebrouck. 5A.A.3.9/1/2.7.	02/04/1917	02/04/1917
War Diary	Nordausques	03/04/1917	14/04/1917
War Diary	Arques (Hazebrouck 5A D.4.6.8.)	15/04/1917	15/04/1917
War Diary	Hazebrouck 5A.G.4.5.9	16/04/1917	16/04/1917
War Diary	Locre. 28.M.23.5.9	17/04/1917	17/04/1917
War Diary	Nordausques 5.A. A.3.9/1/2.7.	18/04/1917	19/04/1917
War Diary	Nordausques	20/04/1917	27/04/1917
War Diary	Arques Hazebrouck. 5A. D.4 6.8	28/04/1917	28/04/1917

War Diary	Hazebrouck 5A. G.4.5.9/1/2	29/04/1917	29/04/1917
War Diary	Locre 28.M.23.5.9	30/04/1917	30/04/1917
Heading	War Diary For Month Of May, 1917, RAMC 112th Fd. Ambce Volume 18		
War Diary	Locre. 28. M.23 D.3.8	01/05/1917	02/05/1917
War Diary	Westoutre M.9.C.3.4.	03/05/1917	06/05/1917
War Diary	Westoutre	07/05/1917	10/05/1917
War Diary	Locre M.23.D.3.8	11/05/1917	13/05/1917
War Diary	Locre	14/05/1917	31/05/1917
Heading	War Diary For Month Of June, 1917. RAMC 112th Field Ambulance Volume 19.		
Miscellaneous	BEF Summary Of Medical War Diary Of 112th F.A. 16th Div.	22/06/1917	22/06/1917
Miscellaneous	112th F.A. 16th Div 8th Corps. 5th Army. Officer Commanding-Lt.Col. P. Houghton.		
Miscellaneous	16th Div. Summary Of Medical War Diaries Of 112th F.A./8th	22/06/1917	22/06/1917
Miscellaneous	112th F.A. 16th Div 8th Corps. 5th Army. Officer Commanding-Col. P. Houghton.		
War Diary	Locre 28. M.23.d.3.8.	01/06/1917	05/06/1917
War Diary	Locre	05/06/1917	05/06/1917
War Diary	Brulooze Walking Wounded Dressing Station M.24.d.3.8.	06/06/1917	06/06/1917
War Diary	W.W. Dr Stn M 24 D.3.8	06/06/1917	09/06/1917
War Diary	Locre M 23 D.3.8	10/06/1917	10/06/1917
War Diary	Locre	11/06/1917	12/06/1917
War Diary	Fletre 24. W.e.9.7	13/06/1917	13/06/1917
War Diary	Fletre	14/06/1917	16/06/1917
War Diary	Haegedoorne 28.S.4.D.2.8.	17/06/1917	17/06/1917
War Diary	Fletre 24. W.e 9.7	18/06/1917	19/06/1917
War Diary	St Sylvestre Cappel 27. P.17d.7.2	20/06/1917	21/06/1917
War Diary	Rubrouck 27.A.14a. 3.7	22/06/1917	23/06/1917
War Diary	Rubrouck	23/06/1917	30/06/1917
Miscellaneous	Plans of 16th Div W.W.D.S Withdrawn to App Dept		
Heading	War Diary For Month Of July, 1917. 112th Field Ambulance RAMC Volume 20		
Miscellaneous	Summary Of Medical War Diaries Of 112th F.A. 16th Div.	22/08/1917	22/08/1917
Miscellaneous	112th F.A 8th Corps. 5th Army.		
Miscellaneous	112th F.A. 19th Corps. 5th Army.		
Miscellaneous	112th F.A 8th Corps. 5th Army.		
Miscellaneous	112th F.A. 18th Corps. 5th Army.	22/08/1917	22/08/1917
War Diary	Rubrouck 27 H.14.a 3.7	01/07/1917	06/07/1917
War Diary	Rubrouck	07/07/1917	21/07/1917
War Diary	Oudezeele 27. J.8. C Central	22/07/1917	24/07/1917
War Diary	Hilhoek 27.L.20. G Central	25/07/1917	28/07/1917
War Diary	Hilhoek	29/07/1917	31/07/1917
Heading	War Diary For Month Of August, 1917. 112th Field Ambulance Volume 21		
Miscellaneous	Summary Of Medical War Diaries Of 112th F.A. 16th Div.	22/08/1917	22/08/1917
Miscellaneous			
War Diary	Hilhoek 24. L. 20.B Central	01/08/1917	02/08/1917
War Diary	The Mill Vlamertinghe 28. H.8.a 9.8	03/08/1917	03/08/1917
War Diary	The Mill Vlamertinghe	03/08/1917	04/08/1917
War Diary	Vlamertinghe	04/08/1917	18/08/1917

War Diary	The Mill	19/08/1917	19/08/1917
War Diary	Vlamertinghe H.8.a.9.8 Sh. 28. NW	20/08/1917	20/08/1917
War Diary	Wormhouldt C 24.C.4.5 Sh.27 Bel & France	21/08/1917	22/08/1917
War Diary	Courcelles 12 Comte Sh 57 France A.15.D.	23/08/1917	24/08/1917
War Diary	Courcelles Le Comte	24/08/1917	24/08/1917
War Diary	Ervillers Sh. 57c France B 13.d.2.5	25/08/1917	26/08/1917
War Diary	Ervillers	27/08/1917	31/08/1917
Miscellaneous	A Duties of N.C.O i/c Walking. Wounded Potijze Annexe:-		
Miscellaneous	B Duties of N.C.O i/c W.W. Memn Cross Roads (or Gate)		
Miscellaneous	C Duties of N.C.O i/c W.W. at the Asylum.		
Miscellaneous	D Duties of N.C.O i/c Walking Wounded		
Diagram etc	Reserve Ground For Huts Or Tentage.		
Miscellaneous	Pathology. 4. Typhoid And Paratyphoid.		
Heading	War Diary. For Month Of September, 1917 RAMC 112th Field Ambulance Volume 22		
War Diary	Ervillers 5y C B.13 D.2.7	01/09/1917	03/09/1917
War Diary	Ervillers	04/09/1917	30/09/1917
Diagram etc	Dressing Station No 112 F.A. Ervillers Arras-Bapaume Road Appendix I		
Diagram etc	Dressing Station No 112 F.A. Ervillers Arras-Bapaume Road Appendix II		
Diagram etc	Dressing Station No 112 F.A. Ervillers Arras-Bapaume Road Appendix III		
Diagram etc	Dressing Station No 112 F.A. Ervillers Arras-Bapaume Road Appendix IV		
Diagram etc	Dressing Station No 112 F.A. Ervillers Arras-Bapaume Road Appendix V		
Diagram etc	Dressing Station No 112 F.A. Ervillers Arras-Bapaume Road Appendix VI		
Heading	War Diary For Month Of October, 1917. 112th Field Ambce RAMC Volume Number 23		
War Diary	Ervillers 5 Y.C.B.13 D.2.7.	01/10/1917	06/10/1917
War Diary	Ervillers	07/10/1917	31/10/1917
Diagram etc	Appendix I		
Diagram etc	Appendix 2		
Miscellaneous	VI Corps Scabies Station Appendix 3		
Diagram etc	VI Corps Scabies Station-Ervillers Appendix 4		
Heading	War Diary For Month Of November, 1917. 112th Field Ambulance RAMC Volume 24		
War Diary	Ervillers 57. C.B.13 D.2.7.	01/11/1917	06/11/1917
War Diary	Ervillers	07/11/1917	30/11/1917
Heading	War Diary For Month Of December, 1917. 112th Field Ambulance RAMC Volume 25		
War Diary	Achiet Le Grand 57. C. A 9.6 Control	01/12/1917	02/12/1917
War Diary	Maricourt 62. C.A. 15.C 8.3	03/12/1917	03/12/1917
War Diary	Maricourt	04/12/1917	04/12/1917
War Diary	Courcelles 62.C. J.32. A.5.2.	05/12/1917	05/12/1917
War Diary	Courcelles	05/12/1917	07/12/1917
War Diary	Hamed 32.C. K. 18d. 9.3	08/12/1917	14/12/1917
War Diary	Hamel	14/12/1917	18/12/1917
War Diary	Hamel B2c Sh. K.18.D.A 9.3 Map Ref	19/12/1917	21/12/1917
War Diary	Hamel	22/12/1917	31/12/1917
Diagram etc	VI Corps Scabies Station Ervillers.		

Heading	War Diary For Month Of January 1918. 112th Fd Ambce RAMC Volume 26		
War Diary	Hamel Map Ref Sh. B2c K18.a.9.3	01/01/1918	02/01/1918
War Diary	Hamel	02/01/1918	31/01/1918
Heading	War Diary For Month Of February, 1918. 112th Field Ambulance RAMC Volume 24		
War Diary	Hamel 62. C R.18 D. 9.3	01/02/1918	06/02/1918
War Diary	Hamel	07/02/1918	28/02/1918
Miscellaneous	War Diary Of No 112 Field Ambulance From 1.3.18 To 31.3.18 Volume XXVIII		
War Diary	Hamel 62 C. K18.9.3	01/03/1918	07/03/1918
War Diary	Hamel	08/03/1918	21/03/1918
War Diary	College Peronne 62 C. 1 27 D.2.4.	22/03/1918	22/03/1918
War Diary	Near Cappy 62. C G.26.d. 9.9	23/03/1918	23/03/1918
War Diary	Bray Sur Somme 62.D. L.16.7.2	24/03/1918	24/03/1918
War Diary	Near Pont Noyelles 62 D. H. 18d. Central	25/03/1918	25/03/1918
War Diary	62.D. a.3.10	25/03/1918	26/03/1918
War Diary	Near Cross Road S Blangy Tronville	27/03/1918	27/03/1918
War Diary	62. D. N. 27 D.6.6	27/03/1918	31/03/1918
Miscellaneous	No. 112 F.A.		
War Diary	Near Blangy-Tronville 62 D. N 2	01/04/1918	01/04/1918
War Diary	N.26.d. 6.6	02/04/1918	03/04/1918
War Diary	Saleux (Amiens.2. C 8.5)	04/04/1918	04/04/1918
War Diary	Biencourt Chateau. (Dieppe. 16 1.I 37.)	05/04/1918	08/04/1918
War Diary	Hocquelus (Abbeville. 14 10 36. E 50 O 2' N)	09/04/1918	09/04/1918
War Diary	In The Train	10/04/1918	10/04/1918
War Diary	Le. Fay (Hazebrouek 5A 5. A 4.4)	11/04/1918	11/04/1918
War Diary	Le Fay	12/04/1918	12/04/1918
War Diary	Leval Restaut 5.A 5A. 2.F	13/04/1918	13/04/1918
War Diary	Westrehem 5A. 5C. 80.55.	14/04/1918	14/04/1918
War Diary	Les Ciseaux 5A. LI. F. 2.1	15/04/1918	17/04/1918
War Diary	Les Ciseaux	18/04/1918	30/04/1918
Miscellaneous	No. 112 F. A. May 1918		
War Diary	Les Ciseaux	01/05/1918	11/05/1918
War Diary	Lacque	12/05/1918	31/05/1918
Heading	War Diary 112 Field Ambce June 1918 Vol 31		
War Diary	Lacque	01/06/1918	25/06/1918
War Diary	Abbeville	26/06/1918	30/06/1918
War Diary	Cover For Documents. Nature Of Enclosures. War Diary 112 Field Ambulance Vol 32		
War Diary	Affender	01/07/1918	01/07/1918
War Diary	Etaples	02/07/1918	02/07/1918
War Diary	Licques	03/07/1918	31/07/1918
Heading	War Diary 112 Field Ambulance Vol 33		
War Diary	Licques	01/08/1918	03/08/1918
War Diary	Wille au Bois	03/08/1918	22/08/1918
War Diary	Rusty	23/08/1918	31/08/1918
Heading	112th F Amb. Sept 1918		
War Diary	Rusty M.D.S	01/09/1918	10/09/1918
War Diary	Barlin	10/09/1918	24/09/1918
War Diary	Binary	25/09/1918	30/09/1918
Heading	112th F.A Oct 1918		
War Diary	Binary	01/10/1918	15/10/1918
War Diary	Hesdigneul	16/10/1918	19/10/1918
War Diary	Haisnes	20/10/1918	20/10/1918
War Diary	Provin	21/10/1918	21/10/1918

War Diary	Camphin	22/10/1918	22/10/1918
War Diary	Templeux	23/10/1918	31/10/1918
Heading	112th F.A Nov 1918		
War Diary	Templeux	01/11/1919	30/11/1919
Miscellaneous	No 112 Field Ambulance		
War Diary	Templeux	01/12/1919	31/12/1919
Heading	16 Div Box 1674 No 112 Field Ambulance		
War Diary	Templeux	01/01/1919	31/01/1919
Miscellaneous	No 112 Field Ambulance Feb 1919		
War Diary	Templeux	01/02/1919	28/02/1919
Heading	War Diary 112 Field Ambulance March 1919		
War Diary	Templeux	01/03/1919	31/03/1919
Heading	112 F.A. April 1919		
War Diary	Templeux	01/04/1919	30/04/1919
Heading	112th F.A. June 1919		
War Diary	Templeux	01/04/1919	27/04/1919

(2)

WO 95 / 1916

16 Division
Divisional Troops
~~Headquarters Branches of Services~~

Dec 1915 — June 1919

112 FIELD AMBULANCE

16TH DIVISION

112TH FLD AMBULANCE

JAN 1916 - ~~DEC 1918~~

1919 JUN

112 F.A

16 [illegible]

F|14911

112th F.A.
Vol II

Dec 1915

121/7910

Instructions regarding War Diaries and Intelligence Summaries are contained in F. S. Regs., Part II. and the Staff Manual respectively. Title Pages will be prepared in manuscript.

WAR DIARY

~~or~~

~~INTELLIGENCE SUMMARY~~

(Erase heading not required.)

Army Form C. 2118

Place	Date	Hour	Summary of Events and Information	Remarks and references to Appendices
HAVRE	19.12 1915		No: 112. Field Ambulance arrived from ~~TWESELDOWN~~ via FARNBORO' and SOUTHAMPTON, in two parties, unloaded transport, & marched to DOCKS-REST-CAMP. B. Houghton Major RAMC	
"	20.12		Marched to GARE DES MARCHANDISES OC. 112. F. A.	
		10.30 AM	& entrained. Train left HAVRE. B.H.	
HOUCHIN MAP-FRANCE 36B.K.15 G.	21.12.	5.45 AM	Arrived at CHOQUES & detrained. Marched to HOUCHIN to billets. Officers in houses, men in barns, animals & wagons in the open. Barns fairly dry with one exception. Weather - rainy. B.H.	
"	22.12		Cleaned up billets. Readjusted wagons. Improved horse-lines. Weather Rainy, & ground very muddy B.H.	
"	23.12		Obtained slag from "Dump" at NEUX LES MINES (Map 36B K.18) Commenced making paths & improved Horse Lines. Weather rainy and great Storm from S W at night. B.H.	
"	24.12		Obtained straw & unloaded wagons. Continued work on Horse-lines, paths & Sanitary arrangements B.H.	

1875 Wt. W593/826 1,000,000 4/15 J.B.C. & A. A.D.S.S./Forms/C. 2118.

Instructions regarding War Diaries and Intelligence Summaries are contained in F. S. Regs., Part II. and the Staff Manual respectively. Title Pages will be prepared in manuscript.

WAR DIARY
or
~~INTELLIGENCE SUMMARY~~
(Erase heading not required.)

Army Form C. 2118

Place	Date	Hour	Summary of Events and Information	Remarks and references to Appendices
HOUCHIN	25.12		Christmas Day. Necessary Fatigues. Church Parade. R.H.	
"	26.12		Continued improvements to area. Obtained routine orders from ADMS. 16th Divn. R.H.	
"	27.12		Continued improvements. Motor Ambulances arrived R.H.	
"	28.12		Received orders from A.D.M.S to proceed with Advance Guard Officer & Interpreter to NEDON & NEDONCHELLE (Map 36.B. A 12 & B.4) to meet Staff Officer & obtain suitable site for opening Ambulance. Found nothing suitable. Went on to AUCHY-AUX-BOIS where I found an isolated building giving accommodation for about 50 cases & suitable billeting area adjacent. Reported to Divn HdQrs. on return, & received orders to proceed to AUCHY tomorrow. R.H.	
AUCHY AUX BOIS Map 36A T.14.	29.12		Marched to AUCHY without incident. About 16 miles. R.H.	

1875 Wt. W593/826 1,000,000 4/15 J.B.C. & A. A.D.S.S./Forms/C. 2118.

Army Form C. 2118

Instructions regarding War Diaries and Intelligence Summaries are contained in F. S. Regs., Part II. and the Staff Manual respectively. Title Pages will be prepared in manuscript.

WAR DIARY
or
~~INTELLIGENCE SUMMARY~~

(Erase heading not required.)

Place	Date	Hour	Summary of Events and Information	Remarks and references to Appendices
AUCHY AUX BOIS	30.12		Opened Ambulance with 36 beds. Started construction of Sanitary arrangements. Visited by A.D.M.S. & Sanitary Officer. 1 patient admitted in evening — sick.	
"	31.12		Started construction of shower-bath for patients & personnel. Continued other construction. Patients Remaining - sick - 1. Admitted - sick 2. Remaining sick 3.	

R. L. [illegible]
Major RAMC
OC. 112. F. A.

1875 Wt. W593/826 1,000,000 4/15 J.B.C. & A. A.D.S.S./Forms/C. 2118.

16th Division

F/149/2

112th Fa.

Vol 2

Jan 1916

Dec '18

WAR DIARY.

No. 112. Field Ambulance.

1st to 31st January. 1916.

B. S. Hough[illegible]
Major RAMC
OC. 112. Fld Ambce

1.2.16

Instructions regarding War Diaries and Intelligence Summaries are contained in F. S. Regs., Part II. and the Staff Manual respectively. Title Pages will be prepared in manuscript.

WAR DIARY
or
~~INTELLIGENCE SUMMARY~~
(Erase heading not required.)

Army Form C. 2118

112. Field Ambulance.

Place	Date	Hour	Summary of Events and Information	Remarks and references to Appendices
AUCHY AUX BOIS Dep^t PAS DE CALAIS	1st Jan 1916		Patients – Officers – admitted 1. Transferred 1. Other Ranks. Remaining 3. Admitted 1. Remaining 4. On departure of detachment of other unit was enabled to concentrate all horses & mules with ASC Detacht in one farm. Sanitary arrangements for unit proceeding, viz:– Shower baths under cover of wagon covers, latrines on Beveridge plan, destructors modelled on system in use at MAZASSISE. R. J. Hamilton Major RAMC	
"	2nd Jan.		Officers nil. O.R. Remaining 4. Admitted 2. To Cas. Cl. Stn 1. To Duty 1. Rem. 4. 1 Latrine & destructor completed & in use. Received orders changing units from whom sick are to be drawn, i.e. 47th vice 48th Bde. RJH.	
"	3.1.16		Officers. Admitted 1. Transferred 1. O.Rks. Rem 4. Admitted 7. To Cas. Cl. Stn 5. Rem. 6. Second latrine & destructor completed & in use. RJH.	
"	4.1.16		Officers. Admitted 3. Transferred 3. Remaining 0. O.R. Rem. 6. Admitted 7. To Cas Cl Stn 4. Rem. 9. Shower bath completed & used – 3 men. Lieut. A. Muir detailed for Temporary Duty with 6th R.I. Regt. RJH	
"	5.1.16		O.R. Rem. 9. Admitted 4. To Duty 1. Rem. 12. 38 men bathed during day. Baths extended to 3 showers. RJH.	

1875 Wt. W593/826 1,000,000 4/15 J.B.C. & A. A.D.S.S./Forms/C. 2118.

Army Form C. 2118

Instructions regarding War Diaries and Intelligence Summaries are contained in F. S. Regs., Part II. and the Staff Manual respectively. Title Pages will be prepared in manuscript.

WAR DIARY
or
~~INTELLIGENCE SUMMARY~~
(Erase heading not required.)

112 Field Ambulance

Place	Date	Hour	Summary of Events and Information	Remarks and references to Appendices
AUCHY AUX BOIS	6.1.16		O.R. Rem. 12. Ad. 7. To Cas Cl Stn. 1. To Duty 4. Rem. 14. 47 NCO's & men bathed, besides patients. R.H.	
"	7.1.16		O.R. Rem. 14. Ad. 5. To Cas Cl Stn. 2. To Duty. 2. Rem 15. 81. NCO's & men bathed, besides patients. R.H.	
"	8.1.16		O.R. Rem. 15. Adm. 13. To Cas Cl Stn 1. To Duty 2. Rem. 25. 5 NCO's & men bathed R.H.	
"	9.1.16		Officers Adm. 1. Rem. 1. O.R. Rem. 25. Adm. 11. To Cas Cl Stn. 2. To Duty 4. Rem. 30. R.H.	
"	10.1.16		Officers. Rem 1. O.R. Rem 30. Adm 8. To Cas Cl Stn 6. To Duty. 9. Rem. 23. The Ambulance was inspected by G.O.C. Div. R.H.	
"	11.1.16		Officers. Rem 1 Transferred 1. Rem. 0. O.R Rem 23 Adm 4. To Duty 9. Rem 18. R.H.	
"	12.1.16		O.R. Rem. 18. Adm 7. To Cas Cl Stn. 2 To Duty. 1. Rem 22 45 NCO's & men bathed. R.H.	

1875 Wt. W593/826 1,000,000 4/15 J.B.C. & A. A.D.S.S./Forms/C. 2118.

Instructions regarding War Diaries and Intelligence Summaries are contained in F. S. Regs., Par. II. and the Staff Manual respectively. Title Pages will be prepared in manuscript.

WAR DIARY
or
~~INTELLIGENCE SUMMARY~~
(Erase heading not required.)

Army Form C. 2118

112. FA

Place	Date	Hour	Summary of Events and Information	Remarks and references to Appendices
AUCHY AUX BOIS	13/1/16		O.R. Rem. 22. Adm 5. To Duty 2. To Cas Cl Stn 3. Rem 22. 58 NCO's & men bathed. Q.J.H.	
"	14/1/16.		O.R. Rem. 22. Adm 5. To Duty 4. To Cas Cl Stn 1. Rem. 22 64 NCO's & men bathed. Q.J.H.	
"	15/1/16.		O.R. Rem. 22. Adm 11. Rec. Transfers from No 111. FA 9. To Duty 4. To Cas Cl Stn 4. Rem 34. Q.J.H.	
"	16/1/16		O.R. Rem 34. Adm 12. To Duty 10. To Cas Cl Stn 5. Rem 31. Q.J.H.	
"	17/1/16		O.R. Rem 31. Adm 10. To Duty 3. To Cas Cl. Stn. 4. Rem 34. Q.J.H.	
"	18/1/16		O.R. Rem 34 Adm. 4. To Duty 3. To Cas Cl Stn 6. Rem 29. Q.J.H.	
"	19/1/16		O.R. Rem. 29. Adm. 9. To Duty 6. To Cas Cl. Stn. 1. Rem 31 Q.J.H.	

1875 Wt. W593/826 1,000,000 4/15 J.B.C. & A. A.D.S.S./Forms/C. 2118.

Instructions regarding War Diaries and Intelligence Summaries are contained in F. S. Regs., Part II. and the Staff Manual respectively. Title Pages will be prepared in manuscript.

WAR DIARY

~~or~~

~~INTELLIGENCE SUMMARY~~

(Erase heading not required.)

Army Form C. 2118

112. F A

Place	Date	Hour	Summary of Events and Information	Remarks and references to Appendices
AUCHY AUX BOIS.	20/1/16		Officers admitted. 1. To Cas Cl Stn. 1. Rem. 0. O.R. Rem. 31. Adm 12. To Duty. 4. To Cas Cl Stn. 4. Rem. 35. R.H.	
"	21/1/16		O.R. Rem. 35. Adm 12. To Duty. 11. To Cas Cl Stn. 5. Rem. 31 R.H.	
"	22/1/16		O.R. Rem. 31. Adm 5. To Duty. 5. To Cas Cl Stn. 1. Rem. 30. Received instructions from DA & QMG. to supply a Staff & transport for Divisional Baths & Laundry work. R.H.	
"	23/1/16		O.R. Rem. 30. Adm 6. To Duty 8. To Cas Cl Stn 3. Rem. 25. R.H.	
"	24/1/16		O.R. Rem. 25. Adm 11. To Duty. 4. To Cas Cl Stn. 5. Rem. 27. Lieut P. W. Barker left for Temporary duty with 1/3 London Bde R.F.A. R.H.	
"	25/1/16		O.R. Rem. 27. Adm. 8. To Duty 2. To Div Rest Stn. 2. To Cas Cl Stn 2 Rem. 29. R.H.	

1875 Wt. W593/826 1,000,000 4/15 J.B.C. & A. A.D.S.S./Forms/C. 2118.

WAR DIARY
or
~~INTELLIGENCE SUMMARY~~
(Erase heading not required.)

Army Form C. 2118

112 F.A.

Instructions regarding War Diaries and Intelligence Summaries are contained in F. S. Regs., Part II. and the Staff Manual respectively. Title Pages will be prepared in manuscript.

Place	Date	Hour	Summary of Events and Information	Remarks and references to Appendices
AUCHY AUX BOIS.	26/1/16		O.R. Rem 29. Adm 11. To Duty 4. To Div Rest Stn 2 To Cas. Cl. Stn. 5. Rem. 26. R.J.H.	
"	27/1/16		O.R. Rem 26. Adm 11. To Duty 2. To Cas Cl Stn 2. Rem 33. Divisional Baths opened 3 NCO's & Transport furnished. R.J.H.	
"	28/1/16		O.R. Rem 33 Adm 8. To Duty 9 To Cas Cl Stn. 3. Rem 29. 80 NCO's & men bathed. 4 NCO's & extra transport furnished for Div Baths. R.J.H.	
"	29/1/16		O.R. Rem. 29 Adm 9. To Duty 8. To Cas Cl Stn. 3. Rem 27. 86 NCO's & men bathed. Additional transport supplied to O.C. Div Baths for distribution of clothing & laundries R.J.H.	
"	30/1/16		O.R. Rem 27. Adm 8. To Duty 4. To Cas Cl Stn. 4. Rem 27 R.J.H.	
"	31/1/16		Officers. Adm 2. To Div Rest Stn 2. Rem 0. O.R. Rem. 27. Adm 11 To Duty - 5. To Cas Cl Stn 3. Rem 30. R.J. Hunter [?] Major RAMC OC 112 F.A.	

1875 Wt. W593/826 1,000,000 4/15 J.B.C. & A. A.D.S.S./Forms/C. 2118.

Feb 1916 112th Field Ambulance

M. H 125.

A. G at the Base.

Herewith War Diary for February of No 112. Fld Ambce.

R. H. [illegible] Major RAMC
O.C. 112 Fld Ambce

2. 3. 16

Army Form C. 2118

WAR DIARY
~~or~~
~~INTELLIGENCE SUMMARY~~
(Erase heading not required.)

No: 112. FIELD AMBULANCE.

Instructions regarding War Diaries and Intelligence Summaries are contained in F. S. Regs., Part II. and the Staff Manual respectively. Title Pages will be prepared in manuscript.

Place	Date	Hour	Summary of Events and Information	Remarks and references to Appendices
AUCHY aux BOIS Dept PAS DE CALAIS	1/2/1916		Officers. Admitted - 2. To Div Rest Station. 2. Remaining. 0. Other Ranks. Remaining 30. Admitted. 6. To Duty - 6. To Cas Cl Stn. 1. Remaining 29. R. S. Houghton Major R.A.M.C.	
	2/2/16		Other Ranks. Remaining 29. Admitted. 8. To Duty. 6. To Cas Cl Stn. 6. Remaining 25 R.S.H.	
	3/2/16		Other Ranks. Rem. - 25. Adm - 12. To Duty - 6. To C. C. S. - 6. Rem. 25 R.S.H.	
	4/2/16		Other Ranks. Rem. - 25. Adm - 10. To Duty - 1. To C. C. S. - 3. Rem. 31 R.S.H.	
	5/2/16		Other Ranks. Rem. - 31. Adm - 15. To Duty - 8. To C. C. S - 4. Rem 34 R.S.H.	
	6/2/16		Officers. Admitted - 1. To C. C. S. 1. Rem O. Other Ranks. Rem - 34. Adm - 8. To Duty - 6. To C. C. S. 10. Rem. 26. R.S.H.	

1875 Wt. W593/826 1,000,000 4/15 J.B.C. & A. A.D.S.S./Forms/C. 2118.

Instructions regarding War Diaries and Intelligence Summaries are contained in F. S. Regs., Part II. and the Staff Manual respectively. Title Pages will be prepared in manuscript.

WAR DIARY

~~or~~

~~INTELLIGENCE SUMMARY~~

(Erase heading not required.)

Army Form C. 2118

NO. 112 FIELD AMBULANCE

Place	Date	Hour	Summary of Events and Information	Remarks and references to Appendices
AUCHY aux BOIS	7/2/16		Officers. Admitted – 1 To. Cas. Cl Stn 1. Remaining 0. Other Ranks. Remaining 26. Admitted 23 To Duty – 5. To Cas. Cl Stn 7. Remaining 37 R.H.	
	8/2/16		Other Ranks. Admitted – 15. To Duty – 8 To C. C. S. 11. Remaining 33 Remaining 37 R.H.	
	9/2/16		Other Ranks. Remaining 33. Adm – 18 To Duty. 2 To C C S. 19 Rem 30 R.H.	
	10/2/16		Other Ranks. Rem 30. Adm 7 To Duty. 2 To C.C.S. 8. Rem 27. R.H.	
	11/2/16		Other Ranks Rem 27 Adm 11. Transferred from No 111 F.A 9 Total 47. To Duty. 4. To Cas Cl Stn. 5 Remaining 38. R.H.	
	12/2/16		Other Ranks. Rem 38. Adm 15. To Duty. 4 To Cas Cl Stn. 16 Rem 33 R.H.	

1875 Wt. W593/826 1,000,000 4/15 J.B.C. & A. A.D.S.S./Forms/C. 2118.

Instructions regarding War Diaries and Intelligence Summaries are contained in F. S. Regs., Par: II. and the Staff Manual respectively. Title Pages will be prepared in manuscript.

WAR DIARY

~~or~~

~~INTELLIGENCE SUMMARY~~

(Erase heading not required.)

Army Form C. 2118

NO: 112. FIELD AMBULANCE

Place	Date	Hour	Summary of Events and Information	Remarks and references to Appendices
AUCHY aux BOIS	13/2/16		Other Ranks. Remaining 33. Admitted 11. To Duty 4. To Cas Cl Stn 10 Rem. 30 R.H.	
	14/2/16		Other Ranks. Rem 30 Adm 12 To Duty 3 To C.C.S 3 Rem. 36. R.H.	
	15/2/16		Other Ranks. Rem 36. Adm 22. To Duty 7 To C.C.S 9 Rem. 42 R.H.	
	16/2/16		Other Ranks. Rem. 42 Adm 13. To Duty 11. To C.C.S 6 Rem 38 Lieut A.D. MOFFAT RAMC (T.C) reported his arrival for duty vice Lieut A MUIR RAMC. (T.C), struck off strength, as M.O i/c 6th R. Irish Regt. Parties of Officers from Nos 105 & 106 F.A's visited the Ambulance for Demonstration in Sanitary Work & appliances. R.H.	
	17/2/16		Officers. Admitted 1. To Cas Cl Stn. 1 Remaining 0. Other Ranks. Remaining 38. Adm. 20 To Duty 5. To C.C.S. 11 Rem. 42 Parties of Officers from 106 & 107 F.A's visited for demonstration in Sanitation R.H.	

1875 Wt. W593/826 1,000,000 4/15 J.B.C. & A. A.D.S.S./Forms/C. 2118.

Instructions regarding War Diaries and Intelligence Summaries are contained in F. S. Regs., Part II. and the Staff Manual respectively. Title Pages will be prepared in manuscript.

WAR DIARY
or
~~INTELLIGENCE SUMMARY~~
(Erase heading not required.)

Army Form C. 2118

No: 112 FIELD AMBULANCE

Place	Date	Hour	Summary of Events and Information	Remarks and references to Appendices
AUCHY aux BOIS	18/2/16.		Other Ranks. Remaining ~~29~~ 42 Admitted 7 To Duty 2 To Cas Cl Stn 12 Remaining 35. R.H.	
"	19/2/16		Other Ranks. Remaining 35. Adm 12 To Duty 8. To C.C.S 3 Rem 36 R.H.	
"	20/2/16		Other Ranks Rem 36. Adm 20. To Duty 6 To C.C.S. 5. Rem 45 R.H.	
"	21/2/16		Officers. Admitted 1. To Cas Cl Stn 1. Other Ranks. Remaining 45. Admitted. 18. To Duty 6. To C.C.S. 11. Rem 46 R.H.	
"	22/2/16		Other Ranks. Remaining 46. Adm 10. To Duty 10. To C.C.S. 11. Rem 35 R.H.	
"	23/2/16		Other Ranks. Rem 35 Adm 17 To Duty 6. To C.C.S. 12. Rem 34 R.H.	
"	24/2/16		Officers Admitted 1. To Cas Cl Stn. 1. Other Ranks. Remaining 34 Admitted 12. To Duty 6. To C.C.S. 5. Rem 35 R.H.	

1875 Wt. W593/826 1,000,000 4/15 J.B.C. & A. A.D.S.S./Forms/C. 2118.

Army Form C. 2118

Instructions regarding War Diaries and Intelligence Summaries are contained in F. S. Regs., Part II. and the Staff Manual respectively. Title Pages will be prepared in manuscript.

WAR DIARY
or
~~INTELLIGENCE SUMMARY~~
(Erase heading not required.)

No: 112. FIELD AMBULANCE

Place	Date	Hour	Summary of Events and Information	Remarks and references to Appendices
AUCHY aux BOIS.	25/2/16		Officers. Admitted 1. To Cas Cl Stn. 1. Other Ranks. Remaining 35. Admitted 19. To Duty 5. To Cas Cl Stn. 14. Remaining 35 R.J.H.	
"	26/2/16		Other Ranks. Rem 35. Adm 4. To Duty 6. To Cas Cl Stn. 17. Rem 16 Received orders to move to BUSNES 1st Corps Reserve Area, on 27.2.16. R.J.H.	
BUSNES 36.A.1-40000 P.26.C.2.4	27/2/16		Moved to BUSNES, arriving 2.15.P.M. Took up large two storied house with attics on outskirts of town for Ambulance Headquarters. Personnel in outbuildings of farms close by. Other Ranks. Remaining 16. Admitted 1. To Duty 3. To No.113. F.A. 6. Remaining 8 R.J.H.	
"	28/2/16		Officers. Admitted 1. To Cas Cl Stn 1 Other Ranks. Remaining 8. Admitted 6. Remaining 14. R.J.H.	
"	29/2/16		Other Ranks. Remaining 14. Admitted 53 (mostly Scabies from Div Artillery) To Duty - 1. To Cas Cl Stn 3. Remaining 63 R.J. Hungerford Major RAMC O.C. 112. F.A.	

1875 Wt. W593/826 1,000,000 4/15 J.B.C. & A. A.D.S.S./Forms/C. 2118.

March } 1916.
April }

No 112 Fld. Ambulance.

112 F Amb
Vol 4

War Diary
of
No: 112. Field Ambulance
March 1st – 31st.

Mar 1916

Army Form C. 2118

Instructions regarding War Diaries and Intelligence Summaries are contained in F. S. Regs., Part II. and the Staff Manual respectively. Title Pages will be prepared in manuscript.

WAR DIARY

~~or~~

~~INTELLIGENCE SUMMARY~~

(Erase heading not required.)

112. FIELD AMBULANCE

Place	Date	Hour	Summary of Events and Information	Remarks and references to Appendices
BUSNES 36.A. P.26.c.2.4	1/3/16		Officers – nil Other Ranks. Remaining 63. Admitted 30 To Cas. Clg. Stn. 14. Remaining 79 R J Hungleton Major RAMC	
"	2/3/16		O. R. Rem. 49. Adm. 36. To Duty. 11. To C.C.S. 33. Rem. 71 RJH	
"	3/3/16		O. R. Rem. 71 Adm 21. To Duty. 35. To C.C.S. 15. Rem. 42 RJH	
"	4/3/16		Officers. Adm. 1 to C.C.S. 1 O.R. Rem 42. Adm. 6. To Duty 4. To C.C.S. 6. Rem 38. RJH	
"	5/3/16		O. R. Rem. 38. Adm 12. To Duty 9. To C.C.S. 5. Rem 36 RJH	
"	6/3/16		O. R. Rem 36. Adm 12. To Duty 5. To C.C.S. 4 Rem 39 RJH	
"	7/3/16		O. R. Rem 39 Adm 10. To Duty 9. To C.C.S. 6. Rem 34 RJH	

1875 Wt. W593/826 1,000,000 4/15 J.B.C. & A. A.D.S.S./Forms/C. 2118.

Instructions regarding War Diaries and Intelligence Summaries are contained in F. S. Regs., Part II. and the Staff Manual respectively. Title Pages will be prepared in manuscript.

WAR DIARY

~~or~~

~~INTELLIGENCE SUMMARY~~

(Erase heading not required.)

Army Form C. 2118

112. Fd Ambce.

Place	Date	Hour	Summary of Events and Information	Remarks and references to Appendices
BUSNES	8/3/16		O. R. Rem 34. Adm 21. To Duty 4. To C.C.S. 15. Rem 36 RJH	
LILLERS 36.A. U.11.C.3.4.	9/3/16		O. R. Rem 36. Adm 1. To Duty 5. To C.C.S. 2. Rem 30. Moved to New 1st Corps Reserve Area. Ambulance Headquarters as per margin in Place de l'Eglise. Very poor accommodation in a small private house with attic. Accommodation for 38 in house & 8 for Scabies in outhouse. Space for 50 more in loft of a Brewery at U.10.d.8.3. Personnel scattered in billets along Rue des Bourg d'Aval in Rue de Sebastopol. Owing to small accommodation only receiving from Divnl Artillery, Cavalry, & Cyclists. RJH	
"	10/3/16		O.R. Rem 30. Adm 7. To C.C.S. 8. Rem 29. Opened Divisional Baths in vats & tubs at Brewery. U.10.d.8.3 RJH	
"	11/3/16		O. R. Rem 29. Adm 8. To Duty 2. Rem 35. RJH	
"	12/3/16		O. R. Rem 35. Adm 8. To Duty 5. To C.C.S. 4. Rem. 34 RJH.	

1875 Wt. W593/826 1,000,000 4/15 J.B.C. & A. A.D.S.S./Forms/C. 2118.

Army Form C. 2118

Instructions regarding War Diaries and Intelligence Summaries are contained in F. S. Regs., Part II. and the Staff Manual respectively. Title Pages will be prepared in manuscript.

WAR DIARY
or
~~INTELLIGENCE SUMMARY~~
(Erase heading not required.)

1/2 F. Ambce

Place	Date	Hour	Summary of Events and Information	Remarks and references to Appendices
LILLERS	13/3/16		Officers Adm. 1 To C.C.S. 1. O.R. Rem. 34. Adm. 11. To Duty 10. To C.C.S. 1. Rem. 34 Q.J.H.	
"	14/3/16		O.R. Rem 34. Adm 4 To Duty 3. To C.C.S. 2 Rem 33 Q.J.H.	
"	15/3/16		Officers Adm. 1. To C.C.S. 1. O.R. Rem. 33. Adm 9. To Duty 6. To C.C.S. 2. Rem 34 Q.J.H.	
"	16/3/16		O.R. Rem. 34. Adm 9. To Duty 5. To C.C.S. 3. Rem 35. Q.J.H.	
"	17/3/16		O.R. Rem 35 Adm 4. To Duty 2 To C.C.S. 1 Rem 36	
"	18/3/16		O.R. Rem. 36 Adm 9. To Duty 10. To C.C.S. 6. To Divn Rest Stn 1 Rem. 28 Lieut. I. M. Fraser left for temporary duty with 6th R.I.F. Q.J.H.	
"	19/3/16		O.R. Rem 28. Adm 3. To Duty 4 Rem 27 Orders received to hold Ambulance in readiness to move to Forward Area Q.J.H.	

1875 Wt. W593/826 1,000,000 4/15 J.B.C. & A. A.D.S.S./Forms/C. 2118.

Army Form C. 2118

Instructions regarding War Diaries and Intelligence Summaries are contained in F. S. Regs., Part II. and the Staff Manual respectively. Title Pages will be prepared in manuscript.

WAR DIARY
~~or~~
~~INTELLIGENCE SUMMARY~~

(Erase heading not required.)

112. Fld Ambce.

Place	Date	Hour	Summary of Events and Information	Remarks and references to Appendices
LILLERS	20/3/16		O.R. Rem. 27. Adm 3. To Duty 5. To C.C.S. 2. Rem 23. Visited Headquarters & Adv. Dr. Stations in new Area. RJK	
"	21/3/16		O.R. Rem 23. Adm. 6. To Duty 2. To C.C.S. 5. To Div Rest Stn 2. Rem 20 A detachment – Lieuts Ferguson & Barker & O.R. 18 proceeded to report to O.C. No: 45. FA for instruction in the New Area. RJK	
"	22/3/16		O.R. Rem. 20. Adm 3. To Duty 5. To C.C.S. 6. Rem. 12 RJK	
"	23/3/16		Officers. Adm. 1. To C.C.S. 1 O.R. Rem. 12. Adm 3. Duty 4. C.C.S. 2. Rem. 6. RJK	
"	24/3/16		O.R. Rem. 6. To Duty. 2. Rem. 4. RJK	
"	25/3/16		Officers. Adm. 1. To. C.C.S. 1. O.R. Rem. 4. Adm 6. To Duty 2. to C.C.S. 4. Rem. 4 Lieut A.D. Moffat left for Temporary Duty with 1st Machine Gun Squadron. Advance Party from No: 45. FA. arrived. Handed over Div Baths RJK	

1875 Wt. W593/826 1,000,000 4/15 J.B.C. & A. A.D.S.S./Forms/C. 2118.

Instructions regarding War Diaries and Intelligence Summaries are contained in F. S. Regs., Part II. and the Staff Manual respectively. Title Pages will be prepared in manuscript.

WAR DIARY
~~or~~
~~INTELLIGENCE SUMMARY~~
(Erase heading not required.)

Army Form C. 2118

No: 112 Field Ambulance

Place	Date	Hour	Summary of Events and Information	Remarks and references to Appendices
LILLERS	26/3/16		Officers. Adm 2. to CCS. 2 O. Ranks. Rem 4 Admitted 4. to C.C.S. 4. Rem. 4. Detachments proceeded by route march & rail — 1 Officer & 6 OR. to NOEUX LES MINES as Advance Party to take over the BREWERY from No: 45 Field Ambulance. 1 Officer & 42 OR to the NUNNERY. PHILOSOPHE to take over Advance Dressing Stations in conjunction with instructional party The Transport of 1 Section moved by road to the NUNNERY. PHILOSOPHE G.14	
NOEUX LES MINES 36.B. K.18.d.9.8	27/3/16		Main body proceeded by route-march and rail, & Transport of 2 sections by road to new Headquarters at the BREWERY. NOEUX. 36.B. K.18.d.9.8. with main Advanced Dressing Station at the NUNNERY. PHILOSOPHE. 36.C. G.13. d. 1.7 & Dug Outs – St MARY. G.14.b & ST GEORGE G.14.d. Headquarters have complete use of Brewery Premises – giving accommodation for 150, easily extensible to 200, in cellars & stores. Personnel billeted in lofts above The NUNNERY can accommodate 400–600 patients in small houses and a large Chapel. It is liable to be shelled from "The Quarries" & "Hohenzollern Redoubt", & might have to be evacuated. ST GEORGE & ST MARY Dugouts are about 1100 yds from front line, & near Old German Front Line Trench. Each accommodates 14 stretchers. From St MARY wounded are removed after dark, – occasionally in daylight, – via the HULLUCH ROAD, by wheeled stretcher if necessary, to the NUNNERY.	

1875 Wt. W593/826 1,000,000 4/15 J.B.C. & A. A.D.S.S./Forms/C. 2118.

Instructions regarding War Diaries and Intelligence Summaries are contained in F. S. Regs., Part II. and the Staff Manual respectively. Title Pages will be prepared in manuscript.

WAR DIARY
or
~~INTELLIGENCE SUMMARY~~
(Erase heading not required.)

Army Form C. 2118

No: 112 Fld Ambce

Place	Date	Hour	Summary of Events and Information	Remarks and references to Appendices
NOEUX LES MINES	24/3/16		(cont) from St GEORGE, occasionally by day across open country to the NUNNERY, by night by trolley line during a special "marche" to VICTORIA STATION 36.C. G. 20. d. 6. 2, thence by Motor Ambulance Cars to NOEUX.	
			Other Ranks – Wounded	
			Transf. from 45. F A 10. Adm. 36. to C.C.S. 22. Rem. 24.	
			Sick	
			Tr. fr. 45 F A 5. Adm 12. to C.C.S. 2 Rem 19	
			Total 43	
			R.H.	
"	28/3/16		Officers. Sick. Adm. 2. to C.C.S. 2.	
			O.R. Wounded.	
			Rem. 24 Adm 13. To C.C.S. 19 Rem. 18	
			Sick	
			Rem. 19 Adm 60. To C.C.S. 19 Rem 60	
			Visited Adv. Dr Stns with D.A.D.M.S. R.H.	
"	29/3/16		O.R. Wounded. Rem 18. Adm 16. To C.C.S. 9. Rem 25.	
			Sick Rem 60. Adm 30. To Duty 8. To C.C.S. 21 Rem 61	
			Spent the night at Adv Dr Stn The NUNNERY & supervised working.	
			R.H.	

1875 Wt. W593/826 1,000,000 4/15 J.B.C. & A. A.D.S.S./Forms/C. 2118.

Instructions regarding War Diaries and Intelligence Summaries are contained in F. S. Regs., Part II. and the Staff Manual respectively. Title Pages will be prepared in manuscript.

WAR DIARY
~~or~~
~~INTELLIGENCE SUMMARY~~
(Erase heading not required.)

Army Form C. 2118

No: 112. Fld Ambce

Place	Date	Hour	Summary of Events and Information	Remarks and references to Appendices
NOEUX LES MINES	30/3/16		O. R. Wounded. Rem 25. Adm 18. To Duty 1. To C.C.S. 18. Rem 24. Sick. Rem 61. Adm 28. To Duty 7. To C.C.S. 17. Rem 65. Spent night at Adv. Dr. Stn ST GEORGE Dugout & supervised working R.J.H.	
"	31/3/16		O. R. Wounded Rem 24. Adm 13. To C.C.S. 14. Rem 23. Sick Rem 65. Adm 36. To Duty 5. To C.C.S. 29. Rem 67. Total 90. R. J. Hingleton Major RAMC	

1875 Wt. W593/826 1,000,000 4/15 J.B.C. & A. A.D.S.S./Forms/C. 2118.

112 Faml
Vol 5

16th Div

Confidential

War Diary
from
APRIL 1st 1916
to APRIL 30th 1916.
No: 112. Fld Ambce.

G. J. Houghton
Lt Col RAMC

April 1916

Instructions regarding War Diaries and Intelligence Summaries are contained in F. S. Regs., Part II. and the Staff Manual respectively. Title Pages will be prepared in manuscript.

WAR DIARY
or
~~INTELLIGENCE SUMMARY~~
(Erase heading not required.)

Army Form C. 2118

112. Field Ambulance

Place	Date	Hour	Summary of Events and Information	Remarks and references to Appendices
NOEUX LES MINES 36.B. 12.B.d.9.8	1/4/16		Officers. Wounded. Admitted 1 To C.C.S. 1 Sick " 1 " " 1 Other Ranks Wounded. Remaining 23. Admitted 20. To Duty 2. To C.C.S. 13. Rem 28 Sick. " 67. " 30 " " 10 " " 23 " 64 R. S. H[illegible] Major RAMC	
"	2/4/16		Offrs. Wd. Adm. 2 Tr. 2 Sick. Adm. 1 Tr. 1 Other Ranks. Wd. Rem. 28. Adm 16. To Duty 2. To C.C.S. 28. Rem 14. Sick. Rem 64 Adm 22 " " 10 " " 14 " 62 RSH	
"	3/4/16		Officers Sick. Adm. 2. C.C.S. 2. Other Ranks Wounded. Rem 14 Adm. 26 To C.C.S. 12 Rem 28. Sick. Rem 62. Adm 41. To Duty 21. To C.C.S. 12. Rem 40 RSH	

1875 Wt. W593/826 1,000,000 4/15 J.B.C. & A. A.D.S.S./Forms/C. 2118.

Instructions regarding War Diaries and Intelligence Summaries are contained in F. S. Regs., Part II. and the Staff Manual respectively. Title Pages will be prepared in manuscript.

WAR DIARY

or

~~INTELLIGENCE SUMMARY~~

(Erase heading not required.)

Army Form C. 2118

112. F A

Place	Date	Hour	Summary of Events and Information	Remarks and references to Appendices
NOEUX LES MINES.	4/4/16		Other Ranks. W.d. Rem 28. Adm 12. Duty 2. CCS. 21 Rem 17 Sick Rem 40. Adm 14. Duty 9 ✓ CCS 10. Rem 64 Rest Station 1 RJK RJK	
"	5/4/16		Officers Sick. Adm 1. CCS. 1 Other Ranks W.d. Rem 17. Adm 20. Duty 5 To CCS 12. Rem 20 Sick. Rem 64. Adm 21 Duty 1 To CCS 8. Rem 46 Capt E. C. Black. RAMC. No: 111. F.A. reported for temporary duty RJK.	
"	6/4/16		Other Ranks W.d. Rem. 20. Adm 36. Duty 3. To CCS. 26. Rem 27 Sick. " 46. " 13 " 16 ✓RJK " 10. " 60 To Rest Station 3 RJK	

1875 Wt. W593/826 1,000,000 4/15 J.B.C. & A. A.D.S.S./Forms/C. 2118.

Instructions regarding War Diaries and Intelligence Summaries are contained in F. S. Regs., Part II. and the Staff Manual respectively. Title Pages will be prepared in manuscript.

WAR DIARY
or
~~INTELLIGENCE SUMMARY~~ 112 F. A.

(Erase heading not required.)

Army Form C. 2118

Place	Date	Hour	Summary of Events and Information	Remarks and references to Appendices
MOEUX LES MINES.	7/4/16		Other Ranks. Wdd. Rem 27. Adm 11. C.C.S. 20. Rem. 18. Sick. Rem 60. Adm 12. To Duty 16. Rest Stn. 3. CCS. 4. Rem 49 QHK	
"	8/4/16		Officers – Sick. Adm 2. To CCS. 2. O.R. Wdd. Rem 18. Adm 6. To CCS 7 Rem. 17. Sick. Rem 49 Adm 26. To Duty 11. To CCS. 8. Rem 56 QHK.	
"	9/4/16		Officers. Wdd. Adm 1 To CCS. 1. Other Ranks. Wdd. Rem. 17. Adm 24. To Duty 1. To CCS 17. Rem 23. Sick Rem 56 " 15 " 11 " 8 Rem 52 Two High Explosive shells exploded in garden beside Ambulance Headquarters. Urinals damaged by earth shower – No casualties. QHK	
"	10/4/16		Officers. Wdd Adm to CCS. 1. Other Ranks. Wdd. Rem 23. Adm 16. Rest Stn 4. CCS. 17. Rem 18 Sick. Rem 52 " 20. To Duty 1. To Rest Stn. 2. To CCS. 21 Rem. 48 QHK.	

1875 Wt. W593/826 1,000,000 4/15 J.B.C. & A. A.D.S.S./Forms/C. 2118.

Instructions regarding War Diaries and Intelligence Summaries are contained in F. S. Regs., Part II. and the Staff Manual respectively. Title Pages will be prepared in manuscript.

WAR DIARY
or
~~INTELLIGENCE SUMMARY~~
(Erase heading not required.)

Army Form C. 2118

112 F.A

Place	Date	Hour	Summary of Events and Information	Remarks and references to Appendices
NOEUX LES MINES.	11/4/16		Other Ranks. Wded. Rem. 18 Adm 6. To Duty 1. To C.C.S. 14. Rem. 9 Sick. Rem. 48. Adm 6. To Duty 4. To C.C.S. 22. Rem. 48. RJH.	
"	12/4/16		Other Ranks. Wded. Rem. 9. Adm 8. Rest Stn. 2. C.C.S. 11. Rem. 4. Sick. Rem. 48. Adm 32. To Duty. 2. To Rest Stn 4. To C.C.S. 15. Rem. 59. RJH	
"	13/4/16		Officers Sick. Adm. 1. To C.C.S. 1. Other Ranks Wded. Rem. 4. Adm 10. To Rest Stn 1. Transferred. 10. Rem. 3 Sick. Rem. 59. Adm 19. To Duty 9. To Rest Stn 5. Transf. 16 Rem. 48.	
"	14/4/16		Other Ranks. Wded. Rem. 3. Adm. 15. Transf. 9. Rem. 9 RJH. Sick. Rem. 48. Adm 21. To Duty 5. To Rest Stn 6. Tr. 9. Rem. 49 Lieut. I. M. Frazer RAMC reported for duty on completion of temporary duty with 6th R. Irish Fus. RJH	

1875 Wt. W593/826 1,000,000 4/15 J.B.C. & A. A.D.S.S./Forms/C. 2118.

Instructions regarding War Diaries and Intelligence Summaries are contained in F. S. Regs., Part II. and the Staff Manual respectively. Title Pages will be prepared in manuscript.

WAR DIARY

or

~~INTELLIGENCE SUMMARY~~

(Erase heading not required.)

112. F.A.

Army Form C. 2118

Place	Date	Hour	Summary of Events and Information	Remarks and references to Appendices
NOEUX LES MINES	15/4/16		Officers. Wded 1. Tr. 1. Sick Adm 1. Tr. 1. Other Ranks. Wded. Rem 9. Adm. 12. Tr. 14. Rem 7 Sick. Rem 49. Adm 26. To Duty 1. Rest Stn. 6. Tr 15. Rem 53 Q.L.H.	
"	16/4/16		Other Ranks Wded. Rem 7. Adm 17. Rest Stn. 1. Tr 18. Rem 5 Sick. Rem 53. Adm 18. To Duty 2. Tr. 13. Rem 57. Capt 2. C. Black. RAMC returned to No. 111. F.A on completion of temporary duty. QLH	
"	17/4/16		Officers. Sick. Adm 1. Tr 1 O. R. Wded. Rem 5. Adm. 16. Tr 12. Rem. 9 Sick. Rem 57. Adm 24. To Duty 2. Tr 29. Rem 50. Lieut. A. D. Moffat. RAMC reported on completion of temporary duty with No. 1. Machine Gun Squadron. Construction of 4 Branch Advance Dressing Station Dug Outs in X[th] AVENUE commenced. QLH	

Army Form C. 2118

Instructions regarding War Diaries and Intelligence Summaries are contained in F. S. Regs., Part II. and the Staff Manual respectively. Title Pages will be prepared in manuscript.

WAR DIARY
or
INTELLIGENCE SUMMARY
(Erase heading not required.)

Place	Date	Hour	Summary of Events and Information	Remarks and references to Appendices
NOEUX LES MINES.	18/4/16		Other Ranks. Wded. Rem. 9. Adm. 10. Transf 8. Rem. 11. Sick. Rem. 50. Adm. 25. To Duty 6. To Rest Stn 1. Tr. 18. Died 1. Rem. 49. R.J.H.	
"	19/4/16		Other Ranks. Wded. Rem. 11. Adm. 20. To Rest Stn 1. Tr. 7. Rem. 23. Sick. Rem. 49. Adm. 29. To Duty 5. To Rest Stn 4. Tr. 21. Rem. 48. R.J.H.	
"	20/4/16		Officers. Wded. Adm. 1. Tr. 1. Sick. Adm. 1. Tr. 1. Other Ranks. Wded. Rem. 23. Adm. 4. Tr. 6. Rem. 21. Sick. Rem. 48. Adm. 33. To Duty. 3. Tr. 19. Rem. 39. R.J.H.	
"	21/4/16		Officers. Wded. Adm. 2. Tr. 2. Other Ranks. Wded. Rem. 21. Adm. 20. To Duty 1. To Rest Stn 1. Tr. 16. Rem. 23. Sick. Rem. 59. Adm. 18. To Duty. 4. To Rest Stn 2. Tr. 35. Rem. 36. R.J.H.	

1875 Wt. W593/826 1,000,000 4/15 J.B.C. & A. A.D.S.S./Forms/C. 2118.

Instructions regarding War Diaries and Intelligence Summaries are contained in F. S. Regs., Part II. and the Staff Manual respectively. Title Pages will be prepared in manuscript.

WAR DIARY
or
~~INTELLIGENCE SUMMARY~~
(Erase heading not required.)

112. F. A.

Army Form C. 2118

Place	Date	Hour	Summary of Events and Information	Remarks and references to Appendices
NOEUX LES MINES	22/4/16		Officers Wded. Adm 1. Tr 1. Other Ranks Wded. Rem. 23. Adm 13. To Duty 3. Tr. 10. Rem 23. Sick. Rem. 36 Adm 20. To Duty 4. Tr 12. Rem 40. Two new Branch A.D.S. in Xth AVENUE reported completed. RJH.	
"	23/4/16		Officers. Sick. Adm. 1 Tr 1 Other Ranks. Wded. Rem 23. Adm 11 To Duty 3 To Rest Stn. 2. Tr. 11 Rem. 18. Sick Rem. 40. Adm 33 To Duty 4 To Rest Stn 4. Tr 17 Rem. 48 RJH	
"	24/4/16		Officers. Sick. Adm 1. Tr 1. Other Ranks. Wded Rem. 18 Adm 8. Rest Stn 2 Tr. 8 Rem. 16 Sick. Rem 48 Adm 38. To Duty 3. To Rest Stn 4 Tr. 18 Rem. 61. ST. MARY (ABERDEEN) Dug-out. Adv Dr Stn handed over to 12th Div RJH.	

1875 Wt. W593/826 1,000,000 4/15 J.B.C. & A. A.D.S.S./Forms/C. 2118.

Instructions regarding War Diaries and Intelligence Summaries are contained in F. S. Regs., Part II. and the Staff Manual respectively. Title Pages will be prepared in manuscript.

WAR DIARY
or
~~INTELLIGENCE SUMMARY~~
(Erase heading not required.)

112. F.A.

Army Form C. 2118

Place	Date	Hour	Summary of Events and Information	Remarks and references to Appendices
NOEUX LES MINES	25/4/16		Officers – Sick. Adm 1. Tr. 1. Other Ranks – Wded. Rem. 16 Adm 26. To Rest Stn 1. Tr. 15. Rem 26. Sick. Rem. 61. Adm 24. To Duty 7. Rest Stn 5. Tr. 23. Rem. 51 RH	
"	26/4/16		Officers – Wded. Adm 2. Tr 2. Sick. Adm 2. Tr 2. Other Ranks – Wded. Rem. 26. Adm. 10. Rest Stn 1. Tr. 22. Rem. 13. Sick. Rem. 50 Adm 41. Duty 9. Rest Stn 5. Tr. 28. Rem. 49 RH	
"	27/4/16		Report of Gas Alarm & Attack received at 6 am. Evacuated by 12th MAC during morning. Reinforced Detachment in the Trenches at intervals during the Day. Wounded and Gassed men began to arrive early, & were evacuated by 12 M.A.C. at intervals as necessary. Ambulance cleared in Evening in expectation of heavy night evacuation from ST GEORGES ADS. Officers. Wd or Gassed. Adm 3. Tr. 3 O.R. Wd or Gassed. Rem. 13. Adm. 241. Tr 257. Died. 1. Rem. 2. Sick Rem. 49. Adm. 4. To Duty 5. To Rest Stn. 2. Tr 41. Rem 5. RH	

1875 Wt. W593/826 1,000,000 4/15 J.B.C. & A. A.D.S.S./Forms/C. 2118.

Instructions regarding War Diaries and Intelligence Summaries are contained in F. S. Regs., Part II. and the Staff Manual respectively. Title Pages will be prepared in manuscript.

WAR DIARY
or
~~INTELLIGENCE SUMMARY~~
(*Erase heading not required.*)

Army Form C. 2118

112. F.A.

Place	Date	Hour	Summary of Events and Information	Remarks and references to Appendices
NOEUX LES MINES	28/4/16		103 cases arrived during the night, and were evacuated early in this morning. (All figures are shown as from 9. AM on date to 9 AM. following day) Visited trenches in evening & found work progressing well Officers. Wded. Adm. 2. Tr. 1. To Duty 1. Other Ranks Wded. Rem. 2. Adm. 32. Tr 6. Died. 1. Rem 27. Sick Rem 5. Adm. 6. To Duty 1. Rem. 10. R.J.H.	
NOEUX LES MINES	29/4/16		Gas Alarm & attack reported at 4. AM Reinforcements of Officers and men at once despatched to the Trenches & further help applied for & obtained from ADMS. Visited the Trenches in the evening & found Trenches completely cleared of all known cases after careful search. by 8. P.M. Saw 56 wounded remaining at ST GEORGE & vicinity start, before returning to Headquarters. Officers. Wded. Adm 5. Tr 4. Rem. 1 Other Ranks - Wded. Rem 27. Adm 252. Tr. 184. Died. 6. Rem 91 Sick. Rem 10. Adm 25. Tr. 15. Rem. 20. R.J.H.	

1875 Wt. W593/826 1,000,000 4/15 J.B.C. & A. A.D.S.S./Forms/C. 2118.

Army Form C. 2118

Instructions regarding War Diaries and Intelligence Summaries are contained in F. S. Regs., Part II. and the Staff Manual respectively. Title Pages will be prepared in manuscript.

WAR DIARY
or
~~INTELLIGENCE SUMMARY~~
(Erase heading not required.)

112 F.A

Place	Date	Hour	Summary of Events and Information	Remarks and references to Appendices
NOEUX LES MINES	30/4/16		Officers Wded. Rem. 1 Adm. 3 Tr. 4 Rem. 0 Other Ranks. Wded Rem 91 Adm. 16 Tr. 81. Died 5. Rem. 21 Sick. Rem. 20 Adm 16 To Duty 2. Tr. 4 Rem. 30.	
			[illegible signature] Lt Col RAMC OC 112. F.A.	

1875 Wt. W593/826 1,000,000 4/15 J.B.C. & A. A.D.S.S./Forms/C. 2118.

112 F. Amb
Vol 6

WAR DIARY.

from

1st May to 31st May.

1916.

of

No: 112. Field Ambulance.

16th D

June/16

Instructions regarding War Diaries and Intelligence Summaries are contained in F. S. Regs., Part II. and the Staff Manual respectively. Title Pages will be prepared in manuscript.

WAR DIARY
~~or~~
~~INTELLIGENCE SUMMARY~~
(Erase heading not required.)

Army Form C. 2118

No: 112 Field Ambulance

Place	Date	Hour	Summary of Events and Information	Remarks and references to Appendices
NOEUX LES MINES 36.B. K.18.d 9.8	1/5/16		Officers. Wounded. Admitted 1. To Corps Rest Station 1 Sick. " 1. To Casualty Clearing Stn. 1 Other Ranks. Wdd. Remaining 21. Admitted 38. To C.C.S. 34. Died 2. Remaining 23. Sick. " 30. " 23. " 6. To Scabies Hosp 1. " 46 R. J. Houghton Lt Col. RAMC	
"	2/5/16		Other Ranks. W. Rem " 23 Adm " 14 To C.C.S. 17 Rem 20. S. Rem 46 " 24 To Duty 3 To C.C.S. 15 Rem 52 RJH	
"	3/5/16		Officers W. Adm 3. To Rest Stn 1 To C.C.S. 2. O.R. W. Rem 20. Adm 24 To Duty 1. To C.C.S. 19. Died 1 Rem 23. S Rem 52. Adm 29. To Duty 7. To CCS. 23. To Scabies Hosp 3. Rem 48 RJH	
"	4/5/16		O.R. W. Rem. 23. Adm. 12. To Duty 2 To Rest Stn 3. To CCS. 17 Rem 13 S. Rem 48 Adm 26 To Duty 1. To Rest Stn 3. To CCS. 27 To Scabies Hosp 1 Rem 42. RJH	
"	5/5/16		Officers. W. 1 To Duty. 1. O.R. W. Rem. 13. Adm. 26. To CCS 12 Rem 27 S. Rem 42. Adm 32. To Duty. 1 To CCS. 14 To Scab. Hosp 10 Rem 46. RJH.	

1875 Wt. W593/826 1,000,000 4/15 J.B.C. & A. A.D.S.S./Forms/C. 2118.

Army Form C. 2118

Instructions regarding War Diaries and Intelligence Summaries are contained in F. S. Regs., Part II. and the Staff Manual respectively. Title Pages will be prepared in manuscript.

WAR DIARY
~~or~~
~~INTELLIGENCE SUMMARY~~

(Erase heading not required.)

112. F A

Place	Date	Hour	Summary of Events and Information	Remarks and references to Appendices
NOEUX LES MINES	6/5/16		O.R. W. Rem 27. Adm 8. To CCS 22. Rem 13. S. Rem 46 Adm 28 To Duty 3. To Rest Stn. 6. To CCS 15. To Scab. Hosp 2. Rem 48. A ration-party of the Ambulance was struck by a shell at VICTORIA STATION 36.C. 9.20. d. 7.2. at 10.30 P.M. One private was mortally wounded and one Sergeant and two privates wounded. R.H.	
"	7/5/16		O.R. W. Rem. 13. Adm. 19. To CCS 9. Died 1. Remaining 22. S. Rem. 48. Adm. 25. To Duty 4. To C.C.S. 12. To Rest Stn. 1. Scabies Hosp. 2. Rem. 54. R.H.	
"	8/5/16		O.R. W. Rem. 22. Adm. 21. To Duty 4. To CCS. 19. Rem 20. S. Rem. 54. Adm. 13 To Duty 2. To CCS. 19. Scabies Hosp. 1. Rem 45. R.H.	
"	9/5/16		Officers. Sick. Adm. 1. To. C.C.S. 1 O.R. W. Rem 20 Adm 9. To Duty 1. To CCS. 18. Rem 10. S. Rem 45 Adm 15. To Duty 9. To CCS. 12. To Scab. Hosp 1. Rem 38 R.H.	

1875 Wt. W593/826 1,000,000 4/15 J.B.C. & A. A.D.S.S./Forms/C. 2118.

Army Form C. 2118

Instructions regarding War Diaries and Intelligence Summaries are contained in F. S. Regs., Par. II. and the Staff Manual respectively. Title Pages will be prepared in manuscript.

WAR DIARY
or
~~INTELLIGENCE SUMMARY~~
(Erase heading not required.)

112. F. A.

Place	Date	Hour	Summary of Events and Information	Remarks and references to Appendices
NOEUX LES MINES	10/5/16		Officers. S. Adm 2 To CCS. 2 O.R. W. Rem 10. Adm 22. To Duty 2. To C.C.S. 11. Rem 19 S. Rem 38. Adm 16. To Duty 4. To C.C.S. 13. Rem 37 R.J.H.	
"	11/5/16		Officers. W. Adm 3. To CCS. 3. O.R. W. Rem 19. Adm 24. To Duty 1. To C.C.S. 24 Rem 21. S. Rem 37. Adm 21. To Duty 6 To C.C.S. 20. Rem 32. R.J.H.	
"	12/5/16		Other Ranks. W. Rem 21 Adm 11. To Duty 2 To CCS. 18. Rem 12. S. Rem 32 Adm 20. To Duty 3. To CCS. 18. To Scabies Hosp 1. Rem 30 R.J.H.	
"	13/5/16		Officers S. Adm 1. To CCS. 1. O.R. W. Rem 12. Adm 6. To CCS. 9. Rem 9. S. Rem 30. Adm 15. To Duty 5. To CCS. 13. Rem 27 R.J.H.	
"	14/5/16		O.R. W. Rem 9. Adm 17. To Duty 1. To CCS. 9. Rem 16. S. Rem 27. Adm 19. To Duty 3 To CCS 12. Rem 31. A large shell struck the end of a wing of the Adv Dr. Stn The NUNNERY & removed the end wall of the Nuns private chapel & the Detachment Billet overhead. The Nuns decided to leave. R.J.H.	

1875 Wt. W593/826 1,000,000 4/15 J.B.C. & A. A.D.S.S./Forms/C. 2118.

Army Form C. 2118

Instructions regarding War Diaries and Intelligence Summaries are contained in F. S. Regs., Part II. and the Staff Manual respectively. Title Pages will be prepared in manuscript.

WAR DIARY ~~or INTELLIGENCE SUMMARY~~

(Erase heading not required.)

112. F.A.

Place	Date	Hour	Summary of Events and Information	Remarks and references to Appendices
NOEUX LES MINES	15/5/16		Officers. W. Adm 1. To CCS 1. S. Adm 1. To CCS. 1. O.R. W. Rem 16 Adm 4 To CCS. 11. Rem 9. S. Rem 31. Adm 22. To Duty 6. To CCS. 13. To Scabies Hosp 1. Rem 23 Lieut M.H. Embree left for temporary duty with 6th Connaught Rangers. RJH	
"	16/5/16		Officers. W. Adm 1. CCS. 1. S. Adm 1 CCS. 1. O.R. W. Rem 9. Adm 9. To Duty 1. To CCS 4. Rem 6 S. Rem 33. Adm 19. To Duty 4. To CCS. 13. Rem 35 Yesterday the Transfer of the HULLUCH SECTOR to the XVIth Divn was completed including the handing over of the Branch Adv. Dr. Stns in Xth AVENUE between WINGS WAY & VENDIN ALLEY. ST. GEORGE Adv Dr Stn remains in our charge. RJH	
"	17/5/16		O.R. W. Rem 6. Adm 8. Transf from 141 F.A. 1. To CCS. 9. Rem 6 S. Rem 35. Adm 16 To Duty 3 To CCS. 18. To Scabies Hosp 1. Rem 29. RJH	
"	18/5/16		Officers. Sick. Adm 1. To CCS. 1 O.R. W. Rem 6. Adm 6. To Duty 2. To CCS. 3. Rem 7. S. Rem 29. Adm 14. To Duty 7. To CCS. 11. Rem 25. RJH	

1875 Wt. W593/826 1,000,000 4/15 J.B.C. & A. A.D.S.S./Forms/C. 2118.

Army Form C. 2118

Instructions regarding War Diaries and Intelligence Summaries are contained in F. S. Regs., Part II. and the Staff Manual respectively. Title Pages will be prepared in manuscript.

WAR DIARY
or
~~INTELLIGENCE SUMMARY~~
(Erase heading not required.)

112. F. A.

Place	Date	Hour	Summary of Events and Information	Remarks and references to Appendices
NOEUX LES MINES	19/5/16		Officers W. Adm 1. To CCS. 1. S. Adm 3. To CCS. 3 O.R. W. Rem 7. Adm 12. To CCS 11. Rem. 8. S. Rem 28. Adm 12. To Duty 2. To CCS 11. Rem 27. Two new Branch ADS Dr Stns completed and taken over in Xth AVENUE. Can hold lying - 6 - 8 cases & sitting 6 in each. Ref Diagrammatic Trench Map. - 23.B.1.3 & 29.A.2.9 Lieut. A. D. Moffat left for Temporary Duty with 9th R Munster Fusrs. GHH.	
"	20/5/16		Officers Sick Adm. 1. To CCS 1 O.R. W. Rem 8. Adm 4. To Duty 1. To CCS. 2. Rem 9. S. Rem 27. Adm 24. To Duty 4. To CCS. 16. To Scabies Hosp. 1. Rem 30. Received a re-inforcement of 8. privates A shell, - probably German Anti-Aircraft, - came through roof of new billet at NUNNERY. GHH	
"	21/5/16		O.R. W. Rem 9. Adm 27. To CCS. 11. Died ~~[illegible]~~ 3. Rem 22. GHH S. Rem 30. Adm 27. To CCS. 27. Rem 30. A shell, - probably German Anti-aircraft - came through the roof of the store-room - the NUNNERY. NOEUX was shelled in the afternoon. Three O.R. killed (cont)	

Army Form C. 2118

Instructions regarding War Diaries and Intelligence Summaries are contained in F. S. Regs., Part II. and the Staff Manual respectively. Title Pages will be prepared in manuscript.

WAR DIARY or ~~INTELLIGENCE SUMMARY~~

(Erase heading not required.)

112 F.A.

Place	Date	Hour	Summary of Events and Information	Remarks and references to Appendices
NOEUX LES MINES	21/5/16 cont.		& 11. O.R. Wounded were brought in to this F.A. including 1 severely & 1 slightly wounded belonging to this Unit. Lieut L. M. Frazer. RAMC left for Temp. Med. Charge. of 7th Leinster Regt. GJH	
"	22/5/16		O.R. W. Rem 22. Adm 6. To CCS. 13. Rem 15 S. Rem 30. Adm 22. To Duty. 2. To CCS. 22. Rem 28 Work started on fortification of NUNNERY with corrugated steel arches & sandbags. GJH	
"	23/5/16		Officers. S. Adm 1. CCS. 1. O.R. W. Rem 15. Adm 5. To Duty. 2 To CCS. 12. Rem 6 S. Rem 28. Adm 21. To Duty 2. To CCS. 13. Rem 34 GJH	
"	24/5/16		Officers. W. Adm 1. To CCS. 1 O.R. W. Rem 6. Adm 9. To CCS. 6. Rem 9 S. Rem 34. Adm 16. To Duty 1. To CCS. 22. To Scabies Hosp 1. Rem 26 GJH	

Instructions regarding War Diaries and Intelligence Summaries are contained in F. S. Regs., Part II. and the Staff Manual respectively. Title Pages will be prepared in manuscript.

WAR DIARY

~~or~~

~~INTELLIGENCE SUMMARY~~

(Erase heading not required.)

Army Form C. 2118

112. F A.

Place	Date	Hour	Summary of Events and Information	Remarks and references to Appendices
NOEUX LES MINES.	25/5/16		Officers. W. Adm 1. To CCS. 1. S. Adm 1. To Rest Stn. 1. O.R. W. Rem 9 Adm 8. To Duty 4. To CCS 6. Rem 7. S. Rem 26 Adm 16. To Duty. 5. To CCS. 12. To Scabies Hosp. 1. Rem 24. Q.I.K.	
"	26/5/16		O.R. W. Rem 7 Adm 13. To Duty 1. To CCS. 7 Rem 12 S. Rem 24. Adm 16. To Duty 1. To CCS. 10. Rem 29. Received a reinforcement of 18 privates. Q.I.K.	
"	27/5/16		O.R.W. Rem 12. Adm 1 CCS. 6. Rem 7 S. Rem 29. Adm 27. To Duty 4. To CCS. 17. To Scabies Hosp. 1. Rem 34. Lieut M. H. Embree rejoined from Temporary Duty with 6th Connaught Rangers Q.I.K.	
"	28/5/16		Officers W. Adm. 1. To CCS. 1 O.R. W. Rem 7. Adm 17. To CCS. 2 Rem 22 S. Rem 34. Adm 20. To CCS. 8. To Scabies Hosp 3. Rem 43 Lieut. P.W. Barker left for Temp Duty with 9th R. Dublin Fusiliers Q.I.K.	

1875 Wt. W593/826 1,000,000 4/15 J.B.C. & A. A.D.S.S./Forms/C. 2118.

Instructions regarding War Diaries and Intelligence Summaries are contained in F. S. Regs., Part II. and the Staff Manual respectively. Title Pages will be prepared in manuscript.

WAR DIARY
~~or~~
~~INTELLIGENCE SUMMARY~~
(Erase heading not required.)

Army Form C. 2118

112. F.A.

Place	Date	Hour	Summary of Events and Information	Remarks and references to Appendices
NOEUX LES MINES	29/5/16		O.R. W. Rem 22. Adm 21. To Duty 3. To CCS. 24. Rem 16. S. Rem 43. Adm 28. To Duty 11 To CCS. 11 To Scabies Hosp 1. Rem 48. Received a re-inforcement of 1 Sergeant. QKH	
"	30/5/16		Officers Sick Adm 2. To CCS. 2. O.R. W. Rem 16. Adm 11. To Duty 1. To CCS. 12. Rem 14. S. Rem 48. Adm 29. To Duty 5. To CCS. 23 To Scabies Hosp. 2. Rem 47 Lieut A D Moffat returned from Temporary Duty with 9th R. Munster Fus. QKH	
"	31/5/16		Officers S. Adm 1. To CCS. 1. O.R. W. Rem 14. Adm 4. To CCS. 9. Rem 9 S. Rem 47. Adm 29. To Duty 6. To CCS. 23 To Scabies Hosp. 2. Rem 45 Q. Houghton Lt Col RAMC	

112 Amb
Vol 7
June

CONFIDENTIAL

War Diary

7

No: 112. Field Ambulance

from. 1.6.1916. to 30.6.1916

June/16

M.H. 313.

A.G. at the BASE

Herewith War Diary of
No: 112 Field Ambulance
from 1.6.16 to 30.6.16.

[illegible]
Lt Col RAMC
O.C. 112. F.A.

6.7.16

Instructions regarding War Diaries and Intelligence Summaries are contained in F. S. Regs., Part II. and the Staff Manual respectively. Title Pages will be prepared in manuscript.

WAR DIARY
or
~~INTELLIGENCE SUMMARY~~
(Erase heading not required.)

Army Form C. 2118

No: 112 Field Ambulance

Place	Date	Hour	Summary of Events and Information	Remarks and references to Appendices
NOEUX LES MINES 36.B K.18.d.98	1/6/16		Officers - Sick, Admitted 1 To Casualty Clearing Station 1 Other Ranks - Wounded. Remaining 9 Admitted 6 To Duty 3 To Casualty Clearing Station 3 Remaining 9 Sick Rem 45 Adm 36. To Duty 13. To C C S. 15. Rem 53 R.J. Hong[illegible] RAMC.	
"	2/6/16		Officers Sick Adm. 1 To CCS. 1 O.R. W. Rem 9 Adm. 10. To CCS. 12 Rem. 7. S. Rem 53 Adm. 33. To Duty 5. To C.C.S. 16. Rest Station 3 Rem. 62. RJH.	
"	3/6/16		O.R. W Rem. 7. Adm 11. To CCS. 11. Rem 7. S. Rem 62 Adm 23 To Duty. 13. To CCS. 35. Rem. 37 RJH.	
"	4/6/16		Officers. S. Adm 2. CCS. 2 O.R. W. Rem 7 Adm 6. C.C.S. 9 Rem 4 S. Rem 37. Adm 23. To Duty 4. C.C.S. 6. Rem 50. G.O.C. 1st Corps presented ribbons of Military Medal to Sergeant Jones & Private Ward on Divisional Parade. Corpl Pharaoh also awarded Medal, but absent on leave in England RJH	

1875 Wt. W593/826 1,000,000 4/15 J.B.C. & A. A.D.S.S./Forms/C. 2118.

Army Form C. 2118

Instructions regarding War Diaries and Intelligence Summaries are contained in F. S. Regs., Part II. and the Staff Manual respectively. Title Pages will be prepared in manuscript.

WAR DIARY
or
~~INTELLIGENCE SUMMARY~~
(Erase heading not required.)

No. 112. F. A

Place	Date	Hour	Summary of Events and Information	Remarks and references to Appendices
NOEUX LES MINES	5/6/16		Officers S. Adm 1 To C.C.S. 1. O.R. W. Rem 4 Adm 6 To Duty 1 To C.C.S. 1 Rem 8 S. Rem 50 Adm 32 To Duty 3. To C.C.S. 13 To Scabies Hosp 3 Rem. 63 Q.I.H.	
"	6/6/16		Officers. W. Adm 1. To C.C.S. 1 S. Adm 1. To C.C.S. 1 Other Ranks. W. Rem 8. Adm 16. To C.C.S. 10. Rem. 14. S. Rem 63. Adm 15 To Duty 8. To C.C.S. 33. Rem 34 Q.I.H.	
"	7/6/16		O.R. W. Rem 14. Adm 6. To Duty 1. To C.C.S. 10. Rem. 9 S. Rem 37. Adm 19 To Duty 3 To C.C.S. 25. Rem 28 Q.I.H.	
"	8/6/16		Officers. W. Adm 1. To C.C.S. 1 O.R. W. Rem. 9 Adm 6. To C.C.S. 4 Rem. 11 S. Rem 28. Adm 13. To C.C.S. 16 Rem 25 Q.I.H.	

1875 Wt. W593/826 1,000,000 4/15 J.B.C. & A. A.D.S.S./Forms/C. 2118.

Army Form C. 2118

Instructions regarding War Diaries and Intelligence Summaries are contained in F. S. Regs., Part II. and the Staff Manual respectively. Title Pages will be prepared in manuscript.

WAR DIARY
~~or~~
~~INTELLIGENCE SUMMARY~~

(Erase heading not required.)

No: 112. F.A.

Place	Date	Hour	Summary of Events and Information	Remarks and references to Appendices
NOEUX LES MINES	9/6/16		Officers. S Adm 1. To C.C.S. 1 O.R. W. Rem 11. Adm 2. To C.C.S. 6 To Rest Stn 6. Rem 3 S. Rem 25. Adm 10. To Duty 3 To C.C.S. 13 Rem 19 Q1H	
"	10/6/16		O.R. W. Rem 3. Adm 6. To C.C.S. 4 Rem. 5. S. Rem 19. Adm 15. To Duty 2. To C.C.S. 15. Rem 17. Q1H	
"	11/6/16		O.R. W. Rem 5 Adm 11. To C.C.S. 14. Rem. 2. S. Rem 17 Adm 17 To Duty 3 To Rest Station 1 To C.C.S. 9 Rem 21 Q1H	
"	12/6/16		O.R. W. Rem 2. Adm 8 To C.C.S. 6. Rem 4 S. Rem 21 Adm 13. To Duty 2 To C.C.S. 7 Rem 25 Q1H	

1875 Wt. W593/826 1,000,000 4/15 J.B.C. & A. A.D.S.S./Forms/C. 2118.

Instructions regarding War Diaries and Intelligence Summaries are contained in F. S. Regs., Part II. and the Staff Manual respectively. Title Pages will be prepared in manuscript.

WAR DIARY
or
~~INTELLIGENCE SUMMARY~~
(Erase heading not required.)

Army Form C. 2118

No. 112 F.A.

Place	Date	Hour	Summary of Events and Information	Remarks and references to Appendices
NOEUX LES MINES	13/6/16		Officers. W. Adm 1. To CCS. 1. S. Adm 2. To Rest Station 1. Remaining 1. (Lieut T. F. Saunders RAMC) O.R. W. Rem 4. Adm 1. To C.C.S. 1. Rem 4. S. Rem 25. Adm 30. To CCS. 19. Rem. 36 QIK	
"	14/6/16		Officers. Sick. Rem. 1 O.R. W. Rem 4. Adm 3. To C.C.S. 2. Rem 5. S. Rem 36. Adm 24. To Duty 10. To C.C.S. 19. Rem 31 QIK	
"	15/6/16		Officers. W. Adm. 2. To CCS. 2 S. Rem. 1. Adm. 1. To Duty 1. To CCS. 1. Rem 0. O.R. W. Rem 5. Adm. 9. To CCS. 9. Rem 5. S. Rem 31. Adm 24. To Duty 1. To Rest Stn. 3. To CCS. 11. Rem 43. Branch Advanced Dressing Station 350 yards up CHALKPIT ALLEY completed. QIK	
"	16/6/16		Officers W. Adm 2. To CCS. 2 S. Adm 3. To CCS. 3 O.R. W. Rem 5. Adm 11. To CCS. 9. Rem 7. S. Rem 43. Adm 18. To Duty 4. To CCS. 21. Rem 36. Branch Advanced Dr Stn at foot of CHALKPIT ALLEY dismantled for reconstruction QIK	

Instructions regarding War Diaries and Intelligence Summaries are contained in F. S. Regs., Part II. and the Staff Manual respectively. Title Pages will be prepared in manuscript.

WAR DIARY
or
~~INTELLIGENCE SUMMARY~~
(Erase heading not required.)

Army Form C. 2118

No. 112. F A

Place	Date	Hour	Summary of Events and Information	Remarks and references to Appendices
NOEUX LES MINES.	17/6/16		O.R. W. Rem 7. Adm 9 To Duty 1. To CCS. 6. Rem 9 S. Rem 36. Adm 18 To Duty 4. To CCS. 15. Rem 35. Q.H.	
"	18/6/16		Officers. S Adm 2. To CCS. 2 O.R W Rem 9. Adm 1. To CCS. 9 Rem 1 S. Rem 35. Adm 18. To Duty 7. To CCS. 9 To Scabies Hosp 1. Rem 36 Q.H.	
"	19/6/16		Officers. W. Adm 1 To CCS. 1 O.R. W. Rem 1 Adm 10. To CCS. 6 Died 1 Rem 4 S. Rem 36 Adm 26 To Duty 2. To Rest Stn 3. To CCS. 14 To Scabies Hosp 1 Rem 42. Q.H.	
"	20/6/16		O.R. W. Rem 4. Adm 2. To Duty 1 To CCS. 1. Rem 4 S. Rem 42. Adm 26. To Duty 5 To CCS. 19. To Scabies Hosp 1 Rem 43 Q.H.	
"	21/6/16		O.R. W Rem 4 Adm 8 To CCS. 7 Rem 5. S. Rem 43. Adm 39. To Duty 4. To CCS. 25. Rem 53. B Section 137. F.A. arrived for Training with this Unit. strength. 3 offrs. 60 O.R. which was divided up equally in 3 detachments, one at Headqrs, one at NUNNERY A.D.S. & one in the Trenches. each party doing 3 days at each station Q.H.	

1875 Wt. W593/826 1,000,000 4/15 J.B.C. & A. A.D.S.S./Forms/C. 2118.

Army Form C. 2118

Instructions regarding War Diaries and Intelligence Summaries are contained in F. S. Regs., Part II. and the Staff Manual respectively. Title Pages will be prepared in manuscript.

WAR DIARY

~~or~~

~~INTELLIGENCE SUMMARY~~

(Erase heading not required.)

No. 112 F A

Place	Date	Hour	Summary of Events and Information	Remarks and references to Appendices
NOEUX LES MINES	22/6/16		Officers W. Adm 1. CCS. 1. O.R. W. Rem 5. Adm 4. To C.C.S. 4 Rem 5. S. Rem 53. Adm 31. To Duty. 7. To CCS. 34. To Scabies Hosp 1. Rem 42. R.H.	
"	23/6/16		O.R. W. Rem 5. Adm 5. To Duty 1. To CCS. 4. Rem 5. S. Rem 42. Adm 41. To Duty 4. Rest Stn. 3. To C.C.S. 29. To Scabies Hosp 1 Rem 46 R.H.	
"	24/6/16		Officers. W. Adm 1. To CCS. 1. S. Adm 1 To CCS. 1. O.R. W. Rem 5. Adm 10. to Duty 1. To C.C.S. 4 ~~Adm~~ Rem. 10. S. Rem 46. Adm 41. To Duty. 7. To C.C.S. 27. To Scabies Hosp. 1. Rem 52 R.H.	
"	25/6/16.		Officers. S. Adm 1. CCS. 1. O.R W. Rem 10. Adm. 25. To Duty 1. To CCS. 16. Rem 18. S. Rem 52. Adm 34. To Duty 6. To Rest Stn. 1. To CCS. 38 Rem 41. R.H.	

1875 Wt. W593/826 1,000,000 4/15 J.B.C. & A. A.D.S.S./Forms/C. 2118.

Instructions regarding War Diaries and Intelligence Summaries are contained in F. S. Regs., Part II. and the Staff Manual respectively. Title Pages will be prepared in manuscript.

WAR DIARY

~~or~~

~~INTELLIGENCE SUMMARY~~

(Erase heading not required.)

Army Form C. 2118

No: 112. F A.

Place	Date	Hour	Summary of Events and Information	Remarks and references to Appendices
NOEUX LES MINES	26/6/16		Officers. W. Adm 1. CCS. 1 S. Adm 1 To CCS. 1. O.R W. Rem. 18. Adm 8. To CCS. 18. Rem 8. S. Rem 41. Adm 25. To Duty. 7 To CCS 11. To Scabies Hosp. 2. Rem 46. Captains. A.B. Bateman RAMC & J E M Wigley RAMC. reported arrival for Duty R.H.	
"	27/6/16		Officers. W. Adm 1. To CCS. 1 O.R. W. Rem 8 Adm 16. To Duty 3. To CCS. 15. Rem 6. S. Rem 46. Adm 25. To Duty 7 To Rest Stn 3 To CCS. 24. To Scabies Hosp 1 Rem 36. Lieut A.J. Ferguson left for temporary Medical Charge 7th Bn R. Irish Fusiliers. R.H.	
"	28/6/16		Officers. W. Adm. 1. To CCS. 1. O.R W. Rem. 6. Adm 53. To Duty. 1 To CCS. 41. Rem 17. S. Rem 36. Adm 32. To Duty. 4. To CCS 24. Rem 40. R.H.	

1875 Wt. W593/826 1,000,000 4/15 J.B.C. & A. A.D.S.S./Forms/C. 2118.

Instructions regarding War Diaries and Intelligence Summaries are contained in F. S. Regs., Part II. and the Staff Manual respectively. Title Pages will be prepared in manuscript.

WAR DIARY
~~or~~
~~INTELLIGENCE SUMMARY~~
(Erase heading not required.)

Army Form C. 2118

No: 112. F.A.

Place	Date	Hour	Summary of Events and Information	Remarks and references to Appendices
NOEUX LES MINES	29/6/16		Officers. W. Adm 1. To C.C.S. 1. O.R. W Rem 17. Adm 33. To Duty 1. To C.C.S. 29. Rem 22 S. Rem 40. Adm 36 To Duty 8. To C.C.S. 18 To Scabies Hosp. 1. Rem. 49. A.D.M.S. 16th Div presented Divisional Parchment certificates to Sergeant Jones, acting-Sergeant Pharoah & pte (acting Corporal) Ward, and the Military Medal Ribbon to Acting Sergeant Pharoah RJH	
"	30/6/16		Officers. W. Adm 1. To C.C.S. 1. O.R. W. Rem 22. Adm 17 To CCS 27 Died 1. Rem. 11 S. Rem 49. Adm 38. To Duty 4 To C.C.S. 23. To Scabies Hosp. 4. Rem 56. Captain J. E M. Wigley left for Duty with 9th Bn R. Dublin Fusls, vice Lieut. P. W. Barker, who returned to this Unit 137. F.A. B. Section, returned to their own headquarters at the conclusion of their training. Repairs completed to B.A.D.S. at foot of CHALKPIT ALLEY, & B.A.D.S. again taken into use. R. J. Hamilton Lt Col RAMC.	

1875 Wt. W593/826 1,000,000 4/15 J.B.C. & A. A.D.S.S./Forms/C. 2118.

11th Division

112th Field Ambulance

July 1916

16

W A R   D I A R Y

112th Field Amb.
RAMC

1st. July 1916 to 31st. Huly 1916.

VOLUME No. 8.

Army Form C. 2118

Instructions regarding War Diaries and Intelligence Summaries are contained in F. S. Regs., Part II. and the Staff Manual respectively. Title Pages will be prepared in manuscript.

WAR DIARY

~~or~~

~~INTELLIGENCE SUMMARY~~

(Erase heading not required.)

No: 112 Field Ambulance.

Place	Date	Hour	Summary of Events and Information	Remarks and references to Appendices
NOEUX LES MINES 36.B K.18.d.9.8	1/7/16		Routine. B. L. Hamilton Lt Col RAMC	
"	2/7/16		Routine. B.L.H.	
"	3/7/16		Routine. B.L.H.	
"	4/7/16		Routine. B.L.H.	
"	5/7/16		Lieut A. D. Moffat left for temporary Duty with 16th Divnl R. Engineers. B.L.H.	
"	6/7/16		Routine. B.L.H.	

1875 Wt. W593/826 1,000,000 4/15 J.B.C. & A. A.D.S.S./Forms/C. 2118.

Instructions regarding War Diaries and Intelligence Summaries are contained in F. S. Regs., Part II. and the Staff Manual respectively. Title Pages will be prepared in manuscript.

WAR DIARY
~~or~~
~~INTELLIGENCE SUMMARY~~
(Erase heading not required.)

Army Form C. 2118

112. F.A.

Place	Date	Hour	Summary of Events and Information	Remarks and references to Appendices
NOEUX LES MINES.	7/4/16		One Private RAWLE received as re-inforcement. At 11.30 P.M. a raid with Gas was made in 14 bis Sector. The Troops returned to their Trenches at 3. A.M. 50 Battle Casualties passed through 112. F.A. mostly caused by shell-fire. 6 cases of Drift Gas poisoning are included in above, 4 from lying in shell-craters, & 2 accidentally in our own trenches.	
"	8/4/16		Routine. RJH	
"	9/4/16		One of my Motor Ambulance Cars when proceeding through PHILOSOPHE without lights according to Divisional orders, knocked down two soldiers. Neither was much hurt, and both admitted that the Car was going dead slow. RJH	
"	10/4/16		Routine RJH	
"	11/4/16		In view of the large number of P.U.O. cases occurring in the personnel of this Unit, I commenced a complete investigation for possible carriers of Enteric Group. None found at Headquarters. RJH	
"	12/4/16		Routine RJH	

1875 Wt. W593/826 1,000,000 4/15 J.B.C. & A. A.D.S.S./Forms/C. 2118.

Instructions regarding War Diaries and Intelligence Summaries are contained in F. S. Regs., Part II. and the Staff Manual respectively. Title Pages will be prepared in manuscript.

WAR DIARY
or
~~INTELLIGENCE SUMMARY~~
(Erase heading not required.)

Army Form C. 2118

No 112. F.A.

Place	Date	Hour	Summary of Events and Information	Remarks and references to Appendices
NOEUX LES MINES	13/4/16		Lieut A. J. Ferguson returned from Temporary Duty with 9th R. I. Fusls. Report from Adv. D. Stn. — no possible carriers of Enteric group. GJH	
"	14/4/16		Routine GJH	
"	15/4/16		Routine GJH	
"	16/4/16		Routine GJH.	
"	17/4/16		Rev W. McNutt. C.F. (Presbyterian) attached to 112. F.A. left on termination of contract. GJH.	
"	18/4/16		New Branch Advanced Dressing Station in Xth Avenue taken over from R.E. The excavations for all the Branch A.D.S. have been made by the personnel of this F A & the building completed by R.E or Pioneers. Medical Arrangements in 14 Bis Sector are now considered as complete, and are as follows:—	

1875 Wt. W593/826 1,000,000 4/15 J.B.C. & A. A.D.S.S./Forms/C. 2118.

Instructions regarding War Diaries and Intelligence Summaries are contained in F. S. Regs., Part II. and the Staff Manual respectively. Title Pages will be prepared in manuscript.

WAR DIARY
~~or~~
~~INTELLIGENCE SUMMARY~~
(Erase heading not required.)

Army Form C. 2118

112 . F.A.

Place	Date	Hour	Summary of Events and Information	Remarks and references to Appendices
NOEUX LES MINES	18/4/16	Continued	Ref – Diagrammatic Trench MAP. 1 10000. 33.C	
			Regimental AID POSTS.	
			PONT STREET. G.24 A. 1½. 4	
			GUN TRENCH G. 30. A. 8½. 3.	
			Xth AVENUE. G. 29. A. ½. 8.	
			Situation Normal. Distribution of Personnel. Officers. Other Ranks	
			F.A. ADV. Drg STN. DUGOUT ST. GEORGE. G. 23. B. 5. 8. 1 11	
			Branch. A.D.S. Dugouts.	
			Xth AVENUE – POSEN ALLEY. G. 23. B. 1. 3 5	
			Xth AVENUE – CHALKPIT ALLEY. G. 29. A 2. 9½ 5	
			Xth AVENUE RESERVE G. 29. A. 1½. 9 2	
			CHALKPIT ALLEY G. 29. A 9. 8 7	
			Total 1 30	
			ADVANCED DRESSING STATION	
			NUNNERY. PHILOSOPHE Officers O.R.	
			Ref. FRANCE 33.C. (4th Ed)n G. 13. d. 1. 7. 1 30.	
			F.A. HEADQUARTERS.	
			Ref. 33B. K. 18. d. 9. 8.	

1875 Wt. W593/826 1,000,000 4/15 J.B.C. & A. A.D.S.S./Forms/C. 2118.

Instructions regarding War Diaries and Intelligence Summaries are contained in F. S. Regs., Part II. and the Staff Manual respectively. Title Pages will be prepared in manuscript.

WAR DIARY
or
~~INTELLIGENCE SUMMARY~~
(Erase heading not required.)

Army Form C. 2118

112. F.A.

Place	Date	Hour	Summary of Events and Information	Remarks and references to Appendices
NOEUX LES MINES.	18/4/16	Cont.	Of the personnel at the NUNNERY 1 NCO & 14 Bearers are kept there as reserve for re-inforcing the Detachment in the Trenches, & can be obtained at any time on demand of O/c ST GEORGE. Arrangements are also made for a re-inforcement of 1 M.O & 24 Other Ranks from Headquarters for the Trenches & 1 MO for the NUNNERY. On demand of a Regimental M.O or arrival of the first of a series of wounded at the nearest Br. A.D Sh. Dugout the F.A Bearers take up the work of carrying Wounded back from the AID POSTS. Owing to the limited accommodation in ST GEORGE this was previously only possible occasionally until my suggestion of Branch A.D.S's was carried out. Previously far too much work was thrown on the Regimental Stretcher-bearers. Normally all patients pass through ST. GEORGE, but in case of heavy fighting one MO would establish himself in CHALKPIT ALLEY. B.A.D.S & send back walking cases direct from there as from the nature of things those from a very long stretch of Front would all pass this DUGOUT. By day walking cases, & men on wheeled stretchers can be sent across the open plain to the NUNNERY. The main evacuation from ST GEORGE is by trolley-line after dark to KINGSBRIDGE STATION. 36.C.G 20.C 3.3. Cases arriving by trolley normally proceed direct to Headquarters NOEUX by Motor Ambce. Car. Cases requiring to be sent direct to CCS if present are dealt with by special arrangement. In case of heavy casualties all cases pass the NUNNERY and are sorted out there R.H.	

1875 Wt. W593/826 1,000,000 4/15 J.B.C. & A. A.D.S.S./Forms/C. 2118.

Instructions regarding War Diaries and Intelligence Summaries are contained in F. S. Regs., Part II. and the Staff Manual respectively. Title Pages will be prepared in manuscript.

WAR DIARY
or
~~INTELLIGENCE SUMMARY~~
(Erase heading not required.)

Army Form C. 2118

112. F.A.

Place	Date	Hour	Summary of Events and Information	Remarks and references to Appendices
NOEUX LES MINES	19/7/16		Lieuts M. T. Embree & P. Barker RAMC. 112 FA placed on sick list. Lieut A. D. Moffat returned from Temporary Duty with Divl R.E. A reinforcement of 4 ptes. RAMC arrived. R.H.	
"	20/7/16		Rev McConnell C. F. (Presbyterian) arrived and was attached to this Unit. Orders were received to take over the Advanced Dressing Stations of No: 45. F.A. 15th Division as a temporary measure in addition to existing Duties. This new area included —	
			(1) A.D.S. CHATEAU VERNELLES — 1 Officer. 13. Other Ranks. 1/40000. Sheet. 33. C. G. 8. C. 2. 2 (2) ST. MARY (ABERDEEN) — 1 " 9 " Diagram. Trench Map. 33. C G 17. B. 7. 9 (3) TOURNIQUET LODGE. — 2 " G. 11. A 3. 0 (4) STANSFIELD ROAD. DUGOUT. — 9 " G. 10. D. 3. 8. (5) HALFWAY HOUSE. — 9 " G. 9. D. 5. 6 (6) LE RUTOIRE ALLEY DUGOUT. — 2 " G. 17. A. 5. 7. (7) WING'S WAY. — 2 " 33. C. G. 17. B. 8. 7	

1875 Wt. W593/826 1,000,000 4/15 J.B.C. & A. A.D.S.S./Forms/C. 2118.

Instructions regarding War Diaries and Intelligence Summaries are contained in F. S. Regs., Part II. and the Staff Manual respectively. Title Pages will be prepared in manuscript.

WAR DIARY
~~or~~
~~INTELLIGENCE SUMMARY~~
(Erase heading not required.)

Army Form C. 2118

112. F.A.

Place	Date	Hour	Summary of Events and Information	Remarks and references to Appendices
NOEUX LES MINES.	20/4/16	cont.	(8) ESSEX LANE. 33.C.17.B.7 8. — 2 Other Ranks.	
			(9) VENDIN ALLEY 33.C.23.B.4.9. — 2	
			Total 2 Officers 50. Other ranks	
			I issued orders to this effect, drawing (a) Officers, & (b) personnel for (1) from my Headquarters, personnel for (3) (4) (5) (6) mostly from NUNNERY, but for (5) partly from Headquarters, (2) (7) (8) (9) from ST GEORGE which received a reinforcement in exchange from Headquarters. The complete equipment of C. Section was to be utilised. The Officers and the Detachment from the NUNNERY were ordered to arrive at the CHATEAU VERMELLES at 8.30. AM. 21.4.16	
			G.H.	
NOEUX LES MINES.	21/4/16		Orders as issued last night carried out and new area taken over. Move complete by 2.PM	
			Orders received to hand over the new area tomorrow to No: 113. F.A.	
			Lieut M.T. Embree evacuated to No: 33. C.C.S.	
			G.H.	

1875 Wt. W593/826 1,000,000 4/15 J.B.C. & A. A.D.S.S./Forms/C. 2118.

Instructions regarding War Diaries and Intelligence Summaries are contained in F. S. Regs., Part II. and the Staff Manual respectively. Title Pages will be prepared in manuscript.

WAR DIARY

~~or~~

~~INTELLIGENCE SUMMARY~~

(Erase heading not required.)

Army Form C. 2118

112. F.A.

Place	Date	Hour	Summary of Events and Information	Remarks and references to Appendices
NOEUX LES MINES.	22/4/16		Lieut. W. Warburton left for temporary duty with 8th R. Munster Fusrs. Lieut. P. Barker transferred to 1st Corps Rest Station. A case of dog-bite was sent to ST DENIS for Pasteur Treatment. Handed over new area to No: 113. FA with exception of STANSFIELD ROAD & TOURNIQUET LODGE, which were handed over to a F.A. of 8th Divn, & VENDIN ALLEY, retained by me. G.J.H.	
"	23/4/16		Routine G.J.H.	
"	24/4/16		Routine G.J.H.	
"	25/4/16		Routine G.J.H.	
"	26/4/16		Routine G.J.H.	
"	27/4/16		A reinforcement of 1 lce Corpl & 7 ptes arrived. G.J.H.	
"	28/4/16		A reinforcement of 1 pte arrived G.J.H.	

1875 Wt. W593/826 1,000,000 4/15 J.B.C. & A. A.D.S.S./Forms/C. 2118.

Instructions regarding War Diaries and Intelligence Summaries are contained in F. S. Regs., Part II. and the Staff Manual respectively. Title Pages will be prepared in manuscript.

WAR DIARY
~~or~~
~~INTELLIGENCE SUMMARY~~
(Erase heading not required.)

112. F.A.

Army Form C. 2118

Place	Date	Hour	Summary of Events and Information	Remarks and references to Appendices
NOEUX LES MINES.	29/5/16		Routine. QH.	
"	30/5/16		Lieut P Barker returned from Rest Station. QH.	
"	31/5/16		Routine.	
			[illegible] Lt Col RAMC.	

1875 Wt. W593/826 1,000,000 4/15 J.B.C. & A. A.D.S.S./Forms/C. 2118.

Aug 1916

WAR DIARY.

112th Field Ambulance.

MONTH OF AUGUST, 1916.

VOLUME:- 9

16 K Div

140/1734

Instructions regarding War Diaries and Intelligence Summaries are contained in F. S. Regs., Part II. and the Staff Manual respectively. Title Pages will be prepared in manuscript.

WAR DIARY

~~or~~

~~INTELLIGENCE SUMMARY~~

(Erase heading not required.)

Army Form C. 2118

No: 112. Field Ambulance.

Place	Date	Hour	Summary of Events and Information	Remarks and references to Appendices
NOEUX LES MINES. 36.B. K.18.d.9.8	1/8/16		Routine. Q.S. Hoskins Lt Col RAMC.	
"	2/8/16		Routine. Q.S.H.	
"	3/8/16		Routine Q.S.H.	
"	4/8/16		Routine Q.S.H.	
"	5/8/16		Lieut M. T. Embree RAMC. previously evacuated to the Base for Disease of Frontal Sinuses & P.U.O., joined the Division as a Reinforcement, and was detailed for this Unit. Q.S.H.	
"	6/8/16		Routine Q.S.H.	

1875 Wt. W593/826 1,000,000 4/15 J.B.C. & A. A.D.S.S./Forms/C. 2118.

Instructions regarding War Diaries and Intelligence Summaries are contained in F. S. Regs., Part II. and the Staff Manual respectively. Title Pages will be prepared in manuscript.

WAR DIARY
or
~~INTELLIGENCE SUMMARY~~
(Erase heading not required.)

Army Form C. 2118

112. F A.

Place	Date	Hour	Summary of Events and Information	Remarks and references to Appendices
HOEUX LES MINES	7/8/16.		On a redistribution of the Front, we took over from No: 113. FA the Medical Dugouts in the HULLUCH Sector, as follows:– LE RUTOIRE 36.C. G.17. A.5.7 Ref. Diagr. Tr. Map XII AVE & WINGSWAY " " B.8.7 " & ESSEX LANE " " D.6.9. " & VENDIN ALLEY G.23. B.4.9 & increased the personnel in the Trenches to 1. M.O. 2. NCO's & 32 ptes. Having obtained from the British Red Cross Scty 5. 20 gallon water tanks, I distributed them in the Medical Dugouts and arranged for the chlorination of the water personally by the M.O. i/c ST GEORGE ADS. GH.	
"	8/8/16		The rotting of the Sandbags lining ST GEORGE ADS. & their highly probable insanitary condition having occupied my attention for some time, I sent up my workmen to reline the walls, & also to reconstruct the floor with the object of obtaining under-ventilation. The scheme proposed is to thoroughly disinfect the walls, line with expanded metal, & cement over this. The smooth cement can subsequently be whitewashed & if necessary protected from injury from stretchers &c by strips of tarred felt, nailed on the wooden laths used for the expanded metal. GH.	

Instructions regarding War Diaries and Intelligence Summaries are contained in F. S. Regs., Part II. and the Staff Manual respectively. Title Pages will be prepared in manuscript.

WAR DIARY
~~or~~
~~INTELLIGENCE SUMMARY~~
(Erase heading not required.)

112. F.A.

Army Form C. 2118

Place	Date	Hour	Summary of Events and Information	Remarks and references to Appendices
NOEUX LES MINES.	9/8/16		Lieut. M. T. Embree. RAMC. transferred to West Riding CCS for a recurrence of his previous illness. G.H.	
"	10/8/16		Routine G.H.	
"	11/8/16		Routine G.H.	
"	12/8/16		Routine G.H.	
"	13/8/16		Lieut W. Warburton returned sick (P.U.O) from Temporary Duty with 8th Bn R. Munster Fusiliers, and was transferred to No: 113 F A Officers' Ward.	
"			Owing to NOEUX being emptied of the Infantry of the Division, the Field Ambulances have to provide fatigue parties for cleaning the streets. To comply with this order, I have had to strike off their work several men specially employed. G.H.	

1875 Wt. W593/826 1,000,000 4/15 J.B.C. & A. A.D.S.S./Forms/C. 2118.

Instructions regarding War Diaries and Intelligence Summaries are contained in F. S. Regs., Part II. and the Staff Manual respectively. Title Pages will be prepared in manuscript.

WAR DIARY

~~or~~

~~INTELLIGENCE SUMMARY~~

(Erase heading not required.)

Army Form C. 2118

112. F. A.

Place	Date	Hour	Summary of Events and Information	Remarks and references to Appendices
NOEUX LES MINES	14/8/16		Routine BJH.	
"	15/8/16		In order to provide the Fire Picket NOEUX for the ensuing week, I have with the permission of the ADMS withdrawn from the NUNNERY ADS the men held there as a re-inforcement for the Trenches.	
			Lieut W. L. Thomas. RAMC. reported his arrival, & was taken on the strength accordingly. BJH	
"	16/8/16		Routine BJH	
"	17/8/16		Routine BJH.	
"	18/8/16		Routine BJH	
"	19/8/16		Routine. BJH.	

1875 Wt. W593/826 1,000,000 4/15 J.B.C. & A. A.D.S.S./Forms/C. 2118.

Instructions regarding War Diaries and Intelligence Summaries are contained in F. S. Regs., Part II. and the Staff Manual respectively. Title Pages will be prepared in manuscript.

WAR DIARY
or
~~INTELLIGENCE SUMMARY~~

(Erase heading not required.)

Army Form C. 2118

112. F. A.

Place	Date	Hour	Summary of Events and Information	Remarks and references to Appendices
NOEUX LES MINES	20/8/16		Lieut T. F. Saunders left for temporary Duty with 170 & 173 Tunnelling Companies. R.E. R.H.	
"	21/8/16		Last night there were several "raids" made by the Troops in HULLUCH Sector and a comparatively large number of casualties occurred. Up to 5 PM ~~this after~~ (R.H.) today, the following were the numbers passed through us:— 9th R. Dublin. Fus.rs Wounded 4. Gassed (British) 12. 1st R Munster Fus.rs " 20. " " 7. Evacuation worked smoothly. The severe cases were passed back by Trolley in the dark. The slighter cases were sent down during the morning. There was a large proportion of shrapnel wounds of the back. The gas cases were variously caused, some by the enemy front trench being full of gas, others were attributed to the fault of the RE to adjust the cylinders properly R.H.	
"	22/8/16		Routine. R.H.	

1875 Wt. W593/826 1,000,000 4/15 J.B.C. & A. A.D.S.S./Forms/C. 2118.

Instructions regarding War Diaries and Intelligence Summaries are contained in F. S. Regs., Part II. and the Staff Manual respectively. Title Pages will be prepared in manuscript.

WAR DIARY

~~or~~

~~INTELLIGENCE~~ SUMMARY

(Erase heading not required.)

Army Form C. 2118

112. FA

Place	Date	Hour	Summary of Events and Information	Remarks and references to Appendices
NOEUX LES MINES	23/8/16		The Division being ordered out of the Line, evacuation of the ADSs commenced. Today by Order of ADMS, I handed over to 25. FA all ADSs in HULLUCH Sector. The relieving of ST GEORGE being almost complete. RJH.	
"	24/8/16		Handed over to 137. FA the ADSs in 14 bis Sector. Handed over to 25. FA the ADS. The NUNNERY. PHILOSOPHE. All personnel & transport, and all equipment not handed over to the relieving FAs returned during the day to the Headquarters NOEUX. RJH	
ALLOUAGNE 36B. C.7.a.4.7.	25/8/16.		Marched from NOEUX by road, passing Church 7.45 AM, leaving one private as Billet Warden in charge of Brewery. Carried practically only Mobilisation equipment. Left in Brewery all furniture, whether made by my own staff or obtained from Red Cross, with extra blankets, equipment, dressings &c, ready for immediate use by incoming Ambulance. Arrived at ALLOUAGNE at 12.45 PM and opened a small ward in the Patronage. Personnel billeted on the premises; Officers in private houses adjacent. Offices in Ecole de Filles. Weather fine & warm. RJH.	

1875 Wt. W593/826 1,000,000 4/15 J.B.C. & A. A.D.S.S./Forms/C. 2118.

Instructions regarding War Diaries and Intelligence Summaries are contained in F. S. Regs., Part II. and the Staff Manual respectively. Title Pages will be prepared in manuscript.

WAR DIARY
or
~~INTELLIGENCE SUMMARY~~
(Erase heading not required.)

Army Form C. 2118

112. F.A.

Place	Date	Hour	Summary of Events and Information	Remarks and references to Appendices
ALLOUAGNE		26/8/16	Very little work in Ambulance. Sick collected by Motor Ambulance Car from ALLOUAGNE & adjacent villages, also sick received from 111. FA, which did not itself open. All possible personnel sent on Route March to AUCHY AUX BOIS 36 A. T 14. d where this Ambulance spent January & February last. The inhabitants welcomed the Unit most enthusiastically. R.H.	
"		27/8/16	Billet Warden left at NOEUX returned on being relieved by a guard from 40th Div. R.H.	
"		28/8/16	At 11 PM received orders from ADMS, & at 12.30 AM 29.8.16 despatched 3 Motor Ambulance Cars to report at Headquarters 3rd Div, on the march. R.H.	
"		29/8/16	The Foden Lorry left at 7 AM to join Lorries of Div Signals. RE. & proceed with them to new area by road. One Officer (Lieut A.J. Ferguson) & 1 NCO. sent with Hdqrs. 49th Bde as Billeting party for new area. Under Divisional Orders the Ambulance marched by road to FOUQUEREUIL 36.B.E.8.c. to entrain for new Area. Left ALLOUAGNE 9. PM & arrived FOUQUEREUIL 12.15. AM. Lost considerable time on the march through frightened horses, & through being held up at level crossing MARLES LES MINES. All vehicles loaded within 20 minutes of the trucks arrival at the ramp. All animals entrained, after the usual difficulties with mules, and all personnel given a hot meal	

1875 Wt. W593/826 1,000,000 4/15 J.B.C. & A. A.D.S.S./Forms/C. 2118.

Instructions regarding War Diaries and Intelligence Summaries are contained in F. S. Regs., Part II. and the Staff Manual respectively. Title Pages will be prepared in manuscript.

WAR DIARY
or
~~INTELLIGENCE SUMMARY~~
(Erase heading not required.)

Army Form C. 2118

112 F.A.

Place	Date	Hour	Summary of Events and Information	Remarks and references to Appendices
	29/8/16		Cont & entrained before 1.45 AM. Train timed to leave at 3.10 AM, actually left at 2.50 AM. The remainder of the Motor Transport sent from station to O.C. Div Supply Column remaining in old area Note:- I am very sorry to lose an excellent Motor Ambulance Staff, & personally feel that this order bears very hardly on C.O's & Motor Drivers, & will cause the latter to cease to take special interest in the Credit of the Ambulance to which they may be attached. RHT	
CORBIE AMIENS 17.	30/8/16		Arrived LONGUEAU nr AMIENS at 11.30 AM. Detrained and marched out of the station in 40 minutes. Marched in storm of wind & rain. Made a long halt half a mile outside the Town to prepare a hot tea & dinner for the personnel, - a difficult & lengthy proceeding! Arrived CORBIE at 6. PM. Billeted, officers & men in small bad billets in RUE FRANCISCO FERRIER. Nominal Headquarters at Officers' Mess at No: 17. Officers, including O.C, all doubled up in billets. Foden Lorry arrived before us, & was ordered to be handed over to Supply Column RHT	
DIVE COPSE. 62.D.J.24.	31/8/16		Under orders of D.D.M.S. XIVth Corps, the Bearer Division under Capt D.N. Macleod with Lieuts A.D. Moffat & W.L. Thomas, with 3 horse Ambulance Wagons & 1 water-cart, proceeded at 12 noon in rear of 48th Bde to SANDPIT nr MEAULTE. 62.D.E.3.1. Tent Division, under my personal command, with remaining officers & transport marched at 1. PM to ~~Main~~ A.D.S XIVth Corps at DIVE COPSE, arriving 3. PM. Weather fine. Pitched all	

1875 Wt. W593/826 1,000,000 4/15 J.B.C. & A. A.D.S.S./Forms/C. 2118.

Instructions regarding War Diaries and Intelligence Summaries are contained in F. S. Regs., Part II. and the Staff Manual respectively. Title Pages will be prepared in manuscript.

WAR DIARY
or
INTELLIGENCE SUMMARY
(Erase heading not required.)

Army Form C. 2118

Place	Date	Hour	Summary of Events and Information	Remarks and references to Appendices
DIVE COPSE	31/8/16		Cont mobilisation Tentage for officers & men & took over F Block Marquees for patients.	
			G. S. Hamilton Lt Col RAMC. OC. 112. F.A.	

1875 Wt. W593/826 1,000,000 4/15 J.B.C. & A. A.D.S.S./Forms/C. 2118.

Sept 1916

W A R D I A R Y

112th Field Ambulance RAMC 16th Div

FOR MONTH OF SEPTEMBER, 1916.

VOLUME 10

Instructions regarding War Diaries and Intelligence Summaries are contained in F. S. Regs., Part II. and the Staff Manual respectively. Title Pages will be prepared in manuscript.

WAR DIARY
or
~~INTELLIGENCE SUMMARY~~
(Erase heading not required.)

Army Form C. 2118

No: 112. Field Ambulance

Place	Date	Hour	Summary of Events and Information	Remarks and references to Appendices
DIVE COPSE XIV Corps Main Dressing Station. SOMME 62 D. N.E J. 24. b.	1/9/16		The Tent Division Opened for duty in F block from 12 midnight to 6 AM. 2.9.16. 39 wounded received and evacuated. 6 Officers including self available, on duty in 2 hour shifts. Other Ranks in 2 parties – 3 hour shifts. At noon rode to Bearer Division in SANDPITS. E. 18 D 3.2. found them bivouacked. Arranged for additional transport and equipment. P. S. Hungerford Lt Col RAMC	
"	2/9/16		For work in Tent Division – see above. Beavers remained at SANDPITS with 48th Bde. P.S.H.	
"	3/9/16		Tent Division on duty 6 AM to 12. noon 26 cases. Rode out to SANDPITS & accompanied Bearer Division via FRICOURT. 62. C. NW F. 3. d & passing near MAMETZ at F. 10. B. to halt at BILLON FARM. F29 b 7.8. Bearers subsequently moved to BRONFAY FARM. F30. a. On my return to Main Dr Stn Despatched Lieut. A. J. Ferguson to join Bearers. Tent Divn again on duty. 5.30 PM to 6 AM 4. 9. 16. (CAPTURED GUILLEMONT 57. C. SW. T. 19. C.). 213 British Wounded & 8 Germans 73 Fus'r Regt. HANOVERIANS. All cases evacuated dressed, & with boots & socks off, & properly wrapped in blankets on system devised by me & in use throughout in this Ambulance	
"	[illegible]	-	P.S.H.	

1875 Wt. W593/826 1,000,000 4/15 J.B.C. & A. A.D.S.S./Forms/C. 2118.

Instructions regarding War Diaries and Intelligence Summaries are contained in F. S. Regs., Part II. and the Staff Manual respectively. Title Pages will be prepared in manuscript.

WAR DIARY
or
~~INTELLIGENCE SUMMARY~~
(Erase heading not required.)

112. F.A.

Army Form C. 2118

Place	Date	Hour	Summary of Events and Information	Remarks and references to Appendices
DIVE COPSE.	4/9/16		Bearer Divn moved to BERNAFAY WOOD. A.D.S. 57.C S.W. S.22.d.9.1. & HALFWAY HOUSE S.23.2.8.0. & AID POST T.19.C.35. Tent Divn on duty 6. AM to 6 PM. 74 wounded and a few Germans. RJH.	
"	5/9/16.		ADS at BRIQUETERIE. 62 C. N.W. A.4. 6.5.5. taken over by Lieuts A.L. Ferguson & A.D. Moffat. Capt Macleod & Lieut Thomas remained at BERNAFAY WOOD. Lieut Col Bennett O.C. 113. FA placed by ADMS in charge of all Divisional Bearers. Tent Divn on duty 10 AM to 6 PM. 64 wounded & a few Germans. RJH.	
"	6/9/16		Bearers lost 1 pte killed, 4 wounded, one shellshocked. Major Bell O.C. 111 F A was ordered to take over the ADS. CARNOY. 62.C.N.W. A.13.4.9 & hand over command of his Tent Divn to me. To facilitate working I transferred 112. Tent D. to K block, & both FAs went on duty simultaneously. I arranged for identical blanketing & undressing of patients, sending two of my men to show 111 FA & taking 2 of 111 FA for training with my men. 112. FA. on duty 12 noon to 6 PM. 40 wounded. RJH	
"	7/9/16		Bearer Division – Capt DN Macleod & Lieut Moffat returned on relief to BRONFAY. Tent Divn on duty 6 am to 12 noon. 35 wounded – stretcher cases. Ordered to take over "sitting cases" only & went on duty 10 PM ~~to~~ 2 AM 20 Cases. RJH	

1875 Wt. W593/826 1,000,000 4/15 J.B.C. & A. A.D.S.S./Forms/C. 2118.

Instructions regarding War Diaries and Intelligence Summaries are contained in F. S. Regs., Part II. and the Staff Manual respectively. Title Pages will be prepared in manuscript.

WAR DIARY

or

~~INTELLIGENCE SUMMARY~~

(Erase heading not required.)

Army Form C. 2118

112. F.A.

Place	Date	Hour	Summary of Events and Information	Remarks and references to Appendices
DIVE COPSE & CARNOY ADS 62.C.N.W A.13.d.9	8/9/16		Bearer Division. – Lieut Moffat – BRONFAY FARM to BRIQUETERIE in relief of Lieut Ferguson – to BRONFAY. Capt Macleod BRONFAY to BERNAFAY WOOD. Tent Div. – Sitting Wounded. 112. FA 6–10. AM & 2–6 PM & 10 PM to 2 AM. 47 cases Owing to the chance of possible complications, orders issued by DDMS. XIV Corps that no officer other than the Commandant M.D.S, senior in rank of Major, should remain at M.D.S, I received orders to take over the ADS. CARNOY from Major Bell (OC. 111 FA) retaining him as long as necessary, and I proceeded in the evening to CARNOY Though senior to the Commandant M.D.S. absolutely no friction had occurred during my stay at DIVE COPSE. R.H	
CARNOY.	9/9/16		Bearer Division engaged in capture of ~~[illegible]~~ GINCHY Main Dressing station moved to BRONFAY FARM. Work at CARNOY light in the day, but began to get heavy in evening. The ADS. a long steel arched tunnel, was very awkward for work, as only one Acetylene Operation lamp could be used without the staff being poisoned, & even so, the place reeked of Acetylene Gas. The staff consisted of myself, Major Bell & Captain Van der Vigver (113. FA) & the bearer subdivision of 113 FA. At 9 PM Major Bell proceeded to BERNAFAY WOOD in charge of a reinforcement of Bearers (112. FA). R.H	

1875 Wt. W593/826 1,000,000 4/15 J.B.C. & A. A.D.S.S./Forms/C. 2118.

Army Form C. 2118

Instructions regarding War Diaries and Intelligence Summaries are contained in F. S. Regs., Part II. and the Staff Manual respectively. Title Pages will be prepared in manuscript.

WAR DIARY
or
~~INTELLIGENCE SUMMARY~~

(Erase heading not required.)

112. F.A.

Place	Date	Hour	Summary of Events and Information	Remarks and references to Appendices
CARNOY & BRONFAY FARM 62.D.NE F.30.a.	10/9/16.		During the night Capt Van der Vijver & I dressed cases passing through from MONTAUBAN. 57.C.S.W. S.27.D. In addition I regulated the evacuations. The Motor Transport was for some time unsatisfactory, as there were not enough Cars running between MONTAUBAN & CARNOY. this was later remedied. The NCO at CARNOY did all in his power. At about 3.30 AM the rush was over, & I began to pass Cars direct to Main Dressing Station without unloading. Cases in the cars were either all well dressed or there was a case or two of severe injury advisable to be sent on without delay. After 4.30. AM cars were sent on in all cases. At about noon I handed over to a FA GUARDS DIVISION, & all personnel moved to BRONFAY FARM Main Dr. Stn. I was ordered to obtain permission from the Commandant to remain there awaiting orders. Major Bell took over command there of both Tent Division. During the afternoon the Bearer Divisions 111. 112. 113. FAs returned to BRONFAY & thence moved into camp for the night in HAPPY VALLEY about 62.D.N.E. F 4.d. Tent Divn dressed ~~[illegible]~~ 134 sitting cases to 6 AM. 11.9.16. QJK	
BRONFAY FARM	11/9/16		Lieut W.L. Thomas left to take Medical Charge of 8th R Dublin Fusiliers. Bearer Division marched to VILLE sur ETANGS. 62.D.NW. 1.30. QJK	

1875 Wt. W593/826 1,000,000 4/15 J.B.C. & A. A.D.S.S./Forms/C. 2118.

Instructions regarding War Diaries and Intelligence Summaries are contained in F. S. Regs., Part II. and the Staff Manual respectively. Title Pages will be prepared in manuscript.

WAR DIARY
~~or~~
~~INTELLIGENCE SUMMARY~~

(Erase heading not required.)

112. F.A.

Army Form C. 2118

Place	Date	Hour	Summary of Events and Information	Remarks and references to Appendices
VILLA des ETANGS nr CORBIE. 62.D.N.W. I.30.	12/9/16		Under orders from ADMS. I proceeded to VILLA des ETANGS & took over command of the Bearer Division, to rest after late strenuous work. Lieut A. J. Ferguson left for England on completion of his contract. Q.I.H.	
"	13/9/16		Lieut W. Warburton, on completion of 1 years service promoted Temporary Captain Q.I.H.	
"	14/9/16		Routine Q.I.H.	
"	15/9/16		Capt W. Warburton proceeded to England on 14 days leave. Q.I.H	
"	16/9/16		Captain Philip Smith (M.C) reported for duty – attached Tent Division, & took over command from Captain Bateman Q.I.H	
"	17/9/16		A considerable amount of personal equipment had been lost by Bearers in action, some of it buried by shells. The Quartermaster arrived from M. Dr Sti & re-equipped. Transport left at 11 Am under LIEUT Moffat to accompany Transport of 48th Inf Bde. Q.I.H	

1875 Wt. W593/826 1,000,000 4/15 J.B.C. & A. A.D.S.S./Forms/C. 2118.

Instructions regarding War Diaries and Intelligence Summaries are contained in F. S. Regs., Part II. and the Staff Manual respectively. Title Pages will be prepared in manuscript.

WAR DIARY
or
~~INTELLIGENCE SUMMARY~~

(Erase heading not required.)

112. F.A.

Army Form C. 2118

Place	Date	Hour	Summary of Events and Information	Remarks and references to Appendices
ALLERY (ABBEVILLE MAP?) no proper reference obtainable	18/9/16		During stay at VILLA du ETANGS the Bearers were only asked to do the necessary fatigues & a few short route marches, as they were very exhausted after arduous work at GUILLEMONT & GINCHY. Under orders from 48th Bde marched off through CORBIE in rain, by the road through ~~HEILLY~~ VEUVILLE to near DAOURS where got into Lorries & were conveyed via RIVERY, AMIENS, PICQUIGNY, SOUES, AIRAINES to ALLERY. Very heavy rain all day. Met Lt Moffat & Transport at ALLERY. Owing to billeting party having been conducted by a Staff Officer to the wrong village, had to do my own billeting. Met every courtesy from M le Maire. Excellent billets for Officers. Men mostly in large hall of Hotel de la Gare. Horses & Transport in open. GJH	
"	19/9/16		Billeting party turned up in morning, very wet & hungry! Reinforcement 10 ptes, including 2 old members, arrived. GJH	
"	20/9/16		Routine. Made out Billeting documents with M le Maire. Under orders from 48th Bde sent forward Capt Macleod & Bearers A Section as loading-party, & Lieut Moffat & 1 man as Billeting party to LONGPRÉ at 9. PM Lieut Moffat entrained with Bde HQrs at 12. 45. am. 21.9.16 Followed at 10 PM with Transport, followed on road in case of accidents by Bearers B & C Sections. Fairly fine weather, some drizzle at times. Arrived LONGPRÉ 1 am. Started entraining about 2 30. am, assisting 145 Coy A.S.C. Entraining completed 4.15. AM. Train left 4.51 am 21.9.16. GJH	

Instructions regarding War Diaries and Intelligence Summaries are contained in F. S. Regs., Par. II. and the Staff Manual respectively. Title Pages will be prepared in manuscript.

WAR DIARY
or
~~INTELLIGENCE SUMMARY~~
(Erase heading not required.)

Army Form C. 2118

112. F. A.

Place	Date	Hour	Summary of Events and Information	Remarks and references to Appendices
WESTOUTRE Trench Map 28. S.W. M.9.c.3.7.	21/9/16		Detrained, assisting 145 Coy. A.S.C., at GODEWAERSVELDE (HAZEBROUCK 5A) & marched to WESTOUTRE, where received orders to stay at HOSPICE with 113 FA as temporary measure. RJK	
"	22/9/16		Took over HOSPICE from 113 F.A. who remained pending taking over their new site. Building mostly occupied by Nuns & Inmates. Two wards on ground floor, large lofts & some officers' billets available. Stores in temporary huts in grounds. Horse-lines roofed & partially floored. Very disreputable make-shift huts for personnel scattered round Hospice grounds & adjacent field. Also took over 2 schoolrooms and yards &c at M.9.c.9.2. RJK	
"	23/9/16		Nothing of interest in our Ambulance. No: 113. FA left for new pitch. RJK	
"	24/9/16		Tent Division with equipment of two sections arrived. Left BRONFAY FARM. M.D.S. on 22.9.16. Spent two nights at CORBIE & entrained there for BAILLEUL. Had been on duty at M.D.S. alternately with 111. FA & since 9.9.16. (inclusive) had dressed 1013 cases so-called "sitting wounded". Largest numbers in 6 hr periods 156, 127 126 & 110. RJK	
"	25/9/16		Began remodelling sanitary arrangements, path-making &c, clipping hedges to provide brushwood for base for Wagon-lines, carting sand & stone for horse lines &c. Took over Divisional Baths in village. RJK	

1875 Wt. W593/826 1,000,000 4/15 J.B.C. & A. A.D.S.S./Forms/C. 2118.

Instructions regarding War Diaries and Intelligence Summaries are contained in F. S. Regs., Part II. and the Staff Manual respectively. Title Pages will be prepared in manuscript.

WAR DIARY

~~or~~

~~INTELLIGENCE SUMMARY~~

(Erase heading not required.)

112. F A

Army Form C. 2118

Place	Date	Hour	Summary of Events and Information	Remarks and references to Appendices
WESTOUTRE	26/9/16		Continued improvements. Decided to divide sick between Headquarters & Schools according to diet. The Schools to be used for men able to eat rations. Lieut. A.D. Moffat to Div R.E. vice M.O. proceeded on leave to England. R.J.H.	
"	27/9/16		Took over charge of grease-separation tanks in connection with Baths & Divisional laundry. Continued improvements. Began construction of new latrine & incinerator of special pattern (16th Div Sanitary Section). Am making a "Sanitary Area", which will be easily accessible & easily kept clean. R.J.H.	
"	28/9/16		Cleaned out one Separation Tank after 6 weeks use. Much Sludge. Continued work. R.J.H.	
"	29/9/16		Capt W. Warburton returned from leave. Reconstructed filter at Separation Tanks. Former arrangement useless. Other improvements continued. R.J.H.	
"	30/9/16		Tested filter & found it worked admirably with clear effluent. Cleaned second tank & repaired valve. Other work as usual. R.J. Hamilton Lt Col RAMC OC. 112. F.A	

1875 Wt. W593/826 1,000,000 4/15 J.B.C. & A. A.D.S.S./Forms/C. 2118.

Oct. 1916

W A R D I A R Y

MONTH OF OCTOBER, 1916.

VOLUME 11

112th Field Ambulance RAMC

16th Div

140/1814

Instructions regarding War Diaries and Intelligence Summaries are contained in F. S. Regs., Part II. and the Staff Manual respectively. Title Pages will be prepared in manuscript.

WAR DIARY

~~or~~

~~INTELLIGENCE SUMMARY~~

(Erase heading not required.)

Army Form C. 2118

No: 112. Field Ambulance

Place	Date	Hour	Summary of Events and Information	Remarks and references to Appendices
WESTOUTRE French Map 28. S.W. M.9.c.3.7.	1/10/16.		Routine. Finished clipping of hedges for foundation for Wagon-lines. R.J. Hunt Lt Col RAMC.	
"	2/10/16		Routine R.J.H.	
"	3/10/16		Routine. R.J.H.	
"	4/10/16		Routine R.J.H.	
"	5/10/16		Routine. Kitchen for M.T. detachment completed. R.J.H.	
"	6/10/16		Captain A.B. Bateman left for temporary duty with 77th Bde. R.F.A. Wagon lines completed. 6 inches of loamy sand on thick brushwood. R.J.H.	

1875 Wt. W593/826 1,000,000 4/15 J.B.C. & A. A.D.S.S./Forms/C. 2118.

Instructions regarding War Diaries and Intelligence Summaries are contained in F. S. Regs., Par. II. and the Staff Manual respectively. Title Pages will be prepared in manuscript.

WAR DIARY
~~or~~
~~INTELLIGENCE SUMMARY~~
(Erase heading not required.)

Army Form C. 2118

112. F. A.

Place	Date	Hour	Summary of Events and Information	Remarks and references to Appendices
WESTOUTRE	7/10/16		Routine QH	
"	8/10/16		Routine QH.	
"	9/10/16		Lieut A.E. Barr Sim reported for Duty. Large central-cage incinerator finished & taken into use. QH	
"	10/10/16		Routine. QH	
"	11/10/16		Lieut. A.D. Moffat returned from temporary Duty with 16th Div. RE. QH	
"	12/10/16		Lieut P.W. Barker left on leave to England. Double-platform incinerator completed at Divisional Baths QH	

1875 Wt. W593/826 1,000,000 4/15 J.B.C. & A. A.D.S.S./Forms/C. 2118.

Instructions regarding War Diaries and Intelligence Summaries are contained in F. S. Regs., Part II. and the Staff Manual respectively. Title Pages will be prepared in manuscript.

WAR DIARY
~~or~~
~~INTELLIGENCE SUMMARY~~
(Erase heading not required.)

Army Form C. 2118

112. F. A.

Place	Date	Hour	Summary of Events and Information	Remarks and references to Appendices
WESTOUTRE	13/10/16		Captain W Warburton left for temporary duty with 174 Bde R.F.A. G.H.	
"	14/10/16		Routine. G.H.	
"	15/10/16		Concreting of stable floor completed, & to be left for a week before use. G.H.	
"	16/10/16		Living hut for Motor Ambulance Drivers completed & occupied. G.H.	
"	17/10/16		Routine. G.H.	
"	18/10/16		Lieut. A.D. Moffat left on leave to England. G.H.	
"	19/10/16		Capt P. Smith returned from leave. Canvas draining-baths for scum from soap-separation tanks (Baths & Laundry) completed & taken into use. G.H.	

1875 Wt. W593/826 1,000,000 4/15 J.B.C. & A. A.D.S.S./Forms/C. 2118.

Instructions regarding War Diaries and Intelligence Summaries are contained in F. S. Regs., Part II. and the Staff Manual respectively. Title Pages will be prepared in manuscript.

WAR DIARY
or
~~INTELLIGENCE SUMMARY~~
(Erase heading not required.)

Army Form C. 2118

112 . F. A

Place	Date	Hour	Summary of Events and Information	Remarks and references to Appendices
WESTOUTRE	20/10/16		Captain Smith departed for duty under D.D.M.S. HAVRE Lieut F. M. Bishop reported for duty. Burning of scum from tables commenced. This appears to be an impure lime soap which chars leaving a residue of impure lime. R.H.	
"	21/10/16		The covering with tin of all cookhouse chopping tables completed R.H.	
"	22/10/16		Stables completed, ie, concreted (16.10.16), tarred, bars liable to be bitten by horses tinned & bails hung between pairs. R.H.	
"	23/10/16		Letter received from Lieut P. Barker (on leave) announcing his admission to 2. A. Mil Hosp Millbank. Lieut T. F. Saunders left for Temporary Duty with 9th R. Dubl. Fusilrs. Ablution hut reopened after reconstruction & enlargement – accommodation nearly doubled, roofed & walled in partly with Corrugated iron & partly with Canvas & rabbit-wire; tin pipes made for sullage-water & an downward & upward filter in a packing case attached for separating soap. R.H.	

1875 Wt. W593/826 1,000,000 4/15 J.B.C. & A. A.D.S.S./Forms/C. 2118.

Instructions regarding War Diaries and Intelligence Summaries are contained in F. S. Regs., Part II. and the Staff Manual respectively. Title Pages will be prepared in manuscript.

WAR DIARY
or
~~INTELLIGENCE SUMMARY~~
(Erase heading not required.)

Army Form C. 2118

112. F.A.

Place	Date	Hour	Summary of Events and Information	Remarks and references to Appendices
WESTOUTRE	24/10/16		Captain D.N. Macleod left for course of Lectures at IInd Army Gas School nr CASSEL. RJH	
"	25/10/16		New downward & upward filter at Divisional Baths completed & working, with object of filtering stream-water through coke & sand before being used for Baths & Laundry. There was originally a cubic hole lined roughly with timber, forming a tank for the pump, and a rabbit-wire box full of coke. We have lined the tank with brick & rendered with cement, & similarly lined the channel to the stream & fitted this channel as a double filter. RJH	
"	26/10/16		Captain D.N. Macleod returned from Gas School. New brick range for ovens & deck-shies built at the Branch Dressing Station at the Schools. RJH	
"	27/10/16		Routine ~~RJH~~ Capt W. Warburton returned from temporary duty with 177. Bde. R.F.A. RJH	
"	28/10/16		Routine RJH	
"	29/10/16		Routine RJH	

1875 Wt. W593/826 1,000,000 4/15 J.B.C. & A. A.D.S.S./Forms/C. 2118.

Instructions regarding War Diaries and Intelligence Summaries are contained in F. S. Regs., Part II. and the Staff Manual respectively. Title Pages will be prepared in manuscript.

WAR DIARY

~~or~~

~~INTELLIGENCE SUMMARY~~

(Erase heading not required.)

Army Form C. 2118

112 F.A.

Place	Date	Hour	Summary of Events and Information	Remarks and references to Appendices
WESTOUTRE	30/10/16		New system at Divisional Baths in operation. Squads of 40 at a time enter, undress, put the contents of their pockets & their boots, socks & puttees in ~~a~~ numbered sandbags, hang their jackets & trousers, cardigans &c on a cross coat-hanger bearing same number as bag; hand hangers to attendant, who places ~~them~~ in the steam disinfecting room; hand in shirts drawers & vest to another attendant & get clean ones instead; go into another room which has been fitted with seats & racks by us; ~~hang~~ sandbags & clean clothes on ~~[illegible]~~ nail ~~on~~ numbered the same as bag; pass ~~[illegible]~~ into shower-bath room; after bathing return to clean clothes room where disinfected outer garments on hangers are returned to them. 80 men per hour can be managed in this way. Lieut A.D. Moffat returned from leave. Q.K.	
"	31/10/16		Routine Q.K.	

1875 Wt. W593/826 1,000,000 4/15 J.B.C. & A. A.D.S.S./Forms/C. 2118.

Nov 1916

W A R D I A R Y .

F O R

MONTH OF NOVEMBER, 1916.

VOLUME 12

16th Div

112th Field Ambulance R.A.M.C.

Vol 10/12

140/1862

Instructions regarding War Diaries and Intelligence Summaries are contained in F. S. Regs., Part II. and the Staff Manual respectively. Title Pages will be prepared in manuscript.

WAR DIARY

~~or~~

~~INTELLIGENCE SUMMARY~~

(Erase heading not required.)

Army Form C. 2118

No: 112. Field Ambulance

Place	Date	Hour	Summary of Events and Information	Remarks and references to Appendices
WESTOUTRE Trench Map 28. S.W M.9.c.3.7	1/11/16		Hon Lt & Qr Mr C. W. Atkins transferred to No: 2 C.C.S. R. J. Hungerford? Lt Col RAMC	
"	2/11/16		Routine. RJH	
"	3/11/16		Brick & Iron range constructed in personnel-kitchen shed. RJH	
"	4/11/16		Downward & Upward Box Filter placed to take Ward Scullery drainage. A reinforcement of one Driver A.S.C. Horse Tpt arrived. RJH	
"	5/11/16		Routine RJH	
"	6/11/16		O.C. left on leave to England. Capt D. N. Macleod in command. RJH	
"	7/11/16		Routine RJH	

1875 Wt. W593/826 1,000,000 4/15 J.B.C. & A. A.D.S.S./Forms/C. 2118.

Instructions regarding War Diaries and Intelligence Summaries are contained in F. S. Regs., Part II. and the Staff Manual respectively. Title Pages will be prepared in manuscript.

WAR DIARY
~~or~~
~~INTELLIGENCE SUMMARY~~
(Erase heading not required.)

Army Form C. 2118

112. F A.

Place	Date	Hour	Summary of Events and Information	Remarks and references to Appendices
WESTOUTRE	8/11/16		Corduroy standing for two water carts completed. Lieut A D Moffat left for temporary duty with 16th Divn Ammunition Column Lieut T. F. Saunders returned from temporary duty with 9th Bn R. Dublin Fusrs G.H.	
"	9/11/16		Capt D N Macleod transferred sick to No: 113. F.A. Capt W Warburton assumed command G.H.	
"	10/11/16		Wind screens completed on either side of Horse standings. G.H.	
"	11/11/16		Lieut T. F. Saunders proceeded on a fortnights leave at end of a years service Hon Lt & QMr. C. W. Atkins returned to duty from No: 2. C.C.S G.H.	
"	12/11/16		Routine G.H.	
"	13/11/16		Routine G.H.	
"	14/11/16		Concrete floor made at Kitchen at Branch Dr Stn at Schools. WESTOUTRE. G.H.	

1875 Wt. W593/826 1,000,000 4/15 J.B.C. & A. A.D.S.S./Forms/C. 2118.

Instructions regarding War Diaries and Intelligence Summaries are contained in F. S. Regs., Par: II. and the Staff Manual respectively. Title Pages will be prepared in manuscript.

WAR DIARY
~~or~~
~~INTELLIGENCE~~ SUMMARY
(Erase heading not required.)

112. F A

Army Form C. 2118

Place	Date	Hour	Summary of Events and Information	Remarks and references to Appendices
WESTOUTRE	15/11/16		Routine RJH	
"	16/11/16		Reinforcement of 11 ptes RAMC & 1 Driver ASC arrived RJH	
"	17/11/16		Routine RJH.	
"	18/11/16		Routine. RJH	
"	19/11/16		O.C. returned from leave in England, having been delayed 1 night at BOULOGNE going, & 1 night at BOULOGNE & 1 night at HAZEBROUCK returning. Capt D.N Macleod returned from No: 113. FA 1 Driver ASC arrived as reinforcement. RJH	
"	20/11/16		Large hut for ASC. H.T. personnel completed & occupied. RJH.	
"	21/11/16		Floor of Personnel-Cookhouse Shed concreted. RJH	
"	22/11/16		Owing to bad quality of materials available for concreting floor of stables, the horses have broken the concrete badly. Have begun to fill in all broken patches with bricks. Lieut AD Moffat returned from temporary Duty with 16th Div. A. C Capt D.N Macleod proceeded on leave to England. Lieut. A.E. Barr-Lim proceeded for duty for 1 month to 16th Div School 1 Driver ASC arrived as reinforcement RJH.	

1875 Wt. W593/826 1,000,000 4/15 J.B.C. & A. A.D.S.S./Forms/C. 2118.

Instructions regarding War Diaries and Intelligence Summaries are contained in F. S. Regs., Part II. and the Staff Manual respectively. Title Pages will be prepared in manuscript.

WAR DIARY
or
~~INTELLIGENCE SUMMARY~~
(Erase heading not required.)

Army Form C. 2118

112. F.A.

Place	Date	Hour	Summary of Events and Information	Remarks and references to Appendices
WESTOUTRE	23/11/16		Corduroying of road between Stables & Wagon-lines commenced. 1 NCO & 2 ptes RAMC arrived as reinforcement. 1 M.T. Driver ASC arrived, replacing one sent to 9th Supply Column. Orders received to strike off strength Lieut P. Barker, as on sick-leave granted in England. RH	
"	24/11/16		Experiments conducted on precipitation of Laundry & Bath effluents with lime. I found that 40grs to 1 gallon when added as lime-water, precipitated all grease & dirt as a sludge, with no surface scum. RH	
"	25/11/16		Farriers shop abandoned for new one constructed close to horse-lines. Capt A.B. Bateman reported for duty. In order to fit in two new screw-valves in the Precipitation Tanks, both tanks & the filter were emptied & cleaned out. Work began at 2 PM. By 6 PM one tank & the filter were ready, & my bricklayers under direction of 2.M.S. R.E. began work. The second tank could not be touched till 8 PM & was clear by 11 PM when the second valve was fitted. This was a very good performance by the squads working. RH	
"	26/11/16		Routine. RH	
"	27/11/16		The lime-process started at the Tanks. As a beginning a quantity largely in excess of absolute requirements was added. i.e. lbs 200 instead of 80; with the object of obtaining an excess for purposes of solution. The filter was reconstructed with a flooring of 3 inch agricultural pipes, very little coke, & 8 inches of cinders topped with 8 inches clean sand. RH	
"	28/11/16		ASC. H.T. NCO's hut completed & occupied. Effluent from tanks distinctly good. RH	

1875 Wt. W593/826 1,000,000 4/15 J.B.C. & A. A.D.S.S./Forms/C. 2118.

Instructions regarding War Diaries and Intelligence Summaries are contained in F. S. Regs., Part II. and the Staff Manual respectively. Title Pages will be prepared in manuscript.

WAR DIARY
~~or~~
~~INTELLIGENCE SUMMARY~~
(Erase heading not required.)

112. F.A.

Army Form C. 2118

Place	Date	Hour	Summary of Events and Information	Remarks and references to Appendices
WESTOUTRE	29/11/16		Commenced to add reduced quantity of slaked lime to contents of tank - i.e. 40 lbs to 3000 galls. This is twice experimental quantity, but I think, is necessary as [illegible] in suspension. The tanks are violently stirred while lime is being added. Carpenters began to build "Cocoa bar" at Divisional Baths. G.H.	
"	30/11/16		Lime process working well. Water fairly clear & greenish colour. Effluent excellent. The last shacks & one fairly decent hut occupied lately by A.S.C. personnel pulled down, bench-boards removed & field N.W. of stables abandoned except for horse trough & ablution-tank-pump. The materials of the hut removed to Schools Dr. Stn. for construction of dining-hall. 1 man R.A.M.C. arrived as reinforcement. During the month a great deal of whitewashing & distempering was done throughout the buildings, both of Headquarters & Schools. G. H. ~~Hughes~~ Wm. Lt Col RAMC OC. 112. F.A.	

Dec 1916

WAR DIARY FOR MONTH OF DECEMBER, 1916.

VOLUME 13.

RAMC 112th Field Ambulance

16th Div

14C/1903

Vol 13

Instructions regarding War Diaries and Intelligence Summaries are contained in F. S. Regs., Part II. and the Staff Manual respectively. Title Pages will be prepared in manuscript.

WAR DIARY

~~or~~

~~INTELLIGENCE SUMMARY~~

(Erase heading not required.)

Army Form C. 2118

No: 112. Field Ambce

Place	Date	Hour	Summary of Events and Information	Remarks and references to Appendices
WESTOUTRE 28 S.W M.9 C.3.7	1/12/16		Routine R.J. Houghton Lt Col RAMC.	
"	2/12/16		Captain W. Warburton proceeded on temporary duty with 7th Bn The Leinster Regt. Work commenced on Dining-Hall shed at Schools A.D.S. Lieut F. M. Bishop left for England on Termination of contract. R.J.H.	
"	3/12/16		Captain D. N. Macleod returned from leave in England. R.J.H.	
"	4/12/16		Captain D. N. Macleod proceeded on temporary duty with 7th Bn R. Irish Rifles. Hon Lieut and 2r Mr C. W. Atkins proceeded on leave to England. R.J.H.	
"	5/12/16		Whitewashing of all wards & billets completed R.J.H.	
"	6/12/16		Routine R.J.H.	
"	7/12/16		The first Nissen Bow Hut for personnel completed. R.J.H.	

1875 Wt. W593/826 1,000,000 4/15 J.B.C. & A. A.D.S.S./Forms/C. 2118.

Instructions regarding War Diaries and Intelligence Summaries are contained in F. S. Regs., Part II. and the Staff Manual respectively. Title Pages will be prepared in manuscript.

WAR DIARY
or
~~INTELLIGENCE SUMMARY~~
(Erase heading not required.)

112 F. A

Army Form C. 2118

Place	Date	Hour	Summary of Events and Information	Remarks and references to Appendices
WESTOUTRE	8/12/16		A large Skylight completed in the attic-ward. Urine soak-pit extended R.J.H.	
"	9/12/16		A rope-ladder, to act as a fire-escape, fitted in an Attic-Ward R.J.H.	
"	10/12/16		Capt D N Macleod returned from temporary duty with 7th R. Irish Rifles. Lieut. A.D. Moffat proceeded on temporary duty with 6th R. Irish Regt R.J.H.	
"	11/12/16		At the Divisional Baths, an issue of half-a-pint of hot cocoa to each man after bathing, commenced. R.J.H.	
"	12/12/16		Second NISSEN Bow Hut completed R.J.H.	
"	13/12/16		Routine R.J.H.	
"	14/12/16		Extensive repairs to main approach commenced. Capt C. H DENYER. RAMC (Reg) & Capt W. TURNER RAMC. (T C) reported for Duty. Capt W. Warburton returned from Temporary duty with 7th Leinsters Capt T. F. Saunders struck off the strength, as granted sick-leave in England. R.J.H.	

1875 Wt. W593/826 1,000,000 4/15 J.B.C. & A. A.D.S.S./Forms/C. 2118.

Instructions regarding War Diaries and Intelligence Summaries are contained in F. S. Regs., Part II. and the Staff Manual respectively. Title Pages will be prepared in manuscript.

WAR DIARY

~~or~~

~~INTELLIGENCE SUMMARY~~

(Erase heading not required.)

Army Form C. 2118

112. F.A

Place	Date	Hour	Summary of Events and Information	Remarks and references to Appendices
WESTOUTRE	15/12/16		A second skylight completed in another attic. Hon Lt & QrMr Atkins returned from leave in England. QJK.	
"	16/12/16		Lieut. A. D. Moffat returned from Temporary Duty with 6th R Irish Regt. QJK.	
"	17/12/16		Capt. D. N. Macleod proceeded on temporary duty with 177. Bde. RFA. Capt A. B. Bateman proceeded on temporary duty with 7/8 R Irish Fusiliers QJK	
"	18/12/16		Routine QJK.	
"	19/12/16		Routine QJK.	
"	20/12/16		Shed built to cover stationary Engine & boilerman at Divl. Baths. Capt. W. Warburton proceeded on Temporary Duty with 2nd R. Irish Regt. QJK	
"	21/12/16		Routine. QJK	
"	22/12/16		Routine QJK.	

1875 Wt. W593/826 1,000,000 4/15 J.B.C. & A. A.D.S.S./Forms/C. 2118.

Army Form C. 2118

Instructions regarding War Diaries and Intelligence Summaries are contained in F. S. Regs., Part II. and the Staff Manual respectively. Title Pages will be prepared in manuscript.

WAR DIARY
or
~~INTELLIGENCE~~ SUMMARY

(Erase heading not required.)

112. F.A.

Place	Date	Hour	Summary of Events and Information	Remarks and references to Appendices
WESTOUTRE	23/12/16		Routine. G.H.	
"	24/12/16		Captain A.B. Bateman returned from temporary duty with 7/8 R. Irish Fusiliers G.H.	
"	25/12/16		Christmas Day. Usual celebrations. G.H.	
"	26/12/16		Capt D.H. Macleod placed on sick list and relieved i/c 177 Bde R.F.A. by Lieut. A.D. Moffat. G.H.	
"	27/12/16		Routine. G.H.	
"	28/12/16		Routine G.H.	
"	29/12/16		At special conference with D.D.M.S. IX th Corps, I was appointed to construct the necessary buildings for a Corps Dressing Station near LOCRE. G.H.	
"	30/12/16		Inspected site of Corps Dressing Station with D.D.M.S. & D.A.D.M.S. IX th Corps & A.D.M.S. 16 th Div. G.H.	

1875 Wt. W593/826 1,000,000 4/15 J.B.C. & A. A.D.S.S./Forms/C. 2118.

Instructions regarding War Diaries and Intelligence Summaries are contained in F. S. Regs., Part II. and the Staff Manual respectively. Title Pages will be prepared in manuscript.

WAR DIARY
or
~~INTELLIGENCE SUMMARY~~
(Erase heading not required.)

Army Form C. 2118

112. F A

Place	Date	Hour	Summary of Events and Information	Remarks and references to Appendices
WESTOUTRE	31/12/16		Routine. During the month daily progress was made in replacing worn-out concrete in the Stable-floors with bricks. This work was necessitated by the poor quality of the sand used for the concrete in the first instance. Work has steadily progressed on the main approach & the space occupied by Motor Ambulance cars when standing or turning. The roadway was never properly made, & is rutted easily in wet weather. Various improvements have been carried out in the Wards &c. A number of chaff-pillows with pillow-cases have been filled & taken into use, and the wards brightened by painting white the trestles. The accommodation in the Pack-Store has been increased &c.	

C. S. Hugh Wm
Lt-Col. RAMC
OC. 112. F A

1875 Wt. W593/826 1,000,000 4/15 J.B.C. & A. A.D.S.S./Forms/C. 2118.

Jan. 1917

W A R   D I A R Y   for month of JANUARY, 1917.

VOLUME 14

RAMC 112th Field Ambulance

16th Div

140/1943

Vol 14

96

Instructions regarding War Diaries and Intelligence Summaries are contained in F. S. Regs., Part II. and the Staff Manual respectively. Title Pages will be prepared in manuscript.

WAR DIARY

~~or~~

~~INTELLIGENCE SUMMARY~~

(Erase heading not required.)

Army Form C. 2118

No: 112. Field Ambulance.

Place	Date	Hour	Summary of Events and Information	Remarks and references to Appendices
WESTOUTRE 28. S.W. M9.c.3.7.	1/1/17		Meriwether Pump at Divisional Baths fitted on new brick pedestal. One Separation-tank pumped out and cleaned. R. J. Houghton Lt Col. RAMC.	
"	2/1/17		"Corps Reserve" posts fixed on site of New IX Corps Main Dressing Station on road from LOCRE to BRULOOZE. 28 M.23.d.3.7. An apparatus for cleaning & disinfecting bed-pans fixed in "Sanitary Area" at FA. Headqrs. Second Separation Tank pumped out & cleaned. RJH	
"	3/1/17		Routine. RJH.	
"	4/1/17		Drew timber for construction of latrines, cookhouse &c at IX Corps M.D.S. Capt D N Macleod came off sick-list. Capt W. Warburton returned from temporary Duty with 2nd. R. Irish. Regt. 1 Pte arrived as reinforcement. RJH	
"	5/1/17		Routine. RJH	
"	6/1/17		The Owner of the site of New IX Corps M.D.S. raised objections to the taking of his land. Ordered Road Material to be deposited there pending result of appeal, & myself visited Roads Officer IX Corps & DDMS. IXth Corps & Z. Branch. IX Corps, who approved. Captain D N Macleod proceeded on temporary Duty. 16th Div School RJH.	

1875 Wt. W593/826 1,000,000 4/15 J.B.C. & A. A.D.S.S./Forms/C. 2118.

Instructions regarding War Diaries and Intelligence Summaries are contained in F. S. Regs., Part II. and the Staff Manual respectively. Title Pages will be prepared in manuscript.

WAR DIARY

or

~~INTELLIGENCE SUMMARY~~

(Erase heading not required.)

Army Form C. 2118

112. F.A.

Place	Date	Hour	Summary of Events and Information	Remarks and references to Appendices
WESTOUTRE	7/1/17		Captain C.H. Denyer left for temporary Duty with 7/8 R. Irish Fusrs. Captain A.B. Bateman left for temporary Duty with 16th Divn Train. Lieut A.C. Barr Sim returned on relief at 16th Divn. School. Filters for bath & laundry water cleaned out. Latrines at Baths recovered with canvas in place of felt destroyed by storm. R.J.H.	
"	8/1/17.		D.A.D.M.S. IX Corps. Rents Officer & I interviewed owner of Land at M.D.S. It was decided that his objection could not be sustained, & that work was to proceed. R.J.H.	
"	9/1/17		Extra steam-pipes having been fitted on the floors of the special disinfecting chambers at Divnl Baths, a wooden frame floor covered with expanded metal was fitted for their protection. R.J.H.	
"	10/1/17		Lieut A.D. Moffat struck off strength on taking over Medical Charge of 177 Bde R.F.A. R.J.H.	
"	11/1/17		Routine R.J.H.	

1875 Wt. W593/826 1,000,000 4/15 J.B.C. & A. A.D.S.S./Forms/C. 2118.

Instructions regarding War Diaries and Intelligence Summaries are contained in F. S. Regs., Part II. and the Staff Manual respectively. Title Pages will be prepared in manuscript.

WAR DIARY
~~or~~
~~INTELLIGENCE SUMMARY~~
(Erase heading not required.)

Army Form C. 2118

112, F.A.

Place	Date	Hour	Summary of Events and Information	Remarks and references to Appendices
WESTOUTRE	12/1/17		A portion of the roofed playground at Schools Dr. Stn enclosed with wood from old "shacks" below & canvas & wire above as billet for 10 men, completed today. R.J.K.	
"	13/1/17		Routine R.J.K.	
"	14/1/17		Capt W. Turner left for temporary duty with 2nd. R. Irish Regt. 1 pte as reinforcement arrived. R.J.K.	
"	15/1/17		Pump of Stationary Engine at Baths repaired. Transport Road at F.A. Hdqrs continued with gravel, allowing horses to leave stables without passing through deep mud. Snow lying on ground after slight falls during past 4 days. 1 pte as reinforcement arrived. R.J.K.	
"	16/1/17		An oildrum stove with long pipe fitted in new dining-hall at schools. This room adjoins the new billet, but is wooden-walled. 1 pte as reinforcement arrived. R.J.K.	
"	17/1/17		Owing to increase in sickness in the Division, turned personnel out of one more attic, & equipped it as a Ward for 20 cases. Men to Operating Tent. R.J.K.	

Instructions regarding War Diaries and Intelligence Summaries are contained in F. S. Regs., Part II. and the Staff Manual respectively. Title Pages will be prepared in manuscript.

WAR DIARY

~~or~~

~~INTELLIGENCE SUMMARY~~

(Erase heading not required.)

Army Form C. 2118

112. F A.

Place	Date	Hour	Summary of Events and Information	Remarks and references to Appendices
WESTOUTRE	18/1/17		Routine R.H.	
"	19/1/17		Capt C. H. Denyer returned from 7/8 R. Irish. Fusrs. Capt. A. B. Bateman struck off strength on reporting to No. 15. C.C.S. Lieut A. S. Barr Sim left for Temporary Duty with Divn Train in relief of Capt. Bateman. 1 P.B. pte arrived as Caretaker at Divisional Baths. R.H.	
"	20/1/17		Worn part of floor of main latrine repaired with Cement. One Separation Tank pumped out & cleaned. Capt W. R. Lidderdale reported for Duty. R.H.	
"	21/1/17		Weather having been cold & snow lying, very hard frost set in. Capt W Turner returned from temporary Duty with 2nd. R.I.Regt, and was at once sent out for temporary Duty with 16th Divn Amm. Column. R.H.	
"	22/1/17		Second tank cleaned out. A "J" pattern hut completed, & personnel from tent transferred thereto. R.H.	

1875 Wt. W593/826 1,000,000 4/15 J.B.C. & A. A.D.S.S./Forms/C. 2118.

Instructions regarding War Diaries and Intelligence Summaries are contained in F. S. Regs., Part II. and the Staff Manual respectively. Title Pages will be prepared in manuscript.

WAR DIARY
or
~~INTELLIGENCE SUMMARY~~
(Erase heading not required.)

Army Form C. 2118

112. F.A.

Place	Date	Hour	Summary of Events and Information	Remarks and references to Appendices
WESTOUTRE	23/1/17		A tap in the Merewether steam-pump at Divisional Baths broke at an old crack & was immediately despatched for repair. Owing to this, & frost no bathing could be done today.	
"	24/1/17		Lieut H.F. Brice-Smith reported for duty. R.J.H. Floor of hut for Merewether pump raised by bricks. It was previously liable to flood from stream. Baths not working. R.J.H.	
"	25/1/17		Routine. R.J.H.	
"	26/1/17		The large (12 seat) latrine for IX. Corps M.D.S. complete except for flap-covers. Woodwork dis-assembled after numbering pieces. Captain C.H. Denyer left for charge of IX. Corps Scabies Station. R.J.H.	
"	27/1/17		The Belgian Engineer at Divn Baths, having been mobilised for the Army, was paid off – 1650 frs, but has procured a substitute, who has been accepted by Q. Branch. Capt W. Turner returned from 16th D.A.C. Capt W.G. Liddesdale left for temporary duty with 2nd. R. Dublin. Fusilrs. R.J.H.	

1875 Wt. W593/826 1,000,000 4/15 J.B.C. & A. A.D.S.S./Forms/C. 2118.

Instructions regarding War Diaries and Intelligence Summaries are contained in F. S. Regs., Part II. and the Staff Manual respectively. Title Pages will be prepared in manuscript.

WAR DIARY

~~or~~

~~INTELLIGENCE SUMMARY~~

(Erase heading not required.)

Army Form C. 2118

112. F.A.

Place	Date	Hour	Summary of Events and Information	Remarks and references to Appendices
WESTOUTRE	28/1/17		Captain A. Massey reported for duty. R.J.H.	
"	29/1/17		Captain A. Massey left for permanent Medical Charge of Divn Train. ~~Lieut~~ A.E. Barr Lim returned from Train on relief. R.J.H.	
"	30/1/17		A second "J" pattern hut completed & occupied by personnel from another attic. On attempting to start the Merewether pump, it was found that its steam-pipes were leaking. Shower-bath pipes at Baths repaired by R.E.	
"	31/1/17		Merewether pump removed for repair. The attic vacated yesterday fitted as a ward and occupied today. The present total "normal" accommodation of the Ambulance buildings for sick is — Headquarters — Ground floor 27 Attics 71. Schools 40. Total 138. The severe frost has frozen nearly every source of water & is causing great inconvenience. R.J. [illegible] Lt Col RAMC	

1875 Wt. W593/826 1,000,000 4/15 J.B.C. & A. A.D.S.S./Forms/C. 2118.

W A R D I A R Y.

FOR MONTH OF FEBRUARY, 1917.

VOLUME 15

UNIT:- 112th Field Ambulance R.A.M.C.

Feb. 1917

16th Div.

140/997

Vol 15

Instructions regarding War Diaries and Intelligence Summaries are contained in F. S. Regs., Part II. and the Staff Manual respectively. Title Pages will be prepared in manuscript.

WAR DIARY
~~or~~
~~INTELLIGENCE SUMMARY~~
(Erase heading not required.)

Army Form C. 2118

No: 112. Field Ambulance.

Place	Date	Hour	Summary of Events and Information	Remarks and references to Appendices
WESTOUTRE 28.S.W M.9.C.3.7	1/2/17		Routine. R. S. Hughes Lt Col RAMC.	
"	2/2/17		Captain H. F. Brice-Smith left for Temporary Duty with 16th Div^l Ammunition Col. R.S.H.	
"	3/2/17		The construction of the framework for the second latrine at IX Corps Main Dressing Station completed, also the under-seat urine troughs. Pack Store racks in construction. R.S.H.	
"	4/2/17		Capt T. F. Saunders RAMC (T.C) reported his return to the Ambulance after prolonged sick leave in England. Capt W. Turner left for temporary duty with 16th Div^l RE. Capt W. G. Liddesdale returned from temporary Duty with 2nd R. Dublin Fusiliers. R.S.H.	
"	5/2/17		Capt W. G. Liddesdale, as surplus to establishment, left for duty with 111 FA. 1 NCO & 5 ptes proceeded to IXth Corps class of Sanitation. R.S.H.	
"	6/2/17		Rev. T. A. McElfatrick 4th Class Chaplain (Presbyterian) attached to the F A. 1 pte. A.S.C. M.T. (Hale) left, proceeding to England to take up a Temporary Commission. R.S.H.	

1875 Wt. W593/826 1,000,000 4/15 J.B.C. & A. A.D.S.S./Forms/C. 2118.

Instructions regarding War Diaries and Intelligence Summaries are contained in F. S. Regs., Part II. and the Staff Manual respectively. Title Pages will be prepared in manuscript.

WAR DIARY
or
~~INTELLIGENCE SUMMARY~~

(Erase heading not required.)

112. F.A.

Army Form C. 2118

Place	Date	Hour	Summary of Events and Information	Remarks and references to Appendices
WESTOUTRE	7/2/17		Routine R.J.H.	
"	8/2/17		A fire occurred in the Brewery beside the Divisional Baths WESTOUTRE but was prevented from spreading to the Baths, where the only damage was some old canvas torn down as a precaution. 1 pte A.S.C. M.T. arrived as reinforcement. R.J.H.	
"	9/2/17		Routine R.J.H.	
"	10/2/17		During the past week the principal repairs to the Stable-floor were completed. At the IX Corps M.D.S. the Switch road was completed by the R.E. All iron Urine troughs were finished, and the seat flaps for the latrines. More pack-store racks made. 1 NCO & 5 ptes returned from Sanitation class Capt W. Turner returned from temporary duty with Div^l RE R.J.H.	
"	11/2/17		Capt W.L. Thomas attached temporarily pending departure for duty under A.D.M.S. CALAIS. R.J.H.	

1875 Wt. W593/826 1,000,000 4/15 J.B.C. & A. A.D.S.S./Forms/C. 2118.

Instructions regarding War Diaries and Intelligence Summaries are contained in F. S. Regs., Part II. and the Staff Manual respectively. Title Pages will be prepared in manuscript.

WAR DIARY
~~or~~
~~INTELLIGENCE SUMMARY~~
(Erase heading not required.)

Army Form C. 2118

112. F.A.

Place	Date	Hour	Summary of Events and Information	Remarks and references to Appendices
WESTOUTRE	12/2/17		Lieut A.E. Barr Sim left for temporary duty with 180 Bde RFA. Q.I.H.	
"	13/2/17		Capt W.L. Thomas left for duty under ADMS CALAIS Q.I.H.	
"	14/2/17		Routine Q.I.H.	
"	15/2/17		The severe frost seems to have ended. Thaw has set in. Q.I.H.	
"	16/2/17		Routine Q.I.H.	
"	17/2/17		During the past week (1) the sandbagging at the base of huts has been practically completed (2) the entrance to the transport lines built up with soling & sand (3) the erection of two large (60' x 20') Nissen Bow huts at IX Corps M.D.S. commenced (4) the frame for the cookhouse for M.D.S. completed (5) Tables & forms made & placed in the Dining-hall at the Schools Dressing Station, & (6) the painting of wagons begun as soon as the thaw permitted. Lieut A.E. Barr Sim returned from temporary duty with 180 Bde RFA, and was immediately placed on the sick-list with P.U.O. Q.I.H.	

1875 Wt. W593/826 1,000,000 4/15 J.B.C. & A. A.D.S.S./Forms/C. 2118.

Instructions regarding War Diaries and Intelligence Summaries are contained in F. S. Regs., Part II. and the Staff Manual respectively. Title Pages will be prepared in manuscript.

WAR DIARY
~~or~~
~~INTELLIGENCE SUMMARY~~
(Erase heading not required.)

Army Form C. 2118

112 F.A.

Place	Date	Hour	Summary of Events and Information	Remarks and references to Appendices
WESTOUTRE	18/2/17		Routine Q.H.	
"	19/2/17		Capt W Warburton proceeded to Second Army Course of Sanitation. Q.H.	
"	20/2/17		All pipes at the Divisional Baths thawed out & repaired when required. This work has been continuous for about 10 days. There were very few bursts, as the water froze in layers rather than in bulk. Q.H.	
"	21/2/17		Commenced to pump water to the Divisional Laundry by "Merryweather". Q.H.	
"	22/2/17		Routine Q.H.	
"	23/2/17		A new Engine having been obtained by the Division, the contract with the Belgian Engineman was concluded, and the old engine removed. Q.H.	

Instructions regarding War Diaries and Intelligence Summaries are contained in F. S. Regs., Part II. and the Staff Manual respectively. Title Pages will be prepared in manuscript.

WAR DIARY

or

~~INTELLIGENCE SUMMARY~~

(Erase heading not required.)

Army Form C. 2118

112 . F.A.

Place	Date	Hour	Summary of Events and Information	Remarks and references to Appendices
WESTOUTRE	24/2/17		Captain W. Warburton returned from Course of Sanitation. During the week (1) the painting of wagons proceeded (2) about 50 slabs of reinforced concrete were made for M.D.S. (3) the two large Nissen Bow huts were completed & camouflage painting begun. The new Engine at the Baths was this day placed in position. The ice has now gone from the Separation tanks and they are working properly again. Great credit is due to the NCO & men in charge of them for keeping up the working as long as possible & getting started when practicable. There were double floes each over 6 inches thick to be broken, & the filter was frozen solid. G.H.	
"	25/2/17		A new P.B man for caretaker at Baths arrived Capt H.F. Brice Smith returned from Duty with D A C.	
"	26/2/17		Capt W Turner proceeded to Course of Sanitation 1 NCO & 5 ptes went to IX Corps Course of Sanitation G.H.	

1875 Wt. W593/826 1,000,000 4/15 J.B.C. & A. A.D.S.S./Forms/C. 2118.

Instructions regarding War Diaries and Intelligence Summaries are contained in F. S. Regs., Part II. and the Staff Manual respectively. Title Pages will be prepared in manuscript.

WAR DIARY
or
INTELLIGENCE SUMMARY
(Erase heading not required.)

Army Form C. 2118

Place	Date	Hour	Summary of Events and Information	Remarks and references to Appendices
WESTOUTRE	27/2/17		Routine R.H.	
"	28/2/17		Frame of ablution shed for M.D.S. completed A new pattern of Ward Urinal of my own design has been made & taken into use; it consists of a cowled funnel fitting into the detachable lid of an oil drum. During the month 7 NCOs & men were evacuated for Measles or German Measles, of whom 5 have returned	

R. S. Hunt[?] Lt Col RAMC

W A R D I A R Y

FOR MONTH OF MARCH, 1917.

VOLUME 16

U N I T :- 112th Field Ambulance R.A.M.C.

Army Form C. 2118

Instructions regarding War Diaries and Intelligence Summaries are contained in F. S. Regs., Part II. and the Staff Manual respectively. Title Pages will be prepared in manuscript.

WAR DIARY
or
~~INTELLIGENCE SUMMARY~~

(Erase heading not required.)

No: 112. Field Ambulance

Place	Date	Hour	Summary of Events and Information	Remarks and references to Appendices
WESTOUTRE 28. S.W. M.9.C.3.7.	1/3/17		1 corporal returned from No: 7. General Hospital. G.J. Houghton Lieut Col RAMC	
"	2/3/17		One separation tank cleaned out. GJH	
"	3/3/17		During the week the repainting of trestles to complete those of two wards was carried on, also painting of wagons. For the Main Dr Stn more slabs of reinforced concrete were made and the high trestles (twelve) for dressing-rooms completed. A temporary latrine was also set up at the M.D.S. for the use of the Guard. GJH	
"	4/3/17		Lieut A E Barr Ctm proceeded on temporary duty with 2nd R Dublin Fusiliers. 1 pte returned from No: 7. Gen. Hosp. GJH	
"	5/3/17		Routine GJH	

1875 Wt. W593/826 1,000,000 4/15 J.B.C. & A. A.D.S.S./Forms/C. 2118.

Instructions regarding War Diaries and Intelligence Summaries are contained in F. S. Regs., Part II. and the Staff Manual respectively. Title Pages will be prepared in manuscript.

WAR DIARY
~~or~~
~~INTELLIGENCE SUMMARY~~
(Erase heading not required.)

Army Form C. 2118

112. F A

Place	Date	Hour	Summary of Events and Information	Remarks and references to Appendices
WESTOUTRE	6/3/17		The Ambulance Carpenters & Bricklayers were sent up to the M D S to live there & erect the various structures already prepared. One Separation tank cleaned out. Visited by Sanitary Officer 55th Division for purpose of studying the working of the Separation tanks. R.H.	
"	7/3/17		Capt H.F. Brice Smith left for temporary duty with 1st Entrenching Battalion Capt D H. Weir reported for temporary Duty. R.H.	
"	8/3/17		Routine. R.H.	
"	9/3/17		Work progressing at Main Dr. Stn. Frames & roofs of both latrines up, also Ablution Shed. Cookhouse partially roofed. Large Latrine & Ablution Shed partially floored. Handed over to Capt W. Turner preparatory to early start for 21 days leave in England. R. Hughes[?] Wm Lt Col RAMC.	

1875 Wt. W593/826 1,000,000 4/15 J.B.C. & A. A.D.S.S./Forms/C. 2118.

Instructions regarding War Diaries and Intelligence Summaries are contained in F. S. Regs., Part II. and the Staff Manual respectively. Title Pages will be prepared in manuscript.

WAR DIARY
or
INTELLIGENCE SUMMARY
(Erase heading not required.)

Army Form C. 2118

112 Field Ambulance

Place	Date	Hour	Summary of Events and Information	Remarks and references to Appendices
WESTOUTRE	10/3/17		Lt. Col G.J. Houghton RAMC proceeded on 21 days' leave in England. Capt D.H. Weir RAMC T. proceeded to 113th F.A. 64427 Pte Glasgey W.J. evacuated to No 1 Canadian C.C.S. 43554 Pte Thomas D evacuated to No 2 C.C.S. W Turner Capt. RAMC	
	11/3/17		1 G.S. Wagon on loan to 47th Mobile Veterinary Section 1 Water Cart on loan to 1st Royal Munster Fusiliers W.T.	
	12/3/17		1 Water Cart returned from 1st Royal Munster Fusiliers Repainting of Horse & Motor Ambulance - G.S Wagons. Water Cart etc in progress Laying of water pipe from Tank thro' Transport lines to Ablution Shed in progress. W.T.	
	13/3/17		Col. J.B. Wilson ADMS visited work at Main Dressing Station and expressed satisfaction at progress made. Repainting of ward-tents continued W.T.	
	14/3/17		Capt D.N. Macleod RAMC returned from Temporary Duty at Divisional School 64386 Pte Scott R 64401 Pte Skadden J } returned from Main Dressing Station 88901 Pte Ritchie S 64352 Pte Huggett E returned from Divisional School Handed over to Capt D N Macleod RAMC W Turner Capt RAMC	

1875 Wt. W593/826 1.000.000 4/15 J.B.C. & A. A.D.S.S./Forms/C. 2118.

Instructions regarding War Diaries and Intelligence Summaries are contained in F. S. Regs., Part II. and the Staff Manual respectively. Title Pages will be prepared in manuscript.

WAR DIARY
or
~~INTELLIGENCE SUMMARY~~
(Erase heading not required.)

Army Form C. 2118

112th Field Ambulance

Place	Date	Hour	Summary of Events and Information	Remarks and references to Appendices
WESTOUTRE	15/3/17		Routine — D.N. Macleod Capt R.A.M.C.	
	16/3/17		64471 Pte. Carmichael T. proceeded for duty with D.D.M.S. 9th Corps. 37861 Pte. Pearce J. reported for duty with this ambulance. D.N.M.	
	17/3/17		Repainting of Horse Ambulances completed: repainting of water carts in progress. Work at M.D.S. suspended owing to lack of material. D.N.M.	
	18/3/17		Routine	
	19/3/17		1 Sergeant + 5 men proceeded to School of Sanitation 9th Corps. D.N.M.	
	20/3/17		101097 Pte. Marr S.; 102257 Pte. Matthews G.; 101734 Pte. Meiklejohn T. } reported for duty with this ambulance. Repainting of water carts completed. D.N.M.	
	21/3/17		Lieut A.E. Barr-Sim returned from 2nd R. Dub. Fus. D.N.M.	

1875 Wt. W593/826 1,000,000 4/15 J.B.C. & A. A.D.S.S./Forms/C. 2118.

Army Form C. 2118

Instructions regarding War Diaries and Intelligence Summaries are contained in F. S. Regs., Part II. and the Staff Manual respectively. Title Pages will be prepared in manuscript.

WAR DIARY
or
~~INTELLIGENCE SUMMARY~~
(Erase heading not required.)

112th Field Ambulance

Place	Date	Hour	Summary of Events and Information	Remarks and references to Appendices
WESTOUTRE	22/3/17		Capt W. Warburton proceeded for Temporary duty with 16th Divisional Train Work at M.D.S. completely suspended. All portable material handed over to 113th Field Ambulance. D.N.M.	
	23/3/17		Routine Improvement of drains in progress. DNM.	
	24/3/17		Routine DNM	
	25/3/17		Routine DNM	
	26/3/17		Wards rewhitewashed. Improvement of drains completed. D.N.M.	
	27/3/17		Whitewashing of wards in progress. New horse trough erected. DNM	
	28/3/17		Routine DNM	
	29/3/17		Routine D.N.M. Whitewashing of wards & corridors completed.	

1875 Wt. W593/826 1,000,000 4/15 J.B.C. & A. A.D.S.S./Forms/C. 2118.

Instructions regarding War Diaries and Intelligence Summaries are contained in F. S. Regs., Part II. and the Staff Manual respectively. Title Pages will be prepared in manuscript.

WAR DIARY
or
~~INTELLIGENCE SUMMARY~~
(Erase heading not required.)

Army Form C. 2118

112th Field Ambulance

Place	Date	Hour	Summary of Events and Information	Remarks and references to Appendices
WESTOUTRE	30/3/17		Preparations for departure of 112th F.A. Advance Party of 59th F.A. arrived. DNM.	
HAZEBROUCK Sheet 27. (1.20.000) V. 16 a.b	31/3/17		112th Field Ambulance moved with 48th Inf. Bgde. to HAZEBROUCK. Billets & Horse lines at Sheet 27 (1/20.000) V. 16 a.b.	

D N Macleod
Capt RAMC.

1875 Wt. W593/826 1,000,000 4/15 J.B.C. & A. A.D.S.S./Forms/C. 2118.

April 1917

WAR DIARY FOR MONTH OF APRIL, 1917.

VOLUME:- 14

UNIT:- 112th Fd Ambce R.A.M.C.

Vol 17

Instructions regarding War Diaries and Intelligence Summaries are contained in F. S. Regs., Part II. and the Staff Manual respectively. Title Pages will be prepared in manuscript.

WAR DIARY

~~or~~

~~INTELLIGENCE SUMMARY~~

(Erase heading not required.)

Army Form C. 2118

No: 112 Field Ambulance

Place	Date	Hour	Summary of Events and Information	Remarks and references to Appendices
ARQUES. HAZEBROUCK 5A D-4. 6.8.	1/4/17		Ambulance marched to ARQUES, where I rejoined on return from leave. Officers billeted between Canal Bridge & Grande Place. Personnel in attics of Hotel de Ville. Transport on Quay W of Canal. 83 cases, including morning-sick & route-casualties had been carried during the day, and were sorted out after arrival. 22 were sent to No: 10 Sty. Hosp. & 61 returned by Motor Lorry to their Units. On my recommendation the Bde issued orders that the Regimental Lorries were to start early next morning, unload, & return for these cases. Cases mostly abrasion & dermatitis of feet. 2 RAMC 112 FA. both old cases of fractured ankle, fell out. I took over command from Capt D K Macleod at 5 PM. G. S. Hamilton Lt Col RAMC F.A.	
NORDAUSQUES HAZEBROUCK 5A A.3. 9½.7.	2/4/17		Under orders from Bde, all Horse Ambulance Wagons were detached to follow OC 112 Battalions on the march. Besides this, I arranged for Motor Ambulance Cars to remain behind at Batt. Hqrs & follow on a couple of hours later to relieve Horse Amb. Wagons if necessary of surplus sick. Units were moving at their own time, so the Ambulance marched off from the Grande Place at 9.15 AM, so as to follow the last Battalion. Progress was repeatedly checked between ARQUES & ST MARTIN au LAERTS, where I made a prolonged halt to allow the road in front to clear. Weather old & raw but no rain &c, till 1 mile from NORDAUSQUES when during a gale of wind a sharp cutting snow fell, changing to heavy rain & later large flakes of snow. Arrived NORDAUSQUES 4 PM. Opened Dressing Station at once in disused factory, very cobwebby & generally dirty, but capable of improvement & very good accommodation for 60 cases at least. Only 11 cases to be accommodated on arrival. 1 RAMC fell out — flat feet & broken boots. Officers billeted in houses, Personnel in barns, Horses in sheds. Later I arranged with 48th Bde for the collection of sick by Horse & Motor Amb cars, including an M.O. to visit RESQUES daily. The Brigadier is appointing me SMO Bde. G.H.	

1875 Wt. W593/826 1,000,000 4/15 J.B.C. & A. A.D.S.S./Forms/C. 2118.

Instructions regarding War Diaries and Intelligence Summaries are contained in F. S. Regs., Part II. and the Staff Manual respectively. Title Pages will be prepared in manuscript.

WAR DIARY

~~or~~

~~INTELLIGENCE SUMMARY~~

(Erase heading not required.)

Army Form C. 2118

112 F.A.

Place	Date	Hour	Summary of Events and Information	Remarks and references to Appendices
NORDAUSQUES	3/4/17		Large fatigue-parties required for cleaning Dressing Station, stores & offices, transport & main road & for sanitary duties. Remainder Squad Drill &c. 3 inches of snow fell during the night & drifted into billets rather badly. Sanitary condition of area fair except near Dressing Station where accumulations of filth existed. The existing latrines are not quite sufficient & approachable only through deep mud. They are of the deep-pit type with more or less fly-proof box seats, & have no overhead cover. Water is obtained from a farmyard pump. It is extraordinarily good to the Chloride of Lime test, but I am adding one measure per cent. In the afternoon I despatched the interpreter to purchase Lime for whitewashing. I myself visited & advised M.O's of 3 Battalions, all of whom reported Sanitary Conditions as fair or good. All Water reported good. I also inspected the T.M.B. area & suggested improvements. This unit was taking interest & getting on well. Weather raw & cold but no rain. R.H.	
"	4/4/17		Capt D N Macleod proceeded to 16th Div School on duty in connection with Mess Accounts, to which he had lent a considerable sum of his own money. R.H.	
"	5/4/17		No: 53603 Pte Gray D.M. despatched for testing for Commission in R.A. R.H.	

1875 Wt. W593/826 1,000,000 4/15 J.B.C. & A. A.D.S.S./Forms/C. 2118.

Instructions regarding War Diaries and Intelligence Summaries are contained in F. S. Regs., Part II. and the Staff Manual respectively. Title Pages will be prepared in manuscript.

WAR DIARY
~~or~~
~~INTELLIGENCE~~ SUMMARY

(Erase heading not required.)

Army Form C. 2118.

112 F.A.

Place	Date	Hour	Summary of Events and Information	Remarks and references to Appendices
NORDAUSQUES	6/4/17		Captain D.N. Macleod returned from Divisional School. Rev R. Bird. Major. C.F. attached temporarily. R.H.	
"	7/4/17		Routine R.H.	
"	8/4/17		Held meeting of Regimental & Ambulance MOs & discussed problems of Open Warfare and March Discipline R.H.	
"	9/4/17		Submitted scheme for Medical Arrangements on Attack Exercise to Brigadier & went over ground with him. R.H.	
"	10/4/17		Routine R.H.	
"	11/4/17		Practised Pitching Tents for Dressing-Stations in high gale & snow. R.H.	
"	12/4/17		Repeated Tent-Pitching in gale with rain & hail R.H.	

2449 Wt. W14957/M90 750,000 1/16 J.B.C. & A. Forms/C.2118/12.

Instructions regarding War Diaries and Intelligence Summaries are contained in F. S. Regs., Part II. and the Staff Manual respectively. Title Pages will be prepared in manuscript.

WAR DIARY
or
~~INTELLIGENCE SUMMARY~~

(Erase heading not required.)

Army Form C. 2118.

112 . F A

Place	Date	Hour	Summary of Events and Information	Remarks and references to Appendices
NORDAUSQUES	13/4/17		Attack Exercise. Medical arrangements worked admirably, & bearers could not have done better under bad ground & weather conditions – High Gale & hail. R.H.	
"	14/4/17		Routine.	
ARQUES HAZEBROUCK 5A D.4.6.8.)	15/4/17		Under orders from ADMS. left 1 Section to look after new Brigade (49th) arriving. 112. FA less 1 section marched with 49th Bde to ARQUES. R.H.	
HAZEBROUCK 5A G.4.5.9.	16/4/17		Marched to HAZEBROUCK. Heavy falling out among infantry. Very inconvenient billet 2 miles outside town. R.H.	
LOCRE. 28.M.23.5.9	17/4/17		Marched to LOCRE. & camped on site of intended Main Dressing Station Map. 28. M. 23. 5. 9. R.H.	
NORDAUSQUES 5A.A.3.9&7	18/4/17		Returned by Car with ADMS to NORDAUSQUES, leaving 2 sections at LOCRE. Lieut. A.E. Barclim reported his return from leave. R.H.	
"	19/4/17		Routine R.H.	

2449 Wt. W14957/M90 750,000 1/16 J.B.C. & A. Forms/C.2118/12.

Instructions regarding War Diaries and Intelligence Summaries are contained in F. S. Regs., Part II. and the Staff Manual respectively. Title Pages will be prepared in manuscript.

WAR DIARY
or
~~INTELLIGENCE SUMMARY~~
(Erase heading not required.)

Army Form C. 2118.

112. F.A.

Place	Date	Hour	Summary of Events and Information	Remarks and references to Appendices
NORDAUSQUES	20/4/17		2 Master & 4 Dqrs Staff arrived by M A Car from LOCRE. 2 M.S & 6 Bearers went to LOCRE in their stead. [illegible]	
"	21/4/17		Routine [illegible]	
"	22/4/17		Routine [illegible]	
"	23/4/17		As S M O 49th Bde, held meeting of Regimental & F.A. M.O.s & discussed March & Open Warfare problems [illegible]	
"	24/4/17		Routine [illegible]	
"	25/4/17		Routine [illegible]	
"	26/4/17		Attack Exercise of 49th Bde. Regimental M O's & Bearers worked admirably. No FA display possible [illegible]	
"	27/4/17		Routine [illegible]	

2449 Wt. W14957/M90 750,000 1/16 J.B.C. & A. Forms/C.2118/12.

Instructions regarding War Diaries and Intelligence Summaries are contained in F. S. Regs., Part II. and the Staff Manual respectively. Title Pages will be prepared in manuscript.

WAR DIARY

or

~~INTELLIGENCE SUMMARY~~

(Erase heading not required.)

Army Form C. 2118.

112 . F.A.

Place	Date	Hour	Summary of Events and Information	Remarks and references to Appendices
ARQUES HAZEBROUCK 5A D.4 6.8.	28/4/17		Marched with 49th Brigade to ARQUES. Weather warm. R.H.	
HAZEBROUCK 5A. G.4. 5.7½	29/4/17		Marched to HAZEBROUCK. Arranged for more convenient billet. Rather heavy falling out on road. Weather very warm. R.H.	
LOCRE. 28.M.23.5.9	30/4/17		Marched to LOCRE & rejoined 2 sections there. Received orders for taking over Adv. Dr Stns & Dr Stns from 19th Divn & arranged with C.O's of F.A's concerned. R. Hamilton Lt Col RAMC	

2449 Wt. W14957/M90 750,000 1/16 J.B.C. & A. Forms/C.2118/12.

May 1917

W A R   D I A R Y :

VOLUME:- 18

FOR MONTH OF MAY, 1917.

U N I T :- RAMC 112th Fd. Amba

Vol 78

Instructions regarding War Diaries and Intelligence Summaries are contained in F. S. Regs., Par. II. and the Staff Manual respectively. Title Pages will be prepared in manuscript.

WAR DIARY
~~or~~
~~INTELLIGENCE SUMMARY~~
(Erase heading not required.)

Army Form C. 2118.

No: 112 FIELD AMBULANCE

Place	Date	Hour	Summary of Events and Information	Remarks and references to Appendices
LOCRE. 28. M. 23 d. 3. 8	1/5/17.		Took over A.D.S. Dugout at VIERSTRAAT. 28. N. 10. a 99. & Bearer Posts beside R.A.Ps. at BRASSERIE VIERSTRAAT. N. 11. a. 58. 9 "POPPY LANE" N. 6 a 15. from 58 F.A., the Division now taking over the DIEPENDAL SECTOR. Detachment Offrs. 2 O.R. 28 R.J. H[illegible] Lt Col RAMC	
"	2/5/17		Took over Dr. Stn. LA CLYTTE. N. 4. 5. 6 from No 58 F.A., to be used as an A.D.S. Detach t. 1 Offr. 35 O.R. RJH.	
WESTOUTRE M. 9. c 3. 7.	3/5/17		Took over from 59. F.A. the Dr Stn - the Hospice & Schools - WESTOUTRE as Headquarters RJH.	
"	4/5/17		Routine RJH	
"	5/5/17		Shells struck stables & round 2. M. Stores at LA CLYTTE. Stores damaged slightly. 8. H. D. Horses & 1 mule killed. 3. H.D. 1 Rider, & 5 mules wounded. Capt. W. Turner proceeded on special leave to England. RJH.	
"	6/6/17		LA CLYTTE shelled again during the night. One wall cracked. Capt F. C. Atkinson Fleming reported for temporary duty RJH.	

2449 Wt. W14957/M90 750,000 1/16 J.B.C. & A. Forms/C.2118/12.

Instructions regarding War Diaries and Intelligence Summaries are contained in F. S. Regs., Part II. and the Staff Manual respectively. Title Pages will be prepared in manuscript.

WAR DIARY
~~or~~
~~INTELLIGENCE SUMMARY~~
(Erase heading not required.)

Army Form C. 2118.

112 F.A.

Place	Date	Hour	Summary of Events and Information	Remarks and references to Appendices
WESTOUTRE	7/5/17		A few shells in LA CLYTTE last night. Reduced Staff to 1 Officer & 15 O.R. RJH	
"	8/5/17		Further reduced LA CLYTTE Staff to 1 Offr & 10 O.R. to live in Dug-out. RJH	
"	9/5/17		The DIEPENDAL Sector being again handed over to 19th Division, an Advance Party of 58 F.A. arrived at LA CLYTTE to take over VIERSTRAAT tomorrow. RJH	
"	10/5/17		Dug Outs at VIERSTRAATTE handed over to 58 FA RJH	
LOCRE M.23.d.3.8	11/5/17		Dr Stn LA CLYTTE handed over to 58 FA, & Dr Stn WESTOUTRE to 59 FA. Marched to field at LOCRE. RJH	
"	12/5/17		Routine RJH	
"	13/5/17		Routine RJH	

2449 Wt. W14957/M90 750,000 1/16 J.B.C. & A. Forms/C.2118/12.

Instructions regarding War Diaries and Intelligence Summaries are contained in F. S. Regs., Part II. and the Staff Manual respectively. Title Pages will be prepared in manuscript.

WAR DIARY
or
~~INTELLIGENCE SUMMARY~~
(Erase heading not required.)

Army Form C. 2118.

112. F.A.

Place	Date	Hour	Summary of Events and Information	Remarks and references to Appendices
LOCRE	14/5/17		Capt W. Warburton to temporary duty with 7th Bn The Leinster Regt. RJH	
"	15/5/17		Despatched C Section + 1 Horse Ambulance Wagon & 3 M. A. Cars (Strength 2 Offrs & 55 O.R. RAMC. 4 OR. M.T. ASC. & 14. OR H.T. ASC) to join 47th Infantry Bde en route for 2nd Army Training Area. Large collection of obsolete orders &c destroyed by fire in presence of Capt Atkinson Kenning RAMC. RJH	
"	16/5/17		Routine RJH	
"	17/5/17		6 Mules received from 2nd Army Remount Depot. RJH	
"	18/5/17		C Section arrived at ESCOUILLES in training Area. Consultation with DDMS. IX th Corps & ADMS. 16th Div & OCs 111 & 113 FAs re Dressing Stations for active operations. Afterwards proceeded to inspect "Walking Wounded Route". RJH	

2449 Wt. W14957/M90 750,000 1/16 J.B.C. & A. Forms/C.2118/12.

Instructions regarding War Diaries and Intelligence Summaries are contained in F. S. Regs., Part II. and the Staff Manual respectively. Title Pages will be prepared in manuscript.

WAR DIARY
or
~~INTELLIGENCE SUMMARY~~
(Erase heading not required.)

Army Form C. 2118.

112 FA.

Place	Date	Hour	Summary of Events and Information	Remarks and references to Appendices.
LOCRE	19/5/17		Took over 17 Small Hospital Marquees for Main & Walking Cases Dressing Stations. Measured out ground in garden of HOSPICE LOCRE 23.d.7.0. & commenced pegging out. G.H.	
"	20/5/17		With ADMS visited all Medical Posts in & behind the Trenches, & again inspected parts of Walking Wounded Route. G.H.	
"	21/5/17		Work begun on Walking Wounded Dressing Station M 24.d.3.8. G.H.	
"	22/5/17		Capt W. Turner returned from leave. G.H.	
"	23/5/17		Inspected Detachment & Dressing Station at ESCOUILLES. (24 kilometres beyond ST. OMER on BOULOGNE Road). Everything very satisfactory. Small Farm Brewery. Patients & Offices in rooms. Personnel in good Coy. G.H.	
"	24/5/17		Capt Atkinson Fleming left to take over charge of 8th Bn. R. Inniskilling Fusiliers. Capt G. Buchanan reported for duty. G.H.	

2449 Wt. W14957/M90 750,000 1/16 J.B.C. & A. Forms/C.2118/12.

Army Form C. 2118.

WAR DIARY
or
~~INTELLIGENCE SUMMARY~~
(Erase heading not required.)

Instructions regarding War Diaries and Intelligence Summaries are contained in F. S. Regs., Part II. and the Staff Manual respectively. Title Pages will be prepared in manuscript.

112. F.A.

Place	Date	Hour	Summary of Events and Information	Remarks and references to Appendices
LOCRE	25/5/17		Last evening a working party at S.P. 13 constructing new R.A.P. were severely shelled and 1 man mortally wounded, 1 slightly - remaining at duty, & 1 badly shell-shocked. 73231 pte Doose G.A. died this morning from wounds at No. 53. C.C.S. GJH.	
"	26/5/17		Received 10 privates RAMC as reinforcement. GJH.	
"	27/5/17		Routine GJH	
"	28/5/17		Routine GJH	
"	29/5/17		Capt C H Denyer returned from duty as O.C. IX Corps Scabies Station. GJH.	
"	30/5/17		Routine GJH	

2449 Wt. W14957/M90 750,000 1/16 J.B.C. & A. Forms/C.2118/12.

Instructions regarding War Diaries and Intelligence Summaries are contained in F. S. Regs., Part II. and the Staff Manual respectively. Title Pages will be prepared in manuscript.

WAR DIARY

or

~~INTELLIGENCE SUMMARY~~

(Erase heading not required.)

112 F.A.

Army Form C. 2118.

Place	Date	Hour	Summary of Events and Information	Remarks and references to Appendices
LOCRE	31/5/17		C Section re returned from Training Area. Dressing Stations – Work Done:– Main M.D.S. 10 Marquees stained & pitched. Floors levelled. Two marquees boarded. Walking Cases Dr Stn. Boundaries wired. Dressing hut – painted inside & a door made at closed end. 7 Marquees Pitched & floored with Tarpaulin. Stables re cleaned, whitewashed, disinfected & repaired. Foul ground dug up & quicklimed. Incinerator too close to Ammunition Dump taken down & re-erected in safe place. Latrines rendered fly-proof. P. J. Hamilton[?] Lt Col RAMC OC 112 F.A.	

2449 Wt. W14957/M90 750,000 1/16 J.B.C. & A. Forms/C.2118/12.

June 1917

10

WAR DIARY.

FOR MONTH OF JUNE, 1917.

VOLUME:- 19.

UNIT:- RAMC. 112th Field Ambulance

Vol 19

B.E.F.

SUMMARY OF MEDICAL WAR DIARIES OF 112th F.A./ 16th Div.

8thCorps. 5th ARMY. from 22.6.17.

Western Front Operations - June - 1917.

Officer Commanding - Lt.Col. P. Houghton.

SUMMARISED UNDER THE FOLLOWING HEADINGS:-

Phase "D" - Battle of Messines - June - 1917.

B.E.F.

112th F.A. 16th Div. 8th Corps. 5th ARMY.

Officer Commanding - Lt.Col. P. Houghton.

WESTERN FRONT
June 1917.

PHASE "D" - Battle of Messines - June - 1917.

Headquarters at Rubrouck H. 14.a.3.7. (27).

June 22nd. Division arrived in 5th ARMY.

B.E.F.

16th Div.

SUMMARY OF MEDICAL WAR DIARIES OF 112th F.A./8th

Corps. 5th ARMY. (from June 22nd).

Western Front Operations - June - 1917.

Officer Commanding - Lt.Col. P. Houghton.

SUMMARISED UNDER THE FOLLOWING HEADINGS:-

Phase "D" - Battle of Messines - June - 1917.

B.E.F.

112th F.A. 16th Div. 8th Corps. 5th ARMY. WESTERN FRONT June 1917.

Officer Commanding - Lt.Col. P. Houghton.

PHASE "D" - Battle of Messines - June - 1917.

Headquarters at Rubrouck H. 14.a.3.7. (27).

June 22nd. Division arrived in 5th ARMY.

Instructions regarding War Diaries and Intelligence Summaries are contained in F. S. Regs., Part II. and the Staff Manual respectively. Title Pages will be prepared in manuscript.

WAR DIARY

~~or~~

~~INTELLIGENCE SUMMARY~~

(Erase heading not required.)

Army Form C. 2118.

No: 112. Field Ambulance

Place	Date	Hour	Summary of Events and Information	Remarks and references to Appendices
LOCRE 28. M.23.d.38.	1/6/17		Captain W. Warburton returned from temporary duty with 7th Bn Leinster Regt. In view of probable shelling of area, started work on two large Elephanted dug-outs, one at 23d.3.8, the other beside the future Walking Wounded Dressing Station at 24d.3.8. on which I have started work last month. See — [signature] Lt Col RAMC	Rough plan Appendix 1
"	2/6/17		Routine [initials]	
"	3/6/17		Capt W. Turner & Lieut A Barr Sim detached to No: 113. F.A. [initials]	
"	4/6/17		Personnel & Surgical Equipment B Tent Subdivision sent to Main Dressing Station under Capt D N Macleod, 113. F.A. HOSPICE LOCRE 29. 6. 5 9). Bearers of No 111. F.A. arrived under Capt Macdonald RAMC & temporarily accommodated at Walking Wounded Dr Stn. 3 NCOs & 39 ptes returned from dug-out construction under 157 Coy RE. Capt T F Saunders began work of putting out direction posts for walking wounded route, being interrupted by hostile shell fire at times, one lamp-stand being struck by a shell-fragment. [initials]	
"	5/6/17		Direction Posts on W.W. Route completed. Right flank via PARRAIN FARM N22 d. 6.4. DOCTOR'S HOUSE 21 d. 6.4 & YORK ROAD to 22 A. 7.10. Left Flank via LAITERIE 16 d. 3.4. From 16. d. 3.4 & 22 A. 7.10 tracks across open to about 16C. 4.4 where they join Sluice to 15-C. 2-4 - BEAVER FARM - MILKYWAY to	

2449 Wt. W14957/M90 750,000 1/16 J.B.C. & A. Forms/C.2118/12.

Instructions regarding War Diaries and Intelligence Summaries are contained in F. S. Regs., Part II. and the Staff Manual respectively. Title Pages will be prepared in manuscript.

WAR DIARY
or
~~INTELLIGENCE SUMMARY~~
(Erase heading not required.)

Army Form C. 2118.

112. F.A.

Place	Date	Hour	Summary of Events and Information	Remarks and references to Appendices
LOCRE	5/6/17		Continued 15 c. 1. 9. Field track to 14 d. 3. 2. Road to "Pompier" Corner 14. c. 5. 9 Turn down NUTLANE by BUTTERFLY FARM. 19. a. 7. 9 to junction with BRULOOZE KEMMEL Road at 24. d. 2. 10. Thence a few yards to W.W. Dr St. 24. d. 3. 8 GW	
BRULOOZE WALKING WOUNDED DRESSING STATION M.24 d.3.8	6/6/17		C Tent Subdivision to Main Dressing Stn. (113 FA) under Capt. Q. Buchanan All Bearers handed over to command of Capt Denyer. Commanding 16th Divl. Bearers. LOCRE shelled at 10.30 AM. One shell burst on new road through my camp, and 4.2 Howitzer shell burst in soft ground above me on the slope four yards from me. I sustained no injury whatever. Other shells distributed East of & close to LOCRE In evening moved up to W.W. Dr Stn with A Tent Sub-Division + 13 O.R of No: 111. FA. Everything ready for reception of Wounded by 10. P.M Description of arrangements. – Wounded to enter direct from LOCRE – KEMMEL Road by Trench-board bridge with handrails. Particulars to be taken by staff of Ar D Book in hut on left of entrance. YMCA to issue refreshments at hut on right of entrance. Wounded to pass thence to right of fence to 3 Marquees with Palliasses spread & benches outside, to await Dressing	See APPENDIX I

2449 Wt. W14957/M90 750,000 1/16 J.B.C. & A. Forms/C.2118/12.

Army Form C. 2118.

WAR DIARY
or
~~INTELLIGENCE SUMMARY~~
(Erase heading not required.)

112. FA

Instructions regarding War Diaries and Intelligence Summaries are contained in F. S. Regs., Part II. and the Staff Manual respectively. Title Pages will be prepared in manuscript.

Place	Date	Hour	Summary of Events and Information	Remarks and references to Appendices
W.W. Dr Stn M24 d.3.8	6/6/17		Continued. Thence to Dressing Room (Nissen Bow hut). After dressing to 2nd row of Marquees or to Large stable to await evacuation. One side of stable with straw laid down & other with benches for men wishing to sit & smoke. The seventh Marquee to be temporarily lent to YMCA for refreshments to men awaiting evacuation. Evacuation to be by Lorry or by Train at siding 24 d.3.6. Staff consists of O.C. & 2 M.O's 112 F.A. (Capt W. Warburton & Capt T. F. Saunders) with assistance from M.O. 11th Hants Pioneers (Capt Black RAMC), personnel of A Tent Subdivn 112 F.A. + Clerks from C Section, and 14 O.R. from 111 F.A. 2nd Lieut. Kerr (Railway Ordnance Dept) reported his arrival for purpose of giving all assistance re trains. Two YMCA officials – Rev Mr Rainsford & Mr Nowlings – joined the latter with 2 privates from my staff set up a Refreshment Bar at GARDEN FARM 14 c.1.7. from which point wounded would be as far as possible brought to the Dressing Station by Horse Ambulance Wagon. Pitt	

2449 Wt. W14957/M90 750,000 1/16 J.B.C. & A. Forms/C.2118/12.

Instructions regarding War Diaries and Intelligence Summaries are contained in F. S. Regs., Part II. and the Staff Manual respectively. Title Pages will be prepared in manuscript.

WAR DIARY

~~or~~

~~INTELLIGENCE SUMMARY~~

(Erase heading not required.)

Army Form C. 2118.

112 F.A

Place	Date	Hour	Summary of Events and Information	Remarks and references to Appendices
N.W. Dr. Stn. M.24.d.3.8	7/6/17		Day of Capture of MESSINES Ridge Zero hour – 3.10 AM. The first cases arrived about 5 AM, but very few till 6.30 AM. After that a rush. Wounds were on the whole slight, but very few likely to get well in a few days. When the rush began, it was found impossible to take particulars at the entrance so A.F.W. 3210 were made out by relays of clerks working in the open. No case was allowed to enter the dressing-room without his proper Medical Card so no difficulty arose through overlooked men. As I had rather expected the 3 marquees for reception were early found insufficient, and I used all 6 marquees for this purpose, keeping the large Stable only for those dressed and awaiting evacuation. During the day I received voluntary assistance from M.O's of near-by Units:— Capt Hardy. M.C. 23rd Heavy Group R.G.A. Lieut Liddell (Straggler M.O) & Capt Mitchell. 3rd Br West India Regt. 1 NCO & 20 ptes of a Labour Battalion were placed at my disposal at 11 AM by a near-by Heavy Battery. They were most useful for loading Trains &c & for relieving RAMC on General Duty. I was thus enabled to send an Orderly with each Lorry or Train. I was able to early slow down the supply of Lorries, originally one every half-hour. They were used in the morning. The first Train was despatched at 1.30PM. The rate of dressing cases worked out at about 6 minutes per case, & so was slow at first. Later numbers were practically doubled through the help given by the volunteering Medical Officers.	

2449 Wt. W14957/M90 750,000 1/16 J.B.C. & A. Forms/C.2118/12.

Instructions regarding War Diaries and Intelligence Summaries are contained in F. S. Regs., Part II. and the Staff Manual respectively. Title Pages will be prepared in manuscript.

WAR DIARY
or
INTELLIGENCE SUMMARY
(Erase heading not required.)

112 F.A.

Army Form C. 2118.

Place	Date	Hour	Summary of Events and Information	Remarks and references to Appendices
W.W. Dr Stn M.24.d.3.8	7/6/17		continued. During the morning it was found that a number of walking wounded were ignoring the laid-down track & were coming in through KEMMEL N.21 central, so horse Ambulance Wagons were sent up the LOCRE - KEMMEL Road to assist them.	
			Evacuations were as follows	

	Time	Cases O.R.	By
AM	8.30.	16	by Lorry.
	9.0.	16	"
	9.45	16	"
	10.30.	16	"
	11.15	16	"
	11.45	19	"
P.M	12.45	16	"

115 / 324 / 6 / 445

	Time	Cases	Officers	O.R	By
P.M.	1.15.	Cases	3	4	by M.A.Car
	1.30	"		40	" TRAIN
	4.0	"		75	" "
	4.0	"	2		" M.A.Car.
	5.40	"		34	" LORRIES
	7.30	Germans	1.	22	" Lorry.
	7.45	British		19	" "
	8.0	"		18	" "
	11.30	"		112	" TRAIN
				324	

After 11.30 PM all cases were allowed to sleep after dressing. Cases were loaded into Lorries & Trains by specially made stair-ladders constructed under Capt Saunders supervision by No 4 Div^l Supply Column. About noon was inspected by Surgeon General Macpherson who appeared to be very pleased with the work in progress.

[initials]

Instructions regarding War Diaries and Intelligence Summaries are contained in F. S. Regs., Part II. and the Staff Manual respectively. Title Pages will be prepared in manuscript.

WAR DIARY
or
~~INTELLIGENCE SUMMARY~~

(Erase heading not required.)

Army Form C. 2118.

112 FA

Place	Date	Hour	Summary of Events and Information	Remarks and references to Appendices
WW. Dr Stn M.24d.3.8	8/6/17		The Dressing-room was clear by 1 AM. Only a few British and 25 German wounded arrived during the night. 3 Officers & 25 O.R. British arrived between 10 AM & 6 PM Evacuation A.M. 10.0. British O.R. 66 Germans 25 O.R. by TRAIN 11.0 " Officers 3 O.R. 6 by M.A. Car P.M. 6.0 " O.R. 19 by Lorry. 91 In despatching German wounded, escort was provided by O.C. 3rd Bn British West India Regiment. RH	
"	9/6/17		Evacuation 10 AM Officers 2 by M A Car " O.R 54 } by Train Germans 5 } 2.54 RH	
LOCRE M23d.3.8	10/6/17		Only an occasional case since 10 AM yesterday, which were sent off by M.A. Car. The Dressing Station from this morning was kept open but with only an Orderly M.O. Bearers & Tent Subdivns B.C. returned to Headquarters which moved back to M.23.d.3.5. RH	

2449 Wt. W14957/M90 750,000 1/16 J.B.C. & A. Forms/C.2118/12.

Instructions regarding War Diaries and Intelligence Summaries are contained in F. S. Regs., Part II. and the Staff Manual respectively. Title Pages will be prepared in manuscript.

WAR DIARY
or
~~INTELLIGENCE SUMMARY~~
(Erase heading not required.)

Army Form C. 2118.

No: 112. F.A.

Place	Date	Hour	Summary of Events and Information	Remarks and references to Appendices
LOCRE	11/6/17		Captain Denyer returned to IXth Corps Scabies Station. B.I.K.	
"	12/6/17		Closed W.W. Dressing Station in the afternoon. A Tent Subdivn's MO returned to Hdqrs. In the 3 days, 7 8 9 June 10 Officers & 670 OR (British) passed through the Dr Stn, as Walking Wounded, of whom all but 32 OR were properly dressed before leaving. Besides these about 20 cases were dressed, but converted into stretcher cases, & passed to No: 113 F.A. as direct admissions. 1 Officer & 52 OR (Germans) were dressed & evacuated. B.I.K.	
FLETRE 27.W.C.9.7	13/6/17		On the Division going into rest, marched at 9.15 AM to farms near FLETRE. Map 27 W 11 C.6.7 & C.9.7 & a. 4.2. Dressing station not opened. Collected sick from 47th Bde & sent in to No: 111 F.A at METEREN X.15 d. Personnel billeted in farms. B.I.K.	

2449 Wt. W14957/M90 750,000 1/16 J.B.C. & A. Forms/C.2118/12.

Army Form C. 2118.

WAR DIARY
or
~~INTELLIGENCE SUMMARY~~
(Erase heading not required.)

Instructions regarding War Diaries and Intelligence Summaries are contained in F. S. Regs., Part II. and the Staff Manual respectively. Title Pages will be prepared in manuscript.

112 FA

Place	Date	Hour	Summary of Events and Information	Remarks and references to Appendices
FLETRE	14/6/17		Capt D N Macleod left for Temporary Duty with 9th R. Dubl. Fusilrs. RH	
"	15/6/17		Lieut A E Barrison left for Temporary Duty with 8th R. Dubl Fusilrs. RH	
"	16/6/17		Routine RH	
HAEGEDOORNE 28.S.4.d.2.8.	17/6/17		Marched to camp near BAILLEUL. All personnel under canvas. Weather very hot. RH	
FLETRE. 27.W.c.9.7	18/6/17		Returned by march in very hot weather to previous camp. RH	
"	19/6/17		Routine RH	

2449 Wt. W14957/M90 750,000 1/16 J.B.C. & A. Forms/C.2118/12.

Instructions regarding War Diaries and Intelligence Summaries are contained in F. S. Regs., Part II. and the Staff Manual respectively. Title Pages will be prepared in manuscript.

WAR DIARY
or
~~INTELLIGENCE SUMMARY~~
(Erase heading not required.)

Army Form C. 2118.

112 FA.

Place	Date	Hour	Summary of Events and Information	Remarks and references to Appendices
ST SYLVESTRE CAPPEL	20/6/17		Marched to farm outside ST SYLVESTRE CAPPEL. Personnel in Tents & Barns.	
27.P.17d.4.2			Capt Denyer returned from IX Corps Scabies Station. Q.H.	
"	21/6/17		Routine. Q.H.	
RUBROUCK 27.H.14a.3.7	22/6/17		Marched mostly in rain to RUBROUCK. Inspected en route by G.O.C. Second Army. Dressing Station in old Estaminet Buildings. Two good wards & good Dressing Room & Dispensary, and good reception-room. Kitchen bad. Small rooms upstairs & attics as billets for 2/3 A Section. Remainder of A in attic over Sergeants' Mess at 14a 6.6. B & C in barn in farm 8.C.3.3. Water from pumps in village. 1 scoop. Washing water from ponds. Q.H.	
"	23/6/17		As SMO 48th Bde inspected Billets & Sanitation of 8th R. Dub. Fus. at LA CLOCHE in B.18.a & 9th R.D.F. in H.4 & 8 & interviewed MOs of 7th R.I.R & 2nd R.D.F. re sanitation. (accompanied by Sub Area Commandant) I am greatly concerned about water-supplies in this area & fear that the wells will soon be polluted by drawing from wider areas including Middens. Have sent an Officer to locate better supplies & myself have interviewed Water Official at ARNEKE 4.24. and have inspected Q.H.	

Instructions regarding War Diaries and Intelligence Summaries are contained in F. S. Regs., Part II. and the Staff Manual respectively. Title Pages will be prepared in manuscript.

WAR DIARY
or
INTELLIGENCE SUMMARY

(Erase heading not required.)

Army Form C. 2118.

RJK

Place	Date	Hour	Summary of Events and Information	Remarks and references to Appendices
RUBROUCK	23/6/17		Continued. various points on the YSER RIVER with a view to drawing there. River reported as requiring 3 scoops & is very low. At B.25 a.11 there is a good rippling run above the footbridge, and it looks a possible place. RJK	
"	24/6/17		Routine RJK	
"	25/6/17		Received 2. ASC ptes as reinforcement RJK	
"	26/6/17		Capt W Turner to 4th R.I Rifles on Temporary Duty RJK	
"	27/6/17		Routine RJK	

2449 Wt. W14957/M90 750,000 1/16 J.B.C. & A. Forms/C.2118/12.

Instructions regarding War Diaries and Intelligence Summaries are contained in F. S. Regs., Part II. and the Staff Manual respectively. Title Pages will be prepared in manuscript.

WAR DIARY
or
INTELLIGENCE SUMMARY
(Erase heading not required.)

Army Form C. 2118.

112 F A.

Place	Date	Hour	Summary of Events and Information	Remarks and references to Appendices
RUBROUCK	28/6/17		Capt D.N. Macleod returned from temporary duty with 9th R. D. Fusrs. The Sub Area Commdt reports that a well formerly 1 scoop now requires 4! and I have received a report of another well drying up altogether. After recent rain the YSER now requires 8–9 Scoops! This is certainly due to washing of manure etc off the land surface, the river being reported as up about 2 feet. I accompanied the Sub Area Cdt to the VIII Corps C.E. & arranged for an early visit from the R.E. Offr i/c Water with a view to discussion of a scheme of my own for a partial filtration of the YSER at B.28 a.1.1. requiring small material, & to be constructed by my own men. The scheme includes a coke or cinder bed 2' deep, held in place above by a plate of expanded metal, below by a wooden dam raised a couple of inches above river-bottom, and admitting water for upward filtration through sand & outflow over the top of a second wooden dam about 1'6" high. The bed of the river below this to be cleaned out down to the footbridge, & tubs sunk under the latter. RJK	

2449 Wt. W14957/M90 750,000 1/16 J.B.C. & A. Forms/C.2118/12.

Instructions regarding War Diaries and Intelligence Summaries are contained in F. S. Regs., Part II. and the Staff Manual respectively. Title Pages will be prepared in manuscript.

WAR DIARY
or
INTELLIGENCE SUMMARY
(Erase heading not required.)

Army Form C. 2118.

112 FA

Place	Date	Hour	Summary of Events and Information	Remarks and references to Appendices
RUBROUCK	29/6/17		Interviewed Water Officer who approved of scheme & at once sent lorry for necessary timber and expanded metal; also tubs. Later took working party to place & explained scheme. Sentence of Court Martial promulgated on parade in presence of the unit. No 73269 Pte Davidson, sentenced to 2 years I.H.L. for communicating military information inside cover of a green envelope.	
"	30/6/17		Working party set up frame for filter during the morning, but river too high to start filling in. Cinders obtained from railway but held up in readiness for fall in level. Arrangements made for sand. Received information from APM CALAIS that two deserters of my ASC were in his custody. Despatched armed escort.	

[illegible]
O.C. 112 FA

2449 Wt. W14957/M90 750,000 1/16 J.B.C. & A. Forms/C.2118/12.

Plans of 16th Div W.W. D.S.

withdrawn to app Dept

WAR DIARY.

FOR MONTH OF JULY, 1917.

VOLUME :- 20

UNIT :- 112th Field Ambulance
Raml.

July 1917 19

B.E.F.

SUMMARY OF MEDICAL WAR DIARIES OF 112th F.A. 16th Div.

8th Corps. 5th ARMY.

19th Corps from July 22nd.
To 3rd Army on 22.8.17.

Western Front Operations - July - Aug. 1917.

Officer Commanding - Lt.Col. P. Houghton.

SUMMARISED UNDER THE FOLLOWING HEADINGS :-

Phase "D" 1. Passchendaele Operations, "July - Nov.1917"

(a) - Operations commencing 1/7/17.

(b) - Operations commencing 1/10/17.
Canadians attacked Passchendaele, Oct. 30th.
Canadians took Passchendaele, Nov. 6th.

112th F.A. 8th Corps. 5th ARMY. WESTERN FRONT.
July-Aug.1917.

Officer Commanding - Lt.Col. P. Houghton.

19th Corps from July 22nd.

PHASE "D" 1. - Passchendaele Operations, "July - Nov. 1917".

(a) - Operations commencing 1/7/17.

Headquarters at Rubrouck H.14.a.3.7. (27).

July 1st.	Operations R.A.M.C. Water Supply.	Work on filter at B.25.c.0.7. commenced.
16th.	Decorations. a/Sgt. Bathgate. Pte. Hislop. " Spenser.	Awarded M.M.
17th.	Capt. C.H. Denyer awarded M.C.	
22nd.	Moves and Transfer. To OUDERZEELE 19th Corps.	

B.E.F.

112th F.A. 19th Corps. 5th ARMY.

WESTERN FRONT.
July-Aug.1917.

Officer Commanding - Lt.Col. P. Houghton.

To 3rd Army 22.8.17.

PHASE "D" 1. Passchendaele Operations,"July - Nov. 1917."

(a) - Operations commencing 1/7/17.

Headquarters at Rubrouck H.14.a.

July 22nd. Moves and Transfer. To OUDERZEELE 19th Corps.

25th. Moves. To HILLHOEK L.20.b. cen. (27).

30th. Moves. Detachment. 0 & 86 to 19th C.R.S. 2/1st West Lancs. F.A.

B.

WESTERN FRONT.
July-Aug.1917.

112th F.A. 8th Corps. 5th ARMY.

Officer Commanding - Lt.Col. P. Houghton.

19th Corps from July 22nd.

PHASE "D" 1. - Passchendaele Operations, "July - Nov. 1917".

(a) - Operations commencing 1/7/17.

Headquarters at Rubrouck H.14.a.3.7. (27).

July 1st.	Operations R.A.M.C. Water Supply.	Work on filter at B.25.c.0.7. commenced.
16th.	Decorations. a/Sgt. Bathgate. Pte. Hislop. " Spenser.	Awarded M.M.
17th.	Capt. C.H. Denyer awarded M.C.	
22nd.	Moves and Transfer. To OUDERZEELE 19th Corps.	

B.E.F.

2.

112th F.A. 18th Corps. 5th ARMY.

WESTERN FRONT.
July-Aug.1917.

Officer Commanding - Lt.Col. P. Houghton.

To 3rd Army 22.8.17.

PHASE "D" 1. Passchendaele Operations,"July - Nov. 1917."

(a) - Operations commencing 1/7/17.

Headquarters at Rubrouck H.14.a.

July 22nd. Moves and Transfer. To OUDERZEELE 19th Corps.

25th. Moves. To HILLHOEK L.20.b. cen. (27).

30th. Moves. Detachment. 0 & 86 to 19th C.R.S. 2/1st West Lancs. F.A.

Army Form C. 2118.

Instructions regarding War Diaries and Intelligence Summaries are contained in F. S. Regs., Part II. and the Staff Manual respectively. Title Pages will be prepared in manuscript.

WAR DIARY
or
~~INTELLIGENCE~~ SUMMARY

(Erase heading not required.)

No. 112 Field Ambulance.

Place	Date	Hour	Summary of Events and Information	Remarks and references to Appendices
RUBROUCK. 27.H.14.a 3.7	1/7/17		Work on filter at B.25.c 0.7. commenced R H Hamilton [illegible] Lieut Col RAMC	
"	2/7/17		Work on filter practically finished. Filter working on departure with small flow in river. Visited again in evening & found a great flow of water & filter partially washed out. I presume someone further up stream had released a dam. RH	
"	3/7/17		Filter badly washed out & still considerable flow. Capt. A E Barr Sim returned from temporary duty with 9th R.D.F. RH	
"	4/7/17		Capt A E Barr Sim departed for England on contract leave. RH	
"	5/7/17		Routine RH	
"	6/7/17		Having decided to change the site & construction of filter, so as to deal with variable amounts of water, I removed all materials to a spot a few yards above the Ford at B25 a 1.1 & began new construction on principle of filtering on one side (East) of bed, & leaving channel for overflow on West side. First chamber – cinders 3 feet thick for through filtration between sheets of expanded metal. Second Chamber – empty but to be partially filled with sand for downward filtration & Third Chamber sand for upward filtration RH	

Instructions regarding War Diaries and Intelligence Summaries are contained in F. S. Regs., Part II. and the Staff Manual respectively. Title Pages will be prepared in manuscript.

WAR DIARY
or
~~INTELLIGENCE SUMMARY~~
(Erase heading not required.)

112 F.A.

Army Form C. 2118.

Place	Date	Hour	Summary of Events and Information	Remarks and references to Appendices
RUBROUCK	7/7/17		Work on new filter continued. G.S.H.	
"	8/7/17		48th Brigade moved to TILQUES Training Area & still continue to take their sick along with the sick of 46th Brigade 15th Division formerly received by No: 113. F.A. Captain D. N. Macleod left for permanent duty in charge of X Ray Dept. No 64. CCS. & is struck off the strength. G.S.H.	
"	9/7/17		Capt. D. H. Weir & 2 O.R. returned from IXth Corps School. Special new latrine completed for use behind the Dressing Station, where digging urine-pits is out of the question, & space a consideration.	

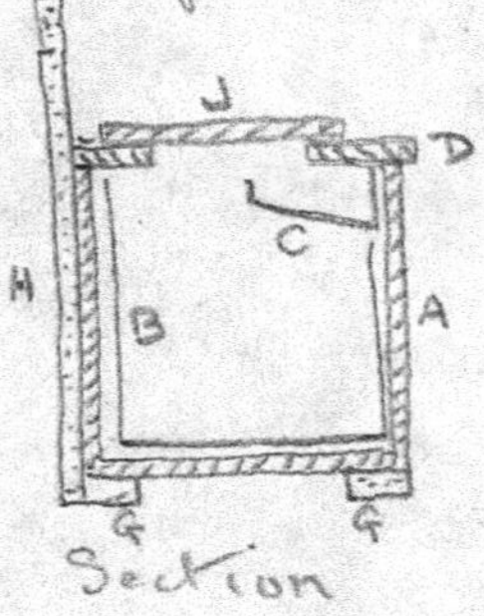

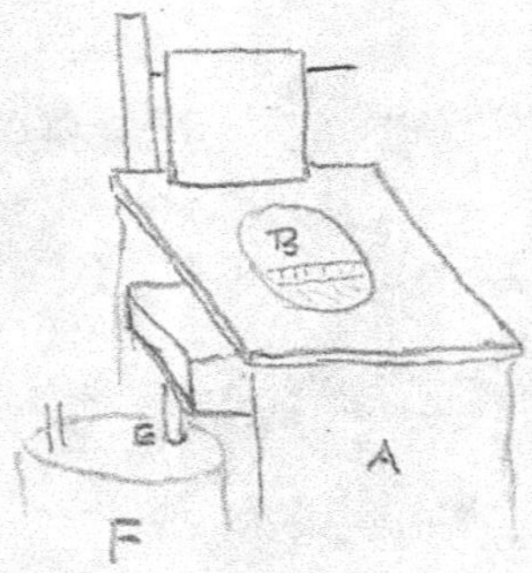

A. Wooden box holding
B. Biscuit tin fitted with wire handle & cut in front
C. for a flat urine-trough attached to
D. Moveable seat-lid.
The trough C is prolonged outside & covered in with a vertical pipe running from the box so
F formed into a covered urine receptacle.
The troughs are adjacent sides of each pair of boxes so that both drain into the one receptacle
G All raised on wooden frame with uprights. H. & back ensuring fall of
J flap lid on rising of user.

G.S.H.

2449 Wt. W14957/M90 750,000 1/16 J.B.C. & A. Forms/C.2118/12.

Army Form C. 2118.

Instructions regarding War Diaries and Intelligence Summaries are contained in F. S. Regs., Part II. and the Staff Manual respectively. Title Pages will be prepared in manuscript.

WAR DIARY
~~or~~
~~INTELLIGENCE SUMMARY~~

(Erase heading not required.)

112 F.A.

Place	Date	Hour	Summary of Events and Information	Remarks and references to Appendices
RUBROUCK	10/7/17		Filter completed but showing some small leaks. The work is interfered with at night, probably by French boys (?), who pull out sandbags from the dam. RJH	
"	11/7/17		I am now dealing with sick of 44th & 46th Bdes. 15th Div. Locally and 48th Bde at TILQUES. Naturally, for lack of accommodation, the vast majority of cases are sent to ST OMER & ARQUES. RJH.	
"	12/7/17		Capt W. Warburton left for temporary duty with 10th R. Dub Fusilrs. Found filter wall defiled with faeces & dam damaged. Repaired, & fitted 2 inch iron pipe from filter to barrel. RJH	
"	13/7/17		Routine. RJH	
"	14/7/17		3 M.A. Cars from 15th Division reported to assist with sick. RJH	
"	15/7/17		Capt T.F. Saunders left for England on leave. Capt G. Buchanan left for England on termination of contract. RJH	

Instructions regarding War Diaries and Intelligence Summaries are contained in F. S. Regs., Part II. and the Staff Manual respectively. Title Pages will be prepared in manuscript.

WAR DIARY

~~or~~

~~INTELLIGENCE SUMMARY~~

(Erase heading not required.)

112. F.A.

Army Form C. 2118

Place	Date	Hour	Summary of Events and Information	Remarks and references to Appendices
RUDROUCK.	16/7/17		Filter again damaged & defiled. Faeces in one of the barrels! 48th Infy Bde returned to vicinity Distributed ribbons of Military Medals to a/Sgt Bathgate & ptes Hislop & Spencer RAMC GH	
"	17/7/17		Cleaned up filter & disinfected barrels. Composite Infy Bde under 46th Bde moved out. Gave ribbon of Military Cross to Capt C. H. Denyer. RAMC. GH	
"	18/7/17		Remade filter & requested French Mission to leave Corps Gendarmerie warned to look after it. Posted Guard of my own men all night. GH	
"	19/7/17		Promulgated sentences of Court Martial - 2 years IHL in each case - on Drivers Richardson & Greaves. Fenced filter with barbed wire. GH	
"	20/7/17		Capt. D.H. Weir & 4 O.R. proceeded to XIV Corps Reinforcement Camp with Medical equipment of a battalion. GH	
"	21/7/17		44th (Composite) Infy Bde moved out. Posted at filter notices signed by Maire & stamped by A.P.M. Held competitions of sports during the day. DDMS VIII Corps distributed Divisional certificates for Gallantry to the Sgt Stanger, Corpl Stewart, ptes Mc Collum, Holdsworth & Gardiner. GH	

1875 Wt. W593/826 1,000,000 4/15 J.B.C. & A. A.D.S.S./Forms/C. 2118.

Instructions regarding War Diaries and Intelligence Summaries are contained in F. S. Regs., Part II. and the Staff Manual respectively. Title Pages will be prepared in manuscript.

WAR DIARY

~~or~~

~~INTELLIGENCE SUMMARY~~

(Erase heading not required.)

Army Form C. 2118

112. F.A.

Place	Date	Hour	Summary of Events and Information	Remarks and references to Appendices
OUDEZEELE 27.J.8.C Central	22/7/17		Marched off at 4.45 AM to OUDEZEELE Weather fine, cool early, hot after 9 AM. Billets for OR in farms. Officers, Messes, &c in tents. GH	
"	23/7/17		4 O.R. despatched to XIX Corps Reinforcement Camp. Special instruction to personnel on weak points shown in competitions on 21.7.17. GH	
"	24/7/17		Special instruction continued. GH	
HILHOEK. 27.L.20.b Central	25/7/17		Marched at 4.45 AM to HILHOEK. Weather dull at first. Extremely heavy thunder-shower caught us one mile from destination. All under canvas in open ground between plantations. GH	
"	26/7/17		Capt A E Barr[illegible] struck off strength (War Office Medical Board — four weeks leave) 5 Ptes arrived as reinforcement. Capt T. F. Saunders returned from leave. Wire received suspending sentence of 142 on Drs Richardson & Greaves. ASC GH	
"	27/7/17		Routine GH	
"	28/7/17		Routine GH	

1875 Wt. W593/826 1,000,000 4/15 J.B.C. & A. A.D.S.S./Forms/C. 2118.

Instructions regarding War Diaries and Intelligence Summaries are contained in F. S. Regs., Part II. and the Staff Manual respectively. Title Pages will be prepared in manuscript.

WAR DIARY

~~or~~

~~INTELLIGENCE SUMMARY~~

(Erase heading not required.)

112 FA

Army Form C. 2118

Place	Date	Hour	Summary of Events and Information	Remarks and references to Appendices
HILHOEK	29/7/17		Attended ADMS' conference of OCs re coming operations. GH	
"	30/7/17		Capt W. Warburton returned from 10th R Dubl Fusrs. Sent available bearers – 86 NCOs & men to XIX Corps Rest Station (2/1 West Lancs FA) GH	
"	31/7/17		Capt A.M. Mitchell & Capt E.E. Lightwood reported for duty & were taken on the strength	

G. J. Houghton
Lieut Col RAMC
OC. 112. F.A.

1875 Wt. W593/826 1,000,000 4/15 J.B.C. & A. A.D.S.S./Forms/C. 2118.

W A R   D I A R Y .

FOR   MONTH   OF   AUGUST,   1917.

VOLUME 21

U N I T 112th Field Ambulance R.A.M.C.

B.E.F.

SUMMARY OF MEDICAL WAR DIARIES OF 112th F.A. 16th Div.

8th Corps. 5th ARMY.

19th Corps from July 22nd.

To 3rd Army on 22.8.17.

Western Front Operations - July - Aug. 1917.

Officer Commanding - Lt.Col. P. Houghton.

SUMMARISED UNDER THE FOLLOWING HEADINGS :-

Phase "D" 1. Passchendaele Operations, "July - Nov.1917"

(a) - Operations commencing 1/7/17.

(b) - Operations commencing 1/10/17.
Canadians attacked Passchendaele, Oct. 30th.
Canadians took Passchendaele, Nov. 6th.

Aug. 3rd. **Moves**. To THE MILL VLAMERTINGHE H.8a.9.8. (28).

9th. **Operations Enemy. Casualties.**) Shell burst in camp Labour Coy, adjoining Hospital.

0 & 5 killed. 0 & 18 wounded.

20th. **Moves**. To WORMHOULDT C.24.c. 4.5 (27).

22nd. **Moves and Transfer**. To BEHAGNIES H.8.b. (57 c) on transfer to 3rd ARMY.

Aug. 3rd. Moves. To THE MILL VLAMERTINGHE H.8a.9.8. (28).

9th. Operations Enemy.) Shell burst in camp Labour Coy,
Casualties.) adjoining Hospital.

0 & 5 killed. 0 & 18 wounded.

20th. Moves. To WORMHOULDT C.24.c. 4.5 (27).

22nd. Moves and Transfer. To BEHAGNIES H.8.b. (57 c) on transfer to 3rd ARMY.

Instructions regarding War Diaries and Intelligence Summaries are contained in F. S. Regs., Par. II. and the Staff Manual respectively. Title Pages will be prepared in manuscript.

WAR DIARY
~~or~~
~~INTELLIGENCE SUMMARY~~
(Erase heading not required.)

Army Form C. 2118

No: 112 . Field Ambulance

Place	Date	Hour	Summary of Events and Information	Remarks and references to Appendices
HILHOEK 27. L. 20. b central	1/8/17		Routine. ~~Heavy~~ Heavy Rain	
			P. J. [illegible] Lt Col RAMC.	
	2/8/17		Capts A M Mitchell & E. E. Lightwood left for temporary duty with No. 113 F.A.	
			Attended meeting of ADMS & F.A. Commanders. Received instructions to take over XIXth Corps Walking Wounded Dressing Station tomorrow	
			More rain.	
			P.J.K.	
The Mill VLAMERTINGHE 28. H. 8. a. 9. 8	3/8/17		Capt W Warburton & 10 OR left at 8 AM as Advance Party to take over W.W. Dr St.	
			Rained practically all day.	
			All arrangements made to march off at 2 PM. All packed but three of [illegible] tents left standing for shelter. At 1 PM received XIXth Corps order [illegible] Relief on 4th. Sent Messenger to ADMS for confirmation. At 3 PM received confirmation of original orders & moved out as rapidly as permitted by mud & other traffic. Joined by 2 Cpts & 38 OR Bearers from XIXth Corps Rest Station. Marched to VLAMERTINGHE Mill, with many holds up on road, especially in POPERINGHE. Arrived 4.15 PM & took over	

1875 Wt. W593/826 1,000,000 4/15 J.B.C. & A. A.D.S.S./Forms/C. 2118.

Instructions regarding War Diaries and Intelligence Summaries are contained in F. S. Regs., Part II. and the Staff Manual respectively. Title Pages will be prepared in manuscript.

WAR DIARY
or
~~INTELLIGENCE SUMMARY~~
(Erase heading not required.)

112 F A.

Army Form C. 2118

Place	Date	Hour	Summary of Events and Information	Remarks and references to Appendices
The Mill VLAMERTINGHE	3/8/17		Continued. Remainder of 47 FA left at once by lorry. 4 Officers (Capts Crosbie, Burton, Rawlings, 110 FA & Sowerby 108 FA) & 58 OR 36th Divl [illegible] remained as reinforcement. Bearers were sent for at 11 PM & left at midnight to reinforce at The PRISON YPRES. 28.I.7.b.2.2. RIV	
"	4/8/17		Reorganised system of duties in Dr. Stn, 4 junior Officers available. Distributed in 6 hour watches, two on duty together by day & one for each night period. Personnel OR. Divided into 3 watches, each section (Tent Subdivn 112 FA) reinforced from 36th Divn staff. Patients are conveyed by Motor Lorries & Char-a-bancs from BELGIAN BATTERY CORNER, H.24.a.5.9 to PRISON YPRES, thence Light Railway lorry service to the W.W. Dr Stn. They are dropped on the East side of the Mill & pass through a range of 4 Marquees fitted with forms, the last having a YMCA bar, open day & night. Thence they pass to 2 waiting room huts, & thence across the lane & enter the Mill-base, reaching the South Entrance of the Clerks' room, where AF W3210 is made out at separate tables according to Divisions. Thence into the Mill Yard & into a hall where A.T. Serum is given by special Nurses. Thence to the Dressing room which accommodates 6 Dressers. Passing out after Dressing by another door, they wait either in another hall or upstairs in a	Appendix I. Plan

Instructions regarding War Diaries and Intelligence Summaries are contained in F. S. Regs., Part II. and the Staff Manual respectively. Title Pages will be prepared in manuscript.

WAR DIARY
or
INTELLIGENCE SUMMARY
(Erase heading not required.)

Army Form C. 2118

112. F.A.

Place	Date	Hour	Summary of Events and Information	Remarks and references to Appendices
VLAMERTINGHE	4/8/17	Continued	Large waiting-room in the floor above the Dressing Room re, and are sorted out by a special NCO i/c Evacuation who despatches them to their proper CCS re as per Corps Orders. A M.T. Officer i/c Lorries lives on the premises. Admissions – 8 am to 12 midnight. O.R. W. 171 S. 190 BH	
"	5/8/17		The Detachments RAMC 36th Div left in the morning under orders of ADMS 36th Div. Duties re-organised with remaining staff, all except reinforcement clerks, 112 F.A. Under previous arrangements the 2/1 Wessex F.A. sent for their AFW.3210 twice daily. Today they did not send, but removed their clerk & forwarded all their AFW3210s to DDMS in the evening. Admissions 12 midnight to 12 midnight. Offrs. W. 3. S. 2 OR. W. 112 S. 199 BH	
"	6/8/17		Under orders ADMS. 16th Div set about making "The Moated Farm" H.2.d.7.2 into a Rest Station for very slight cases. The Station is to be under me but to be worked by Details of 111 FA on their arrival tomorrow from HILHOEK. Started clearing up. With 2 M.O. made out necessary indents on B.R.C. The farm has many rooms on two floors. Two rooms are elephanted, & there is an "elephant" in the middle of the yard, and a sort of basement room heavily protected on top. The place should accommodate about 150 patients with a large room seating 50 as dining hall, and a Tent Sub-Div of F.A.	

1875 Wt. W593/826 1,000,000 4/15 J.B.C. & A. A.D.S.S./Forms/C. 2118.

Instructions regarding War Diaries and Intelligence Summaries are contained in F. S. Regs., Part II. and the Staff Manual respectively. Title Pages will be prepared in manuscript.

WAR DIARY
or
~~INTELLIGENCE SUMMARY~~
(Erase heading not required.)

Army Form C. 2118

112. FA.

Place	Date	Hour	Summary of Events and Information	Remarks and references to Appendices
VLAMERTINGHE	6/8/17		continued. 3 clerks of 36th Div exchanged during the day. No: 30448 pte Clarke. V.W.G. of this Unit, passed through slightly wounded. Admissions	
"	7/8/17.		Capt Marshall Lt & QM Lander & 20 OR 111 FA with transport of the Unit arrived 10 AM & took over Moated Farm. Patients sent there at once. Lieut Chandler arrived in afternoon for duty with No: 111 FA. R.V.	
"	8/8/17		No 64384 pte Whitcross & 66361. pte Holder passed through slightly wounded. Capt. Marshall 111 FA took over Morning Sick Inspection, thereby easing work in Dressing Room. Visited by DDMS XIXth Corps & ordered to arrange for service on Light Railway from KRUISSTRAAT to point close to the Mill. I visited a Railway Telephone & got into touch with S.L.R 2 & C.T.C. An Officer was promised to come to see me tomorrow. The Moated Farm is filling up with 120 patients. I am arranging for treatment there of Scabies. Admissions. Offs. W. 3. S. 2 OR. W. 221. S. 105. (Through Mill) R.V.	

1875 Wt. W593/826 1,000,000 4/15 J.B.C. & A. A.D.S.S./Forms/C. 2118.

Instructions regarding War Diaries and Intelligence Summaries are contained in F. S. Regs., Part II. and the Staff Manual respectively. Title Pages will be prepared in manuscript.

WAR DIARY
or
~~INTELLIGENCE SUMMARY~~
(Erase heading not required.)

Army Form C. 2118

112 FA.

Place	Date	Hour	Summary of Events and Information	Remarks and references to Appendices
VLAMERTINGHE.	9/8/17		Lieut Chandler 111 F.A. took over Morning Sick. Moated Farm = XIX th Corps Advanced Rest Station filled with 164 cases. Scabies Treatment commenced. In afternoon Railway officer from S.L.R. 2 arrived & I took him to see A.D.M.S. 18th Div. who settled preliminaries. A shell burst close to us about 4.45 P.M. in a Labour Coy Camp. 5 killed 18 wounded including 3 fractured thighs. At once collected by us, dressed & passed on. 80608 Pte McCollum – slightly wounded, & 64391 Pte Smith & 484 Pte Cox [illegible] killed, passed through. All slight Admissions. Officers. Sick. 1. Wounded 2. O.R. S. 105. W. ~~15~~ 154 914 RJH.	
"	10/8/17		Routine. Passed through. Officers. S. 1 W. 5. O.R. S. 141 W. 306 RJH.	
"	11/8/17		With 2 M visited Red + Depôt at HAM EN ARTOIS. Passed through. Offrs. S. 1 W. 1 O.R. S. 106. W. 148 RJH	
"	12/8/17		Routine Passed through. Offrs. S. 1. W. 2. O.R. S. 104. W. 94 RJH.	

1875 Wt. W593/826 1,000,000 4/15 J.B.C. & A. A.D.S.S./Forms/C. 2118.

Instructions regarding War Diaries and Intelligence Summaries are contained in F. S. Regs., Part II. and the Staff Manual respectively. Title Pages will be prepared in manuscript.

WAR DIARY
or
~~INTELLIGENCE SUMMARY~~
(Erase heading not required.)

Army Form C. 2118

112 FA

Place	Date	Hour	Summary of Events and Information	Remarks and references to Appendices
VLAMERTINGHE	13/8/17		Sent Lorry to HAM EN ARTOIS for Red Cross Stores, principally for MOATED FARM.	
			Passed through. Offrs. S. 3. W. 2. O.R. S. 91. W. 107.	
			RH	
"	14/8/17		Routine.	
			Passed through. Offrs S. 4. W. 3. O.R. S. 124. W. 114.	
			RH	
"	15/8/17		Cleared all but Light Duty patients out of MOATED FARM. With ADMS took NCOs for Walking Wounded Loading Up Posts at POTIJZE. 28. I. 3. 6. 3, MENINGATE I. 8 central & ASYLUM YPRES H. 12. d. central; gave them written orders & explained their duties. Also later took guides to ATHERLEY JUNCTION H. 3. b. 9. 9 & H. 8. central for off-loading parties.	Appendices A. B. C. D.
			In evening 2. Offrs. Capts Hurst & Wood & 45 O.R. 3/1 Sth Midland FA & Capt Gompertz 2/3 Sth Midld. FA reported for duty.	
			About Midnight sent up the personnel of the Loading-up Posts.	
			Passed through. O. R. S. 150. W. 90.	
			RH	

1875 Wt. W593/826 1,000,000 4/15 J.B.C. & A. A.D.S.S./Forms/C. 2118.

Instructions regarding War Diaries and Intelligence Summaries are contained in F. S. Regs., Part II. and the Staff Manual respectively. Title Pages will be prepared in manuscript.

WAR DIARY
or
~~INTELLIGENCE SUMMARY~~
(Erase heading not required.)

Army Form C. 2118

112. FA

Place	Date	Hour	Summary of Events and Information	Remarks and references to Appendices
VLAMERTINGHE	16/8/17		Heavy fighting. Cases began to come in about 4.30 AM. Crush greatest at Midday. Practically no cases previously dressed at A.D.S's. Visited ATHERLEY JUNCTION with DDMS. XIXth Corps. On my return about noon began to collect slight wounded without dressing here for the Evacuation Train on Broad Gauge beside Mill. (10 trucks – each 14 men on paillasses). Up to this all cases dressed here. Got off first train at 1 PM.	
			Became very dissatisfied with rate of registration owing to crush in the narrow room (Clerks Room on plan) in main building. Opened fresh channels through archway & large billet beside it (Riders on plan), giving three passages for 16th & 36th Divisions & Other Troops respectively. This greatly hastened registration. Second train 3 PM. 140 cases. Third train 5 PM. 150 Cases.	Appendix I Plan.
			At 6 PM dismissed Dressing-room Staffs & brought on fresh reduced Staff. Was quite clear at 8 PM & from that on had only very rare lorry-loads to deal with.	
			At 6 PM. sent up relief for MENIN GATE post, & took off POTIJZE & ASYLUM posts, having obtained consent of DDMS who notified Railways.	
			Lieut Miller. U.S.A. M.S reported for duty at 11. AM.	
			During the day Capts Denyer & Saunders. 112 FA visited Posts.	
			Passed through. Offrs. Wounded. 28. O.R. S. 54. W. 1305. (16th Div 575)	
			R.W.	

1875 Wt. W593/826 1,000,000 4/15 J.B.C. & A. A.D.S.S./Forms/C. 2118.

Instructions regarding War Diaries and Intelligence Summaries are contained in F. S. Regs., Part II. and the Staff Manual respectively. Title Pages will be prepared in manuscript.

WAR DIARY
or
~~INTELLIGENCE SUMMARY~~
(Erase heading not required.)

Army Form C. 2118

112 FA

Place	Date	Hour	Summary of Events and Information	Remarks and references to Appendices
VLAMERTINGHE.	17/8/17		Took off MENINGATE Post in morning. Received reports from NCO's as to working of orders. POTIJZE found some of their original orders unnecessary owing to regular & frequent train service. (15 minutes). MENINGATE & ASYLUM worked perfectly in accordance with orders.	Appendices A.B.C
			Passed through. Offrs. S. 1. O.R. S. 56. W. 159 GSH	
"	18/8/17		Capt Rennie 2/3. Sth Midl. FA. arrived in relief of Capt Bompertz.	
			Capt Lightwood. 112 FA returned from tempy Duty with 113 FA	
			On arrival of Lieut Col Bell D.S.O. handed over charge of Moated Grange to him	
			Passed through. Offrs. S. 5. W. 5. OR. S. 89. W. 63.	
	19/8/17		Passed through Officers. Wounded. 1 O.Rs. Sick 90 Wounded 113	
THE MILL VLAMERTINGHE H.8.a.9.8 Sh.28.NW	20/8/17		Took over Tempy Command of the Unit this day GSH from Lt Col. G.J. Houghton proceeding on 10 days leave to ENGLAND Handed over XIX Corps Walking Wounded Dress. Stn (The MILL Vlamertinghe) to 2/1 S. Midland Fld. Ambce. this day. Marched off at 10.45 am. with Horse Transport*. Personnel proceeded in advance by Motor Lorries Capt. Lightwood detailed for Tempy Duty with 2nd R. Dub. Fusiliers from 21.8.17 Capt SAUNDERS proceeded for Tempy Duty with 180 Bde R.F.A.	G.H. Smyth Capt RAMC
			Passed thro' Officers - Sick - 0 Wounded - 0 OR Sick 2 Wounded 24	
			* Arrived WORMHOULDT at 5 pm.	

1875 Wt. W593/826 1,000,000 4/15 J.B.C. & A. A.D.S.S./Forms/C. 2118.

Instructions regarding War Diaries and Intelligence Summaries are contained in F. S. Regs., Part II. and the Staff Manual respectively. Title Pages will be prepared in manuscript.

WAR DIARY
or
INTELLIGENCE SUMMARY
(Erase heading not required.)

Army Form C. 2118

112 F.A.

Place	Date	Hour	Summary of Events and Information	Remarks and references to Appendices
WORMHOULDT C.24.c.4.5 Sh.27 Bel+France	21/8/17		LtCol. G.J. Houghton - Leave 21/8/17 to 31/8/17 Capt E.E. LIGHTWOOD to 2nd R. Dub. Fus Temporarily. Received orders for Unit to proceed to BAPAUME WEST on 22/8/17. Detailed Billeting Party consisting of S. Sgt HOLLAWAY + 1 OR to report to Bde Billeting Officer at ESQUEBECQ Stn.	A.H.D.
"	22/8/17		Moved from WORMHOULDT to COURCELLES-le-COMTE via ESQUEBECQ + BAPAUME WEST by train. Motor transport proceeded by road via HAZEBROUCK ST POL DOULLENS. ALBERT to report to S.M.T.O. BEHAGNIES Sheet 57c France H.8.b.	
COURCELLES le COMTE Sh 57c France A.15.d.	23/8/17		Arrived at COURCELLES 7.30. am billeted in out-houses of Sugar Refinery. The Refinery itself + rest of village was completely in ruins - having been blown up previously by the Germans. C Section detailed to open up a ward for 12 beds in case of emergency. Motor Ambulances detailed to collect sick from the 48th Infy Bde camped round Courcelles.	A.H.D.
"	24/8/17		"B" Section under Command of CAPT. WARBURTON detailed to take over VI Corps Scabies Stn (South) at ACHIET-le-Grand (Sh. 57c G.10. central) from ~~ACHIET~~ 63rd Fld. Ambce 21st Divn. Motor Transport - 1 Ambulance. Two water carts required for Bullets on account of difficulty of procuring water. Hdqrs A+B Sections marched to ERVILLERS (Sh 57c N.W. B13.d.2.5.) to take over [illegible] Station of 63rd Fld Ambce (West Lancs. T.F.)	~~[illegible]~~ A.H.D.

1875 Wt. W593/826 1,000,000 4/15 J.B.C. & A. A.D.S.S./Forms/C. 2118.

Army Form C. 2118

Instructions regarding War Diaries and Intelligence Summaries are contained in F. S. Regs., Part II. and the Staff Manual respectively. Title Pages will be prepared in manuscript.

WAR DIARY
~~or~~
~~INTELLIGENCE~~ SUMMARY 112th F.A.

(Erase heading not required.)

Place	Date	Hour	Summary of Events and Information	Remarks and references to Appendices
COURCELLES le-COMTE	24/8/17 ctd.		(8) ~~Eight~~ Stretcher Bearers relieved bearers of 63rd Fld Amblce at Relay Posts Shafts 68 + 128 Shaft Trench. Shaft 123 is a short distance from RAP at T.6.d.5.8. Sh.51B France. This is in the old Hindenburg Line. The Relay Posts are at the bottom of the Shaft which is about 45 ft deep. The Ambulance Car (Stand) of 63rd Fld Amblce at T4.b.3.7 Sh.51B was relieved by an Ambulance of this unit. 1 NCO (L/Cpl Gravener) + 7 O.R. returned from Tempy Duty at XIX Corps Reinforcement Camp MERCKINGHEM. Pte Huggett was left behind with following equipment of this unit. No 1 + 2 Fld Med. Panniers, 1 Med. Companion, 1 Surgl Haversack & 2 Water Bottles. Lt Atkins detailed for duty at VI CCS Stn (South) (Achiet-le-Grand) until the latter is in running order re rationing etc.	[initials]
ERVILLERS Sh.57c France B13.d.2.5	25/8/17		Arranged with OC 113th F.A. to collect Sick of 47th Infy. Bde. 6 Connaught Rangers, 6 Roy. Ir. Regt } ERVILLERS	
"	26/8/17		Arranged Collection of Sick from 48th Bde Infy. 2 Roy. Dub. Fus. MOYENVILLE. A.4.a Sh.57c France 8 " " " HAMELINCOURT. A.5.b. " " 9 " " " ERVILLERS B.13.d. " " 10 " " " ERVILLERS " " " " ADMS 16th Divn inspected the Main Dressing Stn. Conference of MO's 48th Infy Bde at 112th F.A. presided over by ADMS re Splints. Motor Cyclist detailed for duty at ADMS's Office. ADMS requires a Special Ward to be devoted to DIARRHOEA CASES. Linen & utensils to be treated as in an Enteric Ward. 12 Reinforcements taken on Strength. Lt. Atkins rejoined H.Qrs at ERVILLERS	[initials]

1875 Wt. W593/826 1,000,000 4/15 J.B.C. & A. A.D.S.S./Forms/C. 2118.

Instructions regarding War Diaries and Intelligence Summaries are contained in F. S. Regs., Part II. and the Staff Manual respectively. Title Pages will be prepared in manuscript.

WAR DIARY
or
~~INTELLIGENCE SUMMARY~~

(Erase heading not required.)

112° F.A.

Army Form C. 2118

Place	Date	Hour	Summary of Events and Information	Remarks and references to Appendices
ERVILLERS	27/8/17		Reclassification for General Service (Class A) – 80 men of 9th Labour Coy Examined. 10 found fit. Arranged for Examination of 353 of 41st Lab. Coy for reclassification also P.B. men attached to Town Major ERVILLERS. Lt. ATKINS returned for duty at Hdqrs	[initials]
"	28/8/17		1st Lt CH. WATT U.S.A. M.O.R.C. reported for Tempy Duty & posted to VI Corps S. Stn (South) 1st Lt. A STRAUSS U.S.A. M.O.R.C " " " " " " " the Head-quarters of the Ambulance. ERVILLERS. Weather bad – raining.	[initials]
"	29/8/17		Commenced the Erection of two Nissen Bow Huts for sick ~~[illegible]~~ Erection of the huts was superintended by Lt. Black R.E. 157 Coy. R.E. Sgt Richards & 6 men detailed to 16th L.Div. Employment Coy under instructions from the A.D.M.S. for Tempy Duty. Weather – inclement, raining most of day.	[initials]
"			A motor Ambulance from 113th F.A. detailed for duty with the unit to clear cases to 113th F.A. (La CAUCHIE) & general duty.	
"	30/8/17			

1875 Wt. W593/826 1,000,000 4/15 J.B.C. & A. A.D.S.S./Forms/C. 2118.

Instructions regarding War Diaries and Intelligence Summaries are contained in F. S. Regs., Part II. and the Staff Manual respectively. Title Pages will be prepared in manuscript.

WAR DIARY
or
~~INTELLIGENCE SUMMARY~~ 112 F.A.

(Erase heading not required.)

Army Form C. 2118.

Place	Date	Hour	Summary of Events and Information	Remarks and references to Appendices
Ervillers	30/8/17		2 motor ambulances detailed by O.C. No 3 MAC Bovry St. Rectrude for duty between hours 9 am & 8 pm. - Evacuating Cases to CCS.	C.H.D.
"	31/8/17		*Plan of Hutting Scheme for accommodation of Sick & personnel submitted to ADMS. Huts required to complete: Nissen Bow 18; Hospl Nissen Bow 1; Recreation Room for Pts 1.	*Plan Attached. Appendix E
			Ambulance tentage erected this day to allow for accommodation of Sick in Nissen Bows at present occupied by personnel.	
			40 of 16th Vol. Employment Coy. examined for reclassification for Class A. B. & C. Reclassification forwarded to ADMS.	
			Lt. Col. J.G. Houghton RAMC returned from leave this evening.	
			[signature] Capt. RAMC, Actg. O.C. 112th Fld Ambce	

2449 Wt. W14957/M90 750,000 1/16 J.B.C. & A. Forms/C.2118/12.

A

Duties of N.C.O i/c Walking wounded POTIJZE ANNEXE:—

1. He will post himself at, or near the point where the rails cross the bye road from Potojze

2. He will send runners to A.D.S. POTIJZE and A.D.S St JEAN to notify the time of train service.

3. Trains must not be delayed unnecessarily. The Railway officials will decide this point. probably 5 minutes will be allowed

4 Groups will not be allowed to stand on POTIJZE ROAD:—

5. He will remind the N.C.O i/c Train to stop at ATHERLEY JUNC:

6. If a train is expected in 20 Minutes or less, and no shelling is going on locally, he can begin to collect men for entraining

AD.

for Lt Col Rawl

A.D.M.S. VI Corps [illegible]

B.

Duties of N.C.O. i/c W.W., MENIN Cross Roads (or GATE).—

1.— He will expect to have to deal with W.W. from POTIJZE and ST JEAN who cannot be entrained. He will, therefore, have halts during entraining periods.

2.— He will, if many cases are arriving, direct the very slight cases to the ASYLUM, only load in lorries the more exhausted.

3.— If few cases are arriving, he will put all into lorries.

4. He will leave a few vacant seats in every third lorry, until he receives orders to discontinue.

5.— He will not delay cases more than 10 minutes to wait for a lorry.

6.— He can "flag" any lorry returning empty, pick it up, and [illegible] whenever possible directing the driver to stop at VLAMERTINGHE Mill.—

[signature]

for Lieut Col RAMC
OC 112 Field Amb[ulance]

C.

Duties of N.C.O. i/c W.W. at the ASYLUM.-

1.- He will expect

(a) Slight W.W. from the whole Corps front arriving on foot when lorries are not available at MENIN GATE.-

(b) Cases from the PRISON, YPRES. with which he must keep in touch.-

(c) Lorries containing W.W. coming from MENIN GATE.-

2.- 20 minutes before departure of a train on the hourly service from the ASYLUM, he will stop all Red + Lorries + will unload them to entrain.- He will not so stop empty ammunition lorries carrying wounded.- He will similarly keep for the train all W.W. from the PRISON, + all cases arriving on foot.-

3.- For the 40 minutes after the departure of a train, he will send his wounded back by lorries, returning empty, directing the driver to stop at VLAMERTINGHE MILL.- He has the right to "flag" all such lorries.

4.- He will not stop Red + Lorries.-

5.- He will send the "third" lorries with a few vacant seats left at MENIN GATE round by KRUISSTRAAT + Belg: Battery Corner, until ordered to discontinue

[signature]

Lieut Col RAMC.
OC. 112 Field Amb^ce

D.

Duties of NCO i/c Walking wounded:-

ATHERLEY Junction and H.S. central

1.- He will have under his command 12 privates for guides and assisting in keeping patients & carrying equipment.-

2.- He & his staff will meet every train arriving from St JEAN.-

3.- He will keep in touch with the Railway officials on the spot & will see that every train carrying wounded is stopped for unloading.-

4.- He will march off the wounded in batches in charge of guides to VLAMERTINGHE MILL.-

5.- If he should find any occupied cases, or cases no longer fit to walk, he will send a runner to the MILL giving the numbers to be carried.-

6. A motor lorry will ply to and from the MILL. Cases will be despatched along the road to meet it.— They will not be kept to wait for it

~~Lieut Col RAMC~~
~~OC 12 Field Amb~~

[signature]

for Lieut Col RAMC,
O.C. XIX Corps [illegible]

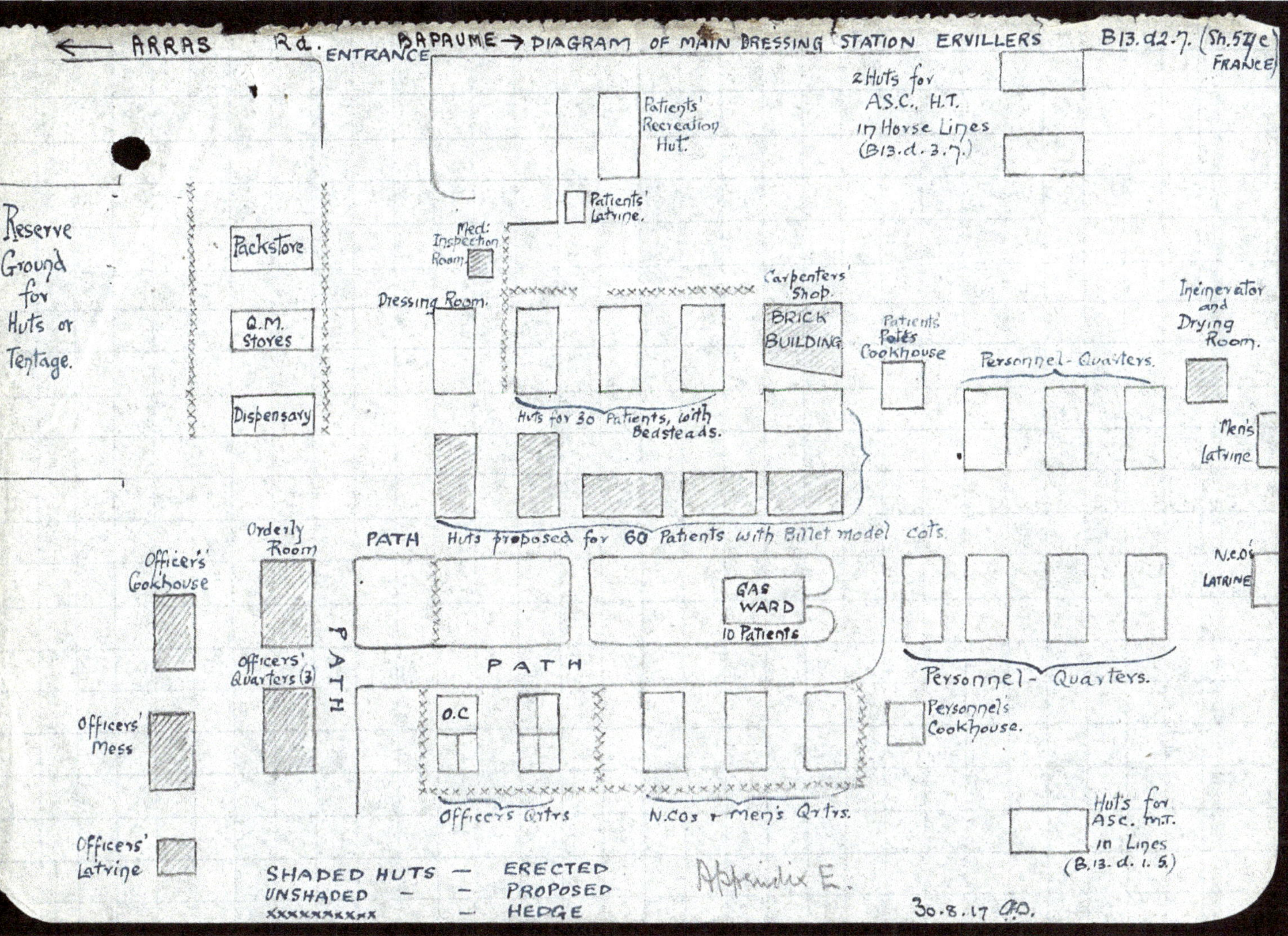

← ARRAS Rd. BAPAUME → DIAGRAM OF MAIN DRESSING STATION ERVILLERS
B13.d2.7. (Sh.57c) FRANCE
ENTRANCE
2 Huts for A.S.C., H.T. in Horse Lines (B13.d.3.7.)
Patients' Recreation Hut.
Patients' Latrine.
Reserve Ground for Huts or Tentage.
Packstore
Q.M. Stores
Dispensary
Med: Inspection Room.
Dressing Room.
Carpenters' Shop.
BRICK BUILDING
Patients' Cookhouse
Incinerator and Drying Room.
Personnel-Quarters.
Men's Latrine
Huts for 30 Patients, with Bedsteads.
PATH Huts proposed for 60 Patients with Billet model cots.
Orderly Room
Officers' Cookhouse
N.C.O's LATRINE
GAS WARD 10 Patients
PATH
Officers' Quarters (3)
Personnel-Quarters.
Personnel's Cookhouse.
Officers' Mess
O.C
Officers Qrtrs
N.C.Os & Men's Qrtrs.
Officers' Latrine
Huts for ASC. M.T. in Lines (B.13.d.1.5.)
SHADED HUTS — ERECTED
UNSHADED — PROPOSED
xxxxxxxxx — HEDGE
Appendix E.
30.8.17

P A T H O L O G Y. 4.

Typhoid and Paratyphoid.

Monthly Inoculation Returns.

Inoculation Returns - 1st Iv. A.D.M.S.

Enteric Group.

The Results of Antityphoid Inoculation in our Army. (Japan)

Sept 1917 16

WAR DIARY.

FOR MONTH OF SEPTEMBER, 1917.

VOLUME 22

UNIT:- RAMC 112th Field Ambulance

Instructions regarding War Diaries and Intelligence Summaries are contained in F. S. Regs., Part II. and the Staff Manual respectively. Title Pages will be prepared in manuscript.

WAR DIARY
or
~~INTELLIGENCE SUMMARY~~
(Erase heading not required.)

Army Form C. 2118.

No: 112 Field Ambulance.

Place	Date	Hour	Summary of Events and Information	Remarks and references to Appendices
ERVILLERS 57.C. B.13 d.2.7.	1/9/17		Took over command on arrival from leave from Capt C.H. Denyer. M.C. Dressing Station among ruins and gardens West of the ARRAS–BAPAUME Road. 5 Nissen Bow Huts erected and in use 3 more started construction since arrival of Unit. Officers' Mess with Kitchen and scullery, C.O's hut, Orderly Room, latrines and Incinerator with Drying Room, and a cookhouse in use. All these require considerable alteration for the Winter. In the afternoon visited VI th Corps Scabies Station i/c Capt Warburton & B Section this F.A. (with Lieut Watt. U.S.A. M.S) – an old brickfield. – Patients in old Brick-drying sheds and Marquees. Officers & stores in chambers of furnace-building, with personnel in upper floor. Dining-room shed & cookhouse, All very sketchy & requiring alteration for Winter ACHIET LE GRAND. 57.C. G.9. b-d G. J. Houghton Lieut Col RAMC.	See Appendices I & II ~~[illegible]~~ GH
"	2/9/17.		With ADMS spent the morning in inspecting Trenches of left Section including my own Bearer Relay Posts at 57.B.T.6.b.3.0. & 5.d.8.8. Went up via ST LEGER. 57.B.T.28 & CROISILLES T.23.b & returned via HENIN sur COJEUL. T.2.b. My bearers have to carry about $1\frac{3}{4}$ miles in HINDENBURG LINE – SHAFT TRENCH & half a mile over the open to CRUCIFIX CORNER. 51 B.N.33 b 3.9. Lieut A. STRAUSS. U.S.A M.S. left for 49. C.C.S. Capt D.H. Weir assumed duties of Transport officer. GH.	
"	3/9/17		Prepared Plan (Appendix I a) of Dressing Station, showing existing arrangements & proposed additions & alterations. Obtained bedsteads for Diarrhoea Ward. GJH.	

2449 Wt. W14957/M90 750,000 1/16 J.B.C. & A. Forms/C.2118/12.

Army Form C. 2118.

Instructions regarding War Diaries and Intelligence Summaries are contained in F. S. Regs., Part II. and the Staff Manual respectively. Title Pages will be prepared in manuscript.

WAR DIARY
or
~~INTELLIGENCE SUMMARY~~
(Erase heading not required.)

112. F.A.

Place	Date	Hour	Summary of Events and Information	Remarks and references to Appendices
ERVILLERS	4/9/17		Visited in the morning by D.M.S. ~~Third~~ Army, D.D.M.S. VIth Corps & ADMS 15th Division. The DMS & DDMS expressed approval of my plan, which allowed for alternative use as a Main Dressing Station. Capt Lightwood returned from temporary duty with 2nd R.Dub.Fusls & was posted to VIth Corps Scabies Station R.J.H.	
"	5/9/17		Capt D. H. Weir & 1 pte returned from XIXth Corps Reinforcement Camp. R.J.H.	
"	6/9/17		Hon Lt & Q.M. C.W. Atkins left on leave to England 10. P.B. men arrived from the Base in place of 10 "Batmen" A.S.C. R.J.H.	
"	7/9/17		7 A.S.C. Batmen (Cat. A) proceeded to H.T. & S. Base Depot. HAVRE. 1 pte (farrier) A.S.C. arrived for permanent duty. Capt A.M. Mitchell returned from temporary duty at 32. C.C.S. R.J.H.	
"	8/9/17		Capt Mitchell posted to VIth Corps Scabies Stn in relief of Capt Lightwood posted to permanent duty with 11th Hants (Pioneers). For progress during week see App. III. R.J.H.	see Appendix III

2449 Wt. W14957/M90 750,000 1/16 J.B.C. & A. Forms/C.2118/12.

Army Form C. 2118.

Instructions regarding War Diaries and Intelligence Summaries are contained in F. S. Regs., Part II. and the Staff Manual respectively. Title Pages will be prepared in manuscript.

WAR DIARY
~~or~~
~~INTELLIGENCE SUMMARY~~

(Erase heading not required.)

112 F A.

Place	Date	Hour	Summary of Events and Information	Remarks and references to Appendices
ERVILLERS	9/9/17		Routine GJK.	
"	10/9/17		Capt W. Mercer joined on return from leave. 14 O.R. (1 NCO & 3 ptes, Nurses, and 10 Bearers) left for temporary duty with 29 C.C.S. Visited Trench Posts and arranged for (a) Re-adjustment of Gas Blankets, (b) Limewashing & Disinfection of Dug Outs & simultaneous change of blankets & underclothing. GJK.	
"	11/9/17		Capt W. Warburton ~~Capt W. [illegible]~~, on completion of 2 Days Anti Gas Instruction, with Capt W Tierney returned from Temporary duty with GJK 7th R. I. Rifles, proceeded on Contract leave. GJK.	
"	12/9/17		Routine GJK	
"	13/9/17		Two men A.S.C. batmen, on return from leave sent to A.S.C. Depot, HAVRE. The remaining man, being on leave, has been warned by letter to proceed direct. GJK	
"	14/9/17		Routine GJK	
"	15/9/17		Routine GJK For progress during Week see Appendix IV. GJK.	See Appendix IV

2449 Wt. W14957/M90 750,000 1/16 J.B.C. & A. Forms/C.2118/12.

Instructions regarding War Diaries and Intelligence Summaries are contained in F. S. Regs., Part II. and the Staff Manual respectively. Title Pages will be prepared in manuscript.

WAR DIARY

~~or~~

~~INTELLIGENCE SUMMARY~~

(Erase heading not required.)

Army Form C. 2118.

112 F.A.

Place	Date	Hour	Summary of Events and Information	Remarks and references to Appendices
ERUILLERS	16/9/17		Routine. G.H.	
"	17/9/17		Visited Trench Bearer-Posts. The lime-washing &c has been carried out, and the Bearers claim to be free from lice. The NCO & 4 men beside the R.A.P. at T.6.d.5.? are moving to a point in the "Shaft" beside the R.A.P. as being more accessible, and are making bed-racks for themselves there. G.H.	
"	18/9/17		1 Ford Car with driver evacuated to the Base. G.H.	
"	19/9/17		Routine. G.H.	
"	20/9/17		Routine. G.H.	
"	21/9/17		Capt C.H. Dunger took over temporary charge of VIth Corps Scabies Stn, on departure to 113 F.A. of Lieut Watt. U.S.A.M.S. G.H.	
"	22/9/17		Routine. For progress during week see Appendix V. G.H.	Appendix V.

2449 Wt. W14957/M90 750,000 1/16 J.B.C. & A. Forms/C.2118/12.

Instructions regarding War Diaries and Intelligence Summaries are contained in F. S. Regs., Part II. and the Staff Manual respectively. Title Pages will be prepared in manuscript.

WAR DIARY
or
INTELLIGENCE SUMMARY
(Erase heading not required.)

Army Form C. 2118.

112 FA.

Place	Date	Hour	Summary of Events and Information	Remarks and references to Appendices
ERVILLERS	23/9/17		Issued orders for special practice in working in box-respirators from 4.00 to 4.15. PM daily during ensuing week. RJK	
"	24/9/17		Inspected Trench Bearer Posts and issued instructions re practice in box-respirators. At HQrs first practice most successful. All trades and offices continued work, & tea was served out to patients. RJK	
"	25/9/17		New Ford Car with Driver arrived. 2. O.R. RAMC. arrived as re-inforcement. RJK	
"	26/9/17		Capt. W. Turner & Capt W. Warburton returned from leave. Capt W. Warburton proceeded to VII Corps Scabies Stn. Stl. RJK	
"	27/9/17		Capt C H Denyer returned from Scabies Stn on relief by Capt W Warburton. Capt Turner left for permanent M.O. of 16th Divn. R.E. A.D.M.S. witnessed Box Respirator Practice. RJK	
"	28/9/17		Routine RJK	

Instructions regarding War Diaries and Intelligence Summaries are contained in F. S. Regs., Part II. and the Staff Manual respectively. Title Pages will be prepared in manuscript.

WAR DIARY
or
~~INTELLIGENCE SUMMARY~~
(Erase heading not required.)

Army Form C. 2118.

112 F.A.

Place	Date	Hour	Summary of Events and Information	Remarks and references to Appendices
ERVILLERS	29/9/16		Routine. For Progress see Appendix VI QIK	Appendix VI
"	30/9/16		Lieuts. F. C. Irving & Wade Wright. U.S.A. M.S were attached for a week's training before going to a CCS. R. S. Hunt... Lieut Col RAMC	

2449 Wt. W14957/M90 750,000 1/16 J.B.C. & A. Forms/C.2118/12.

APPENDIX. I

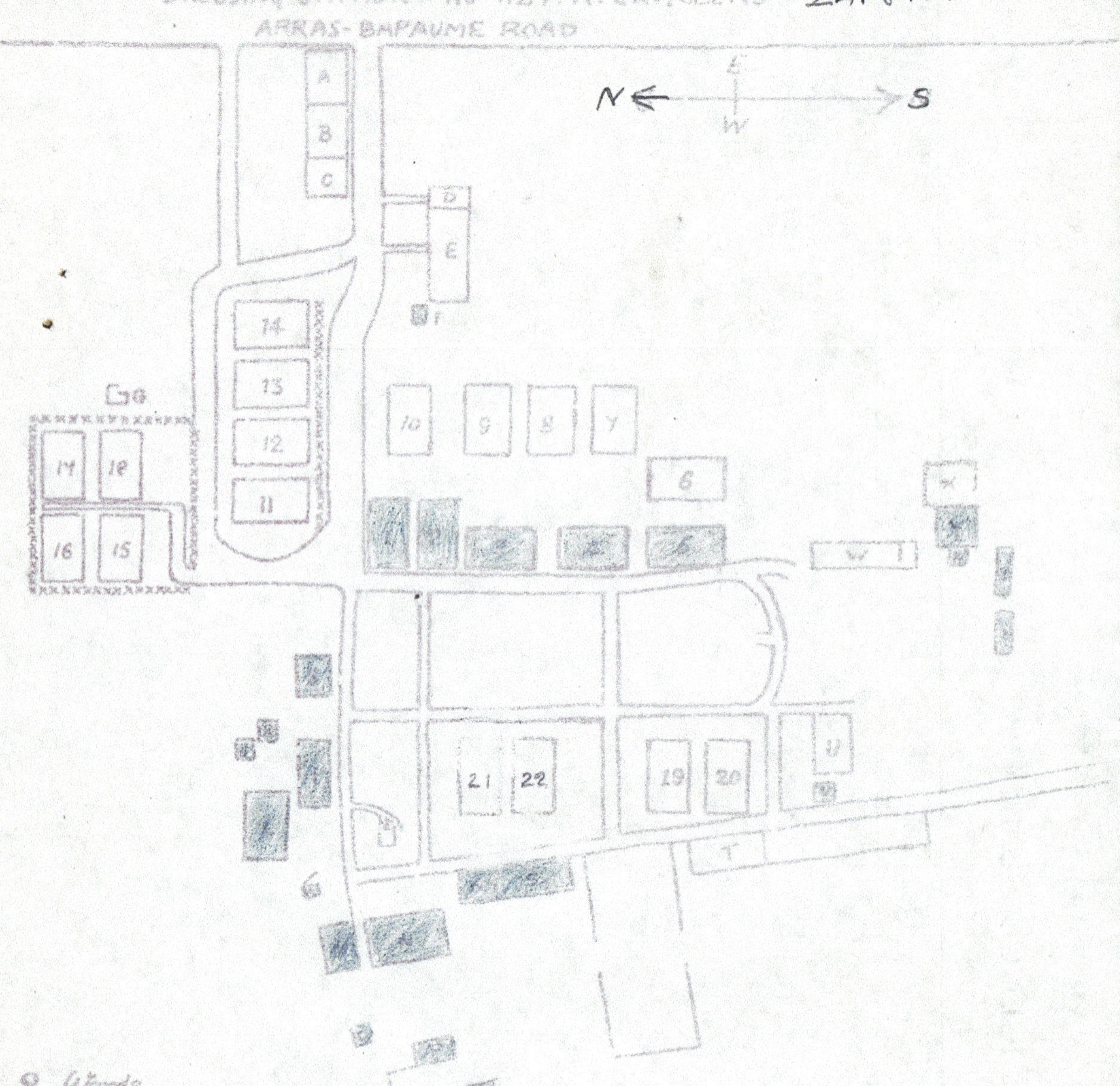

1-9 Wards.

10 Recreation Room

11-13 Wards.

14 Pack Store

15-18 Personnel

19-20 Dining Halls

21-22. Officers Billets

Completed buildings blocked in
In construction – outlined } blue
Present use – (ink.)

A	Medical-Inspection Room.	J	Officers' Kitchen	S	Area Store
B	Dressing Room	K	Scullery.	T	M.T. Billet
C	Orderly Room	L	Officers' Mess	U.	Cookhouse
D	Canteen	M	Sergeants' Mess	V	Cook's store
E	Sergeants	N	Mobilisation Store	W.	Ablution and Baths.
F	Barber's Shop (M.I. Room)	O	Sgts' Mess Kitchen	X	Incinerator + Boilers
G	Night Latrine (Personnel)	P	Billet	Y	Drying Room.
	P.C (Orderly Room)	Q	Provision Store	Z	Latrines.
	Officers	R	Dispensary.	&	Laundry.

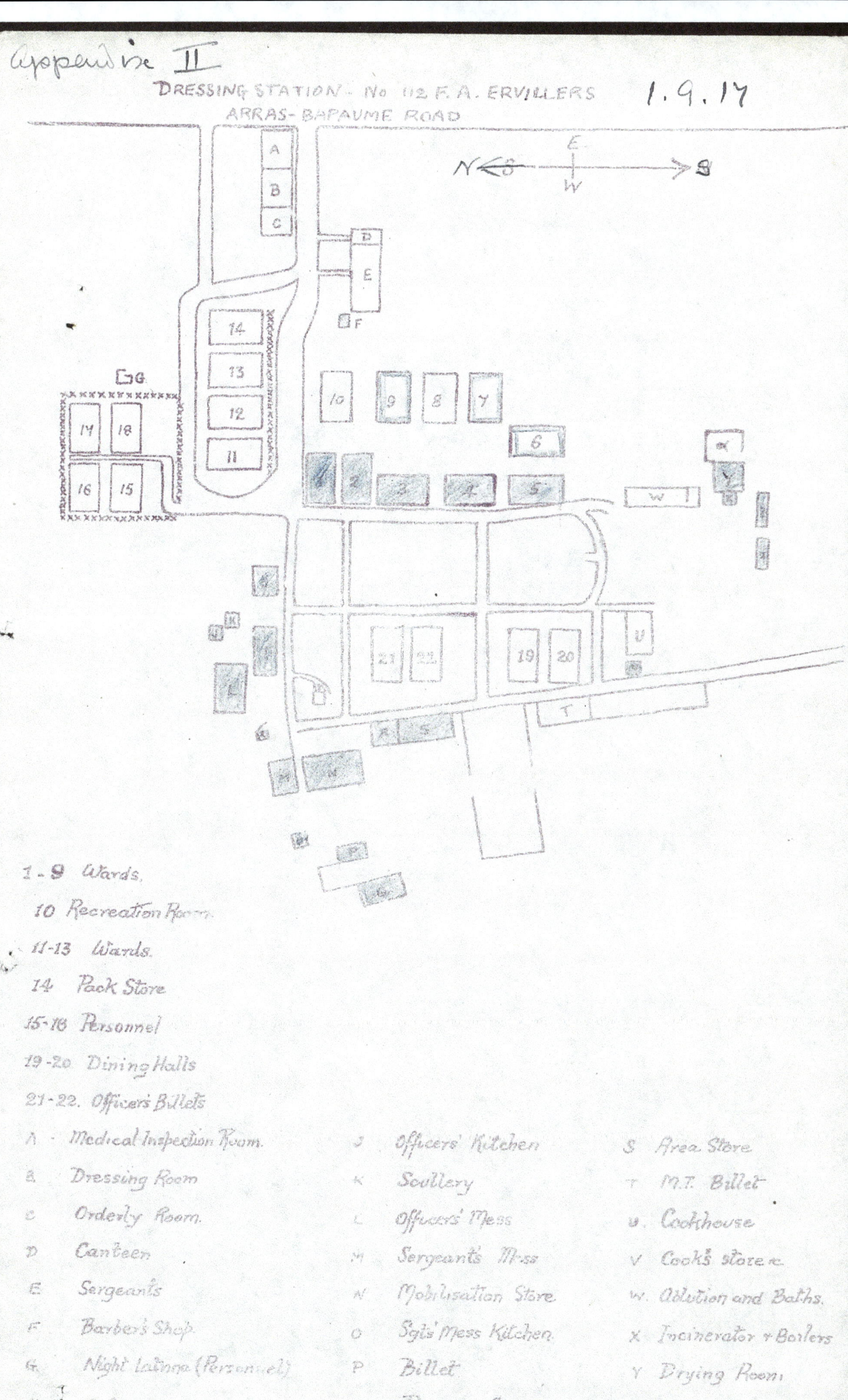

Appendix II
DRESSING STATION - No 112 F.A. ERVILLERS
1.9.17
ARRAS-BAPAUME ROAD
N
E
W
S
A
B
C
D
E
F
G
14
13
12
11
17
18
16
15
10
9
8
7
6
1
2
3
4
5
W
U
19
20
21
22
T
R
S
M
N
P
Q
1-9 Wards.
10 Recreation Room
11-13 Wards.
14 Pack Store
15-16 Personnel
19-20 Dining Halls
21-22. Officers Billets
A - Medical Inspection Room.
B Dressing Room
C Orderly Room.
D Canteen
E Sergeants
F Barber's Shop
G Night Latrine (Personnel)
H P-C
I Officers
J Officers' Kitchen
K Scullery
L Officers' Mess
M Sergeant's Mess
N Mobilisation Store
O Sgts' Mess Kitchen
P Billet
Q Provision Store
R Dispensary.
S Area Store
T M.T. Billet
U. Cookhouse
V Cook's store
W. Ablution and Baths.
X Incinerator & Boilers
Y Drying Room
Z Latrines.
α Laundry

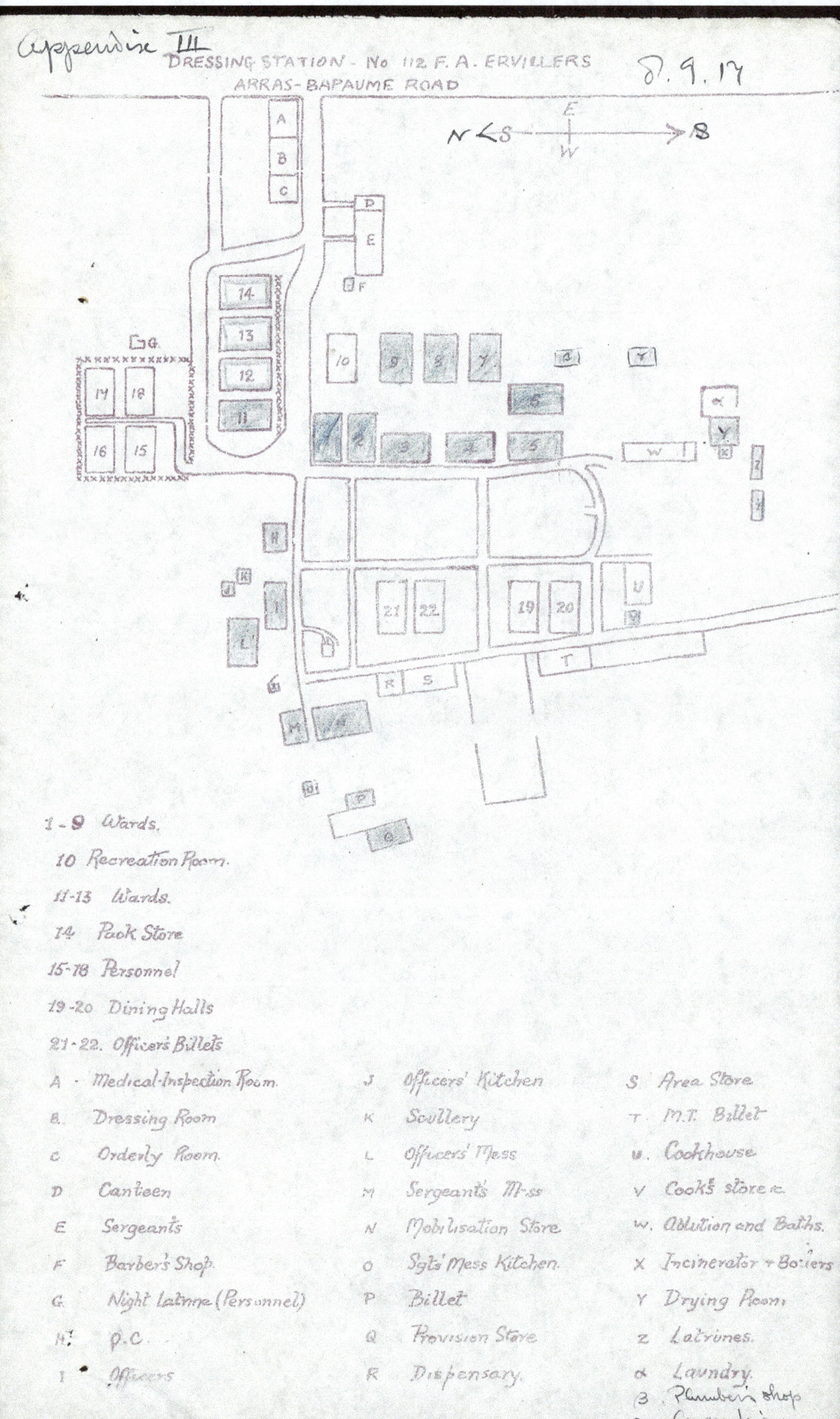
Appendix III
DRESSING STATION - No 112 F. A. ERVILLERS
ARRAS-BAPAUME ROAD
8.9.17
N
S
E
W
A
B
C
D
E
F
G.
14
13
12
11
10
17
18
16
15
21
22
19
20
T
R
S
U
M
P
Q
W
1-9 Wards.
10 Recreation Room.
11-13 Wards.
14 Pack Store
15-18 Personnel
19-20 Dining Halls
21-22. Officer's Billets
A - Medical-Inspection Room.
B. Dressing Room
C Orderly Room.
D Canteen
E Sergeants
F Barber's Shop.
G. Night Latrine (Personnel)
H. P.C.
I Officers
J Officers' Kitchen
K Scullery
L Officers' Mess
M Sergeant's Mess
N Mobilisation Store
O Sgts' Mess Kitchen.
P Billet
Q Provision Store
R Dispensary.
S Area Store
T M.T. Billet
U. Cookhouse
V Cook's store &c.
W. Ablution and Baths.
X Incinerator + Boilers
Y Drying Room.
Z Latrines.
α Laundry.
β Plumber's shop
γ Carpenter's.

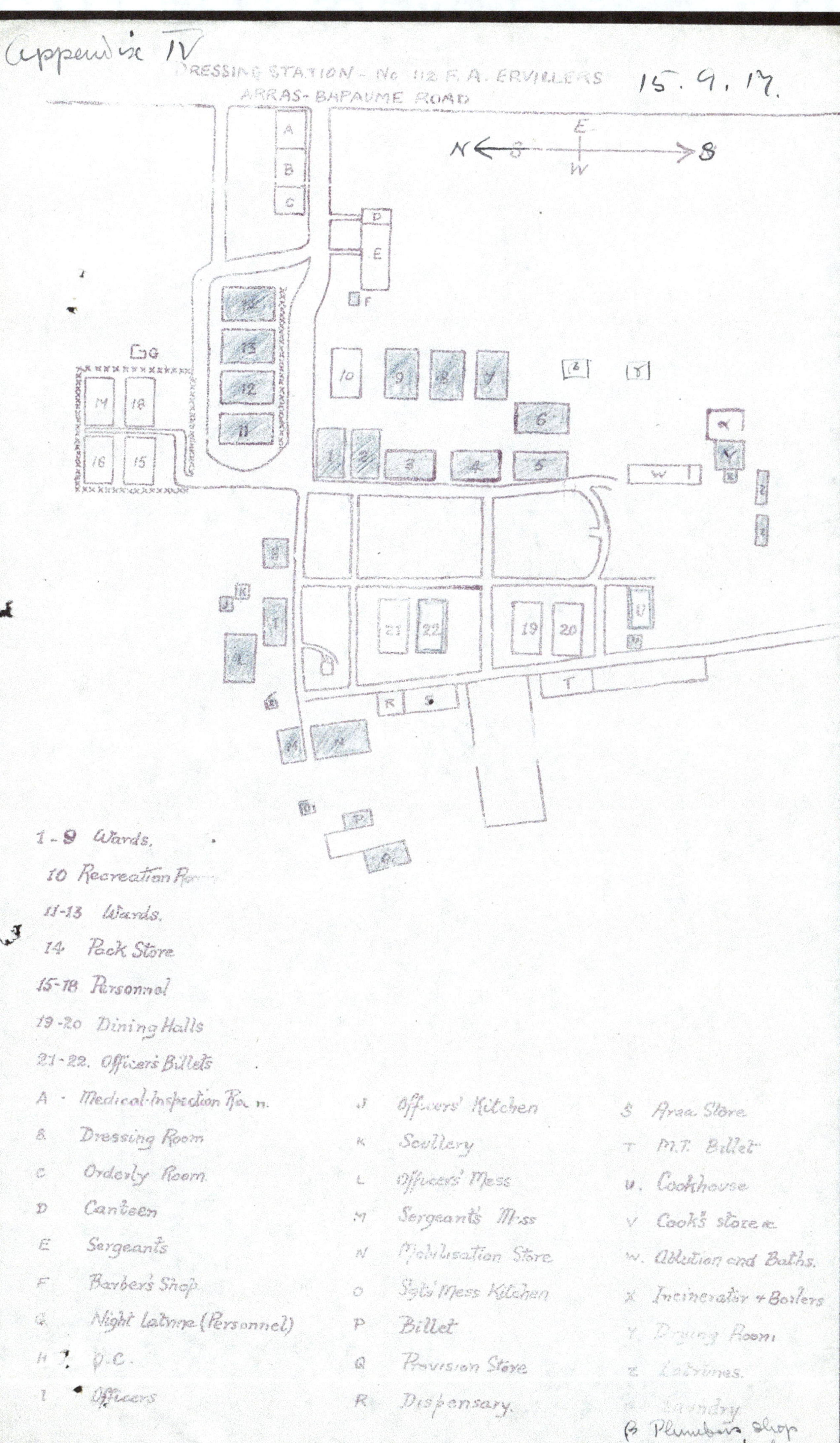

Appendix IV
DRESSING STATION – No 112 F.A. ERVILLERS
ARRAS–BAPAUME ROAD
15.9.17.
N
S
E
W
A
B
C
D
E
F
G
10
9
8
7
6
5
4
3
2
1
13
12
11
14
18
15
16
W
U
21
22
19
20
T
R
S
N
M
L
P
O
1–9 Wards.
10 Recreation Room
11–13 Wards.
14 Pack Store
15–18 Personnel
19–20 Dining Halls
21–22. Officers Billets
A – Medical Inspection Room.
B Dressing Room
C Orderly Room.
D Canteen
E Sergeants
F Barber's Shop
G Night Latrine (Personnel)
H – O.C.
I Officers
J Officers' Kitchen
K Scullery
L Officers' Mess
M Sergeant's Mess
N Mobilisation Store
O Sgts' Mess Kitchen
P Billet
Q Provision Store
R Dispensary.
S Area Store
T M.T. Billet
U. Cookhouse
V Cook's stores.
W. Ablution and Baths.
X Incinerator + Boilers
Y. Drying Room.
Z Latrines.
Laundry
β Plumber's shop
γ Carpenter's shop

Appendix V
DRESSING STATION - No 112 F.A. ERVILLERS
ARRAS-BAPAUME ROAD
22.9.17
N
S
E
W
1-9 Wards.
10 Recreation Room.
11-13 Wards.
14 Pack Store
15-18 Personnel
19-20 Dining Halls
21-22. Officers Billets
A Medical-Inspection Room.
B Dressing Room
C Orderly Room
D Canteen
E Sergeants.
F Barbers Shop
G Night Latrine (Personnel)
H O.C
I Officers
J Officers' Kitchen
K Scullery
L Officers' Mess
M Sergeants' Mess
N Mobilisation Store
O Sgts' Mess Kitchen
P Billet
Q Provision Store
R Dispensary.
S Area Store
T M.T. Billet
U Cookhouse
V Cook's store &c.
W. Ablution and Baths.
X Incinerator & Boilers
Y Drying Room
Z Latrines.
α Laundry.
β Plumber's Shop
γ Carpenter's Shop

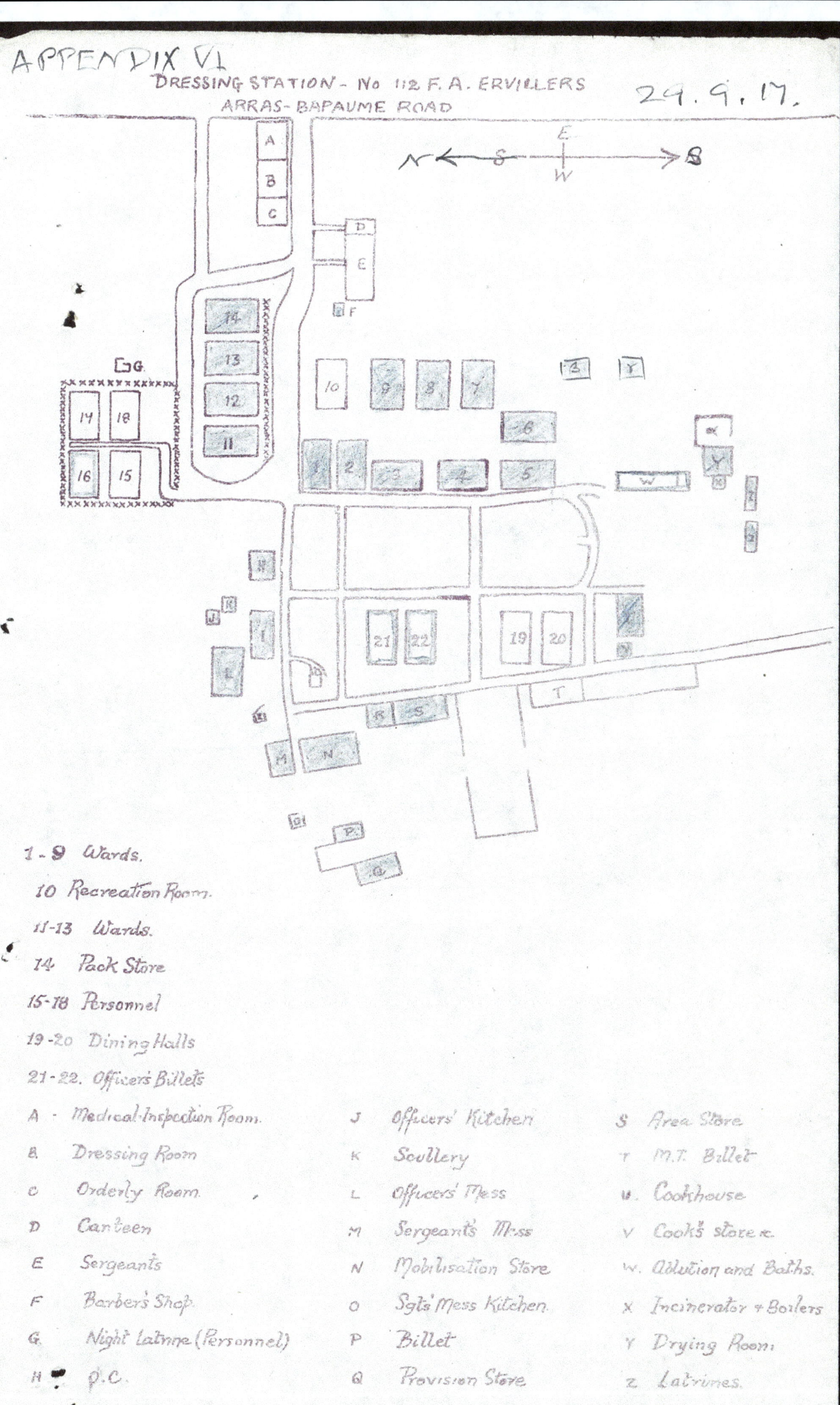
APPENDIX VI
DRESSING STATION - No 112 F. A. ERVILLERS
ARRAS-BAPAUME ROAD
29.9.17.
N
S
E
W
A
B
C
D
E
F
G.
H
I
J
K
L
M
N
O
P
Q
R
S
T
W
1
2
3
4
5
6
7
8
9
10
11
12
13
14
15
16
17
18
19
20
21
22
1-9 Wards.
10 Recreation Room.
11-13 Wards.
14 Pack Store
15-18 Personnel
19-20 Dining Halls
21-22. Officers' Billets
A - Medical Inspection Room.
B Dressing Room
C Orderly Room.
D Canteen
E Sergeants
F Barber's Shop
G. Night Latrine (Personnel)
H Q.C.
I Officers
J Officers' Kitchen
K Scullery
L Officers' Mess
M Sergeant's Mess
N Mobilisation Store
O Sgts' Mess Kitchen
P Billet
Q Provision Store
R Dispensary.
S Area Store
T M.T. Billet
U. Cookhouse
V Cook's store.
W. Ablution and Baths.
X Incinerator + Boilers
Y Drying Room.
Z Latrines.
α Laundry.
β Plumber's Shop
γ Carpenters "

Oct. 1917

16

WAR DIARY

FOR MONTH OF OCTOBER, 1917.

UNIT 112th Field Ambce RAMC

VOLUME NUMBER 23

140/2499

Vol 23

Instructions regarding War Diaries and Intelligence Summaries are contained in F. S. Regs., Part II. and the Staff Manual respectively. Title Pages will be prepared in manuscript.

WAR DIARY
or
~~INTELLIGENCE SUMMARY~~
(Erase heading not required.)

Army Form C. 2118.

No: 112 Field Ambulance

Place	Date	Hour	Summary of Events and Information	Remarks and references to Appendices
ERVILLERS 57.c. B.13 d.2 7.	1/10/17		Visited Trenches in morning Received orders from DDMS VIth Corps to form at F.A Headqrs a Scabies Station for VIth Corps of 300 beds, retaining a few huts for ordinary cases. R.J. Hamilton Lt Col RAMC	
"	2/10/17		No: 30741 a/Sgt Richards awarded Military Medal for gallantry in YPRES salient Prepared plan of new Scabies Station and received approval of ADMS & DDMS RJH	Appendix I
"	3/10/17		Routine RJH.	
"	4/10/17		Visited BARLY & inspected huts at VIth Corps Scabies Stn North and selected those whose transfer to ERVILLERS was to be desired. The attached American Officers sent to accompany MO i/c 9th RDF for instruction RJH	
"	5/10/17		Capt C.H. Denmer left for 21 days leave in England. American Officers sent to accompany MO i/c Divl Train for instruction. RJH	
"	6/10/17		Routine RJH.	

2449 Wt. W14957/M90 750,000 1/16 J.B.C. & A. Forms/C.2118/12.

WAR DIARY

~~or~~

~~INTELLIGENCE SUMMARY~~

(Erase heading not required.)

Army Form C. 2118.

Instructions regarding War Diaries and Intelligence Summaries are contained in F. S. Regs., Part II. and the Staff Manual respectively. Title Pages will be prepared in manuscript.

112. F.A.

Place	Date	Hour	Summary of Events and Information	Remarks and references to Appendices
ERVILLERS	7/10/17		No: 64693 pte Shepperley & No: 74449 pte Cottrell to be unpaid Lce-Corpls. R.J.H.	
"	8/10/17		Lieutenants Irving & Wright. U.S.A.M.C left for No: 43. CCS at the conclusion of a week's instruction. Visited Trenches No: 35040 pte Hislop to be unpaid Lce Corpl. R.J.H.	
"	9/10/17		Ambulance Head Quarters inspected by G.O.C. 16th Divn. 7 Convalescents from VII Corps Scabies Stn. etc arrived in the evening to assist in construction. Up to this I have been dependent on 6–8 men of my own unit for hutting, & 3 or 4 for road-making. My Interpreter – Mch de Logis E B de Fleurac awarded the Croix de Guerre for gallantry & valuable services at FREZENBURG. YPRES SALIENT. No 64712 a/g Sgt Stanger & No 64583 pte Dumbling awarded Military Medal for gallantry in YPRES Salient. R.J.H.	
"	10/10/17		Made out Standing Orders for Reception and Treatment for Scabies Station ~~[illegible]~~ R.J.H. & forwarded to DDMS for approval. 1st/c Staff Sgt Major Ingle left for England for Temporary Commission in A.S.C. 2 more Convalescents ex S.S. Stn arrived for help in construction. R.J.H.	Appendix 2 3
"	11/10/17		DDMS held Sanitary Conference at F.A. HQrs. R.J.H.	

2449 Wt. W14957/M90 750,000 1/16 J.B.C. & A. Forms/C.2118/12.

Army Form C. 2118.

WAR DIARY
~~or~~
~~INTELLIGENCE SUMMARY~~

(Erase heading not required.)

Instructions regarding War Diaries and Intelligence Summaries are contained in F. S. Regs., Part II. and the Staff Manual respectively. Title Pages will be prepared in manuscript.

112 FA.

Place	Date	Hour	Summary of Events and Information	Remarks and references to Appendices
ERVILLERS	12/10/17		Horse Lines sufficiently advanced to be occupable. Started painting interior of huts. GLH	
"	13/10/17		Routine GLH.	
"	14/10/17		Routine GLH	
"	15/10/17		Routine GLH	
"	16/10/17		Routine GLH	
"	17/10/17		Inspected Relay Posts & RAP in Trenches GLH	
"	18/10/17		With ADMS visited Trenches & decided to as early as possible change the "Wounded" Route on left flank of Division, utilising "FIT LANE" & "WIND AVENUE" to the exit near Strong Point C.10. Thence wounded could be conveyed by wheeled stretcher or possibly by trolley to the HENIN-CROISILLES Road where a car could be arranged for. Shaft 68 to be abandoned, & a damaged MEBU near S.P. C10. to be fitted as Relay post instead GLH	

2449 Wt. W14957/M90 750,000 1/16 J.B.C. & A. Forms/C.2118/12.

Army Form C. 2118.

Instructions regarding War Diaries and Intelligence Summaries are contained in F. S. Regs., Part II. and the Staff Manual respectively. Title Pages will be prepared in manuscript.

WAR DIARY ~~or~~ ~~INTELLIGENCE~~ SUMMARY

(Erase heading not required.)

112 FA

Place	Date	Hour	Summary of Events and Information	Remarks and references to Appendices
ERVILLERS	19/10/17		Visited HENIN & searched for and found alternative sites for a shelter & Car-stand. GJH	
"	20/10/17		With ADMS decided on site at 57.B. T 2 b. 77. We subsequently visited HQ of Division in whose AREA HENIN is, & obtained permission to take over the site. GJH	
"	21/10/17		Routine GJH	
"	22/10/17		Sent up ~~[illegible]~~ workmen to HENIN to build shed. Capt R. Stillman U.S.A. M.C reported for instruction for a week. GJH	
"	23/10/17		Capt. E. Lightwood. RAMC reported for Duty on absorption of 9th R. Dub Fus. Visited by DDMS & AA & QMG VIth Corps on question of materials wanted for hutting &c. GJH	
"	24/10/17		Routine GJH	
"	25/10/17		Accompanied by Capt Stillman USAMC visited RAP & Relay Posts in Trenches. Took up workmen to roof in part of MEBU. GJH	

2449 Wt. W14957/M90 750,000 1/16 J.B.C. & A. Forms/C.2118/12.

Instructions regarding War Diaries and Intelligence Summaries are contained in F. S. Regs., Part II. and the Staff Manual respectively. Title Pages will be prepared in manuscript.

WAR DIARY
or
~~INTELLIGENCE SUMMARY~~
(Erase heading not required.)

Army Form C. 2118.

112 FA.

Place	Date	Hour	Summary of Events and Information	Remarks and references to Appendices
ERVILLERS	26/10/17		Routine GJV	
"	27/10/17		Officially occupied MEBU as Relay Post & shed at HENIN. Personally inspected in afternoon, & saw parties in occupation &c. GJV	
"	28/10/17		Capt Stillman U.S.A.M.C. left on conclusion of instructional period. I was sent for by ADMS 16th Division during evening, and informed of his immediate departure, & was handed over necessary information as Acting ADMS GJV	
"	29/10/17		Lieut H.E. Gillett U.S.A.M.C. arrived for duty with 112 F.A. Visited by DDMS VIth Corps & given orders re hot water bottles & for stretcher cases later worked out scheme. GJV	
"	30/10/17		Routine	
"	31/10/17		Capt E Lightwood left for temporary duty with 177 Bde R.F.A. Capt E Aissler ~~[illegible]~~ GJV U.S.A.M.C. reported for a Week's instruction Progress During Month A Workman For the construction of the Dressing Station, up to 11.10.17 I was dependent on some 6-8 Artisans or Handy Men of my own Unit besides 3 or 4 bearers & batmen for road-making	

2449 Wt. W14957/M90 750,000 1/16 J.B.C. & A. Forms/C.2118/12.

Instructions regarding War Diaries and Intelligence Summaries are contained in F. S. Regs., Part II. and the Staff Manual respectively. Title Pages will be prepared in manuscript.

WAR DIARY
or
~~INTELLIGENCE SUMMARY~~
(Erase heading not required.)

Army Form C. 2118.

·112 FA

Place	Date	Hour	Summary of Events and Information	Remarks and references to Appendices
ERVILLERS	31/10/17	Continued.	On 11th inst. 7 convalescent workmen were obtained from VIth Corps Scabies Stn. 8th as extra hands, & their numbers were gradually increased to 16 on the 24th. 11 more arrived between 27th & 31st. On 16th inst a squad of 5-3 men was lent me by the 16th Divl Hutting Coy. The DDMS sent me 1 corpl from a Sanitary Section on 28th, & 2 more arrived on evening of 30th; these men were specially for work on Adrian Huts. The construction of the stables, was, save for the fitting of the roof timbers all done by my ASC Detacht (less B Section) themselves. Throughout the month I was repeatedly held up by want of materials & also by the heavy leave-allotment of the unit.	
			B. Construction During the month the principal works were — (1) Stables for full establishment completed in roof & floor & with temporary sides. (2) A Nissen Bow Hut for ASC Personnel completed. (3) Huts 16-20 completed, & 21 complete save for lining. 27 completed & partitioned, & 28 partitioned but not lined.	Appendix 4
			(4) Huts 1-3 & 16-21 fitted with brick fire-places of special pattern, with domed sheet iron roof, & two tubes crossing inside on the slant for hot air.	

2449 Wt. W14957/M90 750,000 1/16 J.B.C. & A. Forms/C.2118/12.

Army Form C. 2118.

Instructions regarding War Diaries and Intelligence Summaries are contained in F. S. Regs., Part II. and the Staff Manual respectively. Title Pages will be prepared in manuscript.

WAR DIARY
or
INTELLIGENCE SUMMARY

(Erase heading not required.)

112 FA

Place	Date	Hour	Summary of Events and Information	Remarks and references to Appendices
ERVILLERS	31/10/17		continued.	
			(5) Huts 6–14 fitted with iron stoves temporarily	
			(6) " 1.2.3.6.7. painted inside – white with service-colour dado & red line.	
			(7) 1–3. 6–14 & 16–21. nearly all windows fitted with translucent material between two layers of rabbit-wire.	
			(8) Hut 4 & Treatment Hut in construction.	Appendix ii
			(9) Much road- & path-making	
			(10) Ground prepared & planted with vegetables.	
			(11) Officers Dining Room lined by labour of Members of the Mess themselves.	
			(12) Shed constructed at HENIN & portion of MEBU roofed with cement & expanded metal.	
			P. S. [illegible] Lt Col RAMC OC 112 FA	

2449 Wt. W14957/M90 750,000 1/16 J.B.C. & A. Forms/C.2118/12.

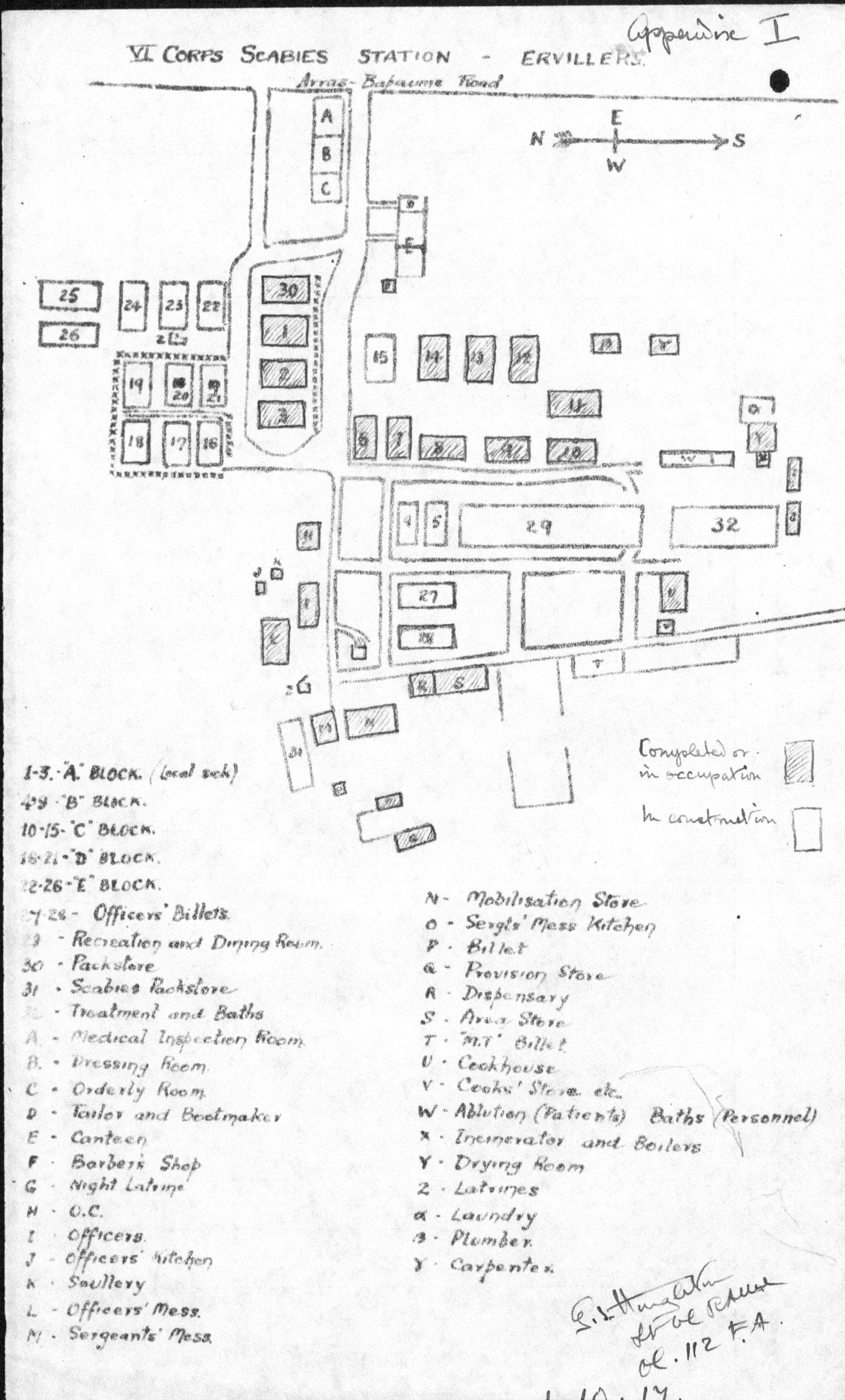
Appendix I
VI CORPS SCABIES STATION - ERVILLERS.
Arras-Bapaume Road
E
N
S
W
Completed or in occupation
In construction
1-3. "A" BLOCK. (local sch)
4-9 "B" BLOCK.
10-15 "C" BLOCK.
16-21 "D" BLOCK.
22-26 "E" BLOCK.
27-28 - Officers' Billets.
29 - Recreation and Dining Room.
30 - Packstore
31 - Scabies Packstore
32 - Treatment and Baths
A - Medical Inspection Room.
B. - Dressing Room.
C - Orderly Room.
D - Tailor and Bootmaker
E - Canteen
F - Barber's Shop
G - Night Latrine
H - O.C.
I - Officers.
J - Officers' Kitchen
K - Scullery
L - Officers' Mess.
M - Sergeants' Mess.
N - Mobilisation Store
O - Sergts' Mess Kitchen
P - Billet
Q - Provision Store
R - Dispensary
S - Area Store
T - "M.T" Billet
U - Cookhouse
V - Cooks' Store etc.
W - Ablution (Patients) Baths (Personnel)
X - Incinerator and Boilers
Y - Drying Room
Z - Latrines
α - Laundry
β - Plumber.
γ - Carpenter.
Lt Col RAMC
OC. 112 F.A.
1.10.17.

Appendix 2.

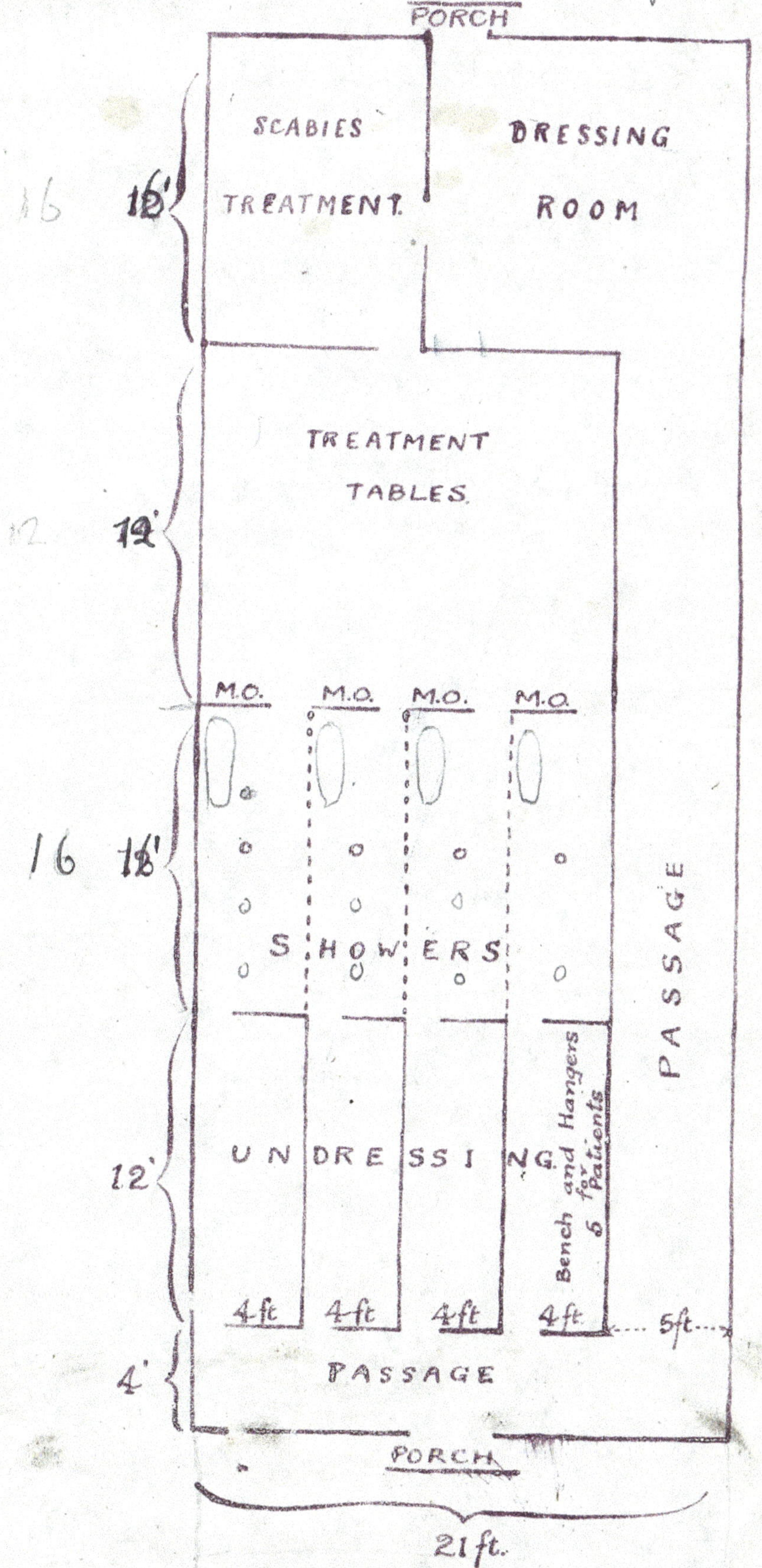

Proposed plan of **BATHS** *and*
TREATMENT ROOM *in* **ADRIAN HUT 60' x 21'.**
32 on Plan.

P. I. Hamilton
Lt Col RAMC
OC. 112 FA

Appendix 3.

VI Corps Scabies Station

Standing Orders for Reception and Routine Treatment of Cases.

A. - Reception:-

(1) All cases arriving will be detained at the Medical Inspection Room till seen and admitted by the Orderly Medical Officer, who will detail them to Blocks according to accommodation.

(2) Unless specially counter-ordered by the O. M. O., all cases will pass direct to the Bathing and Treatment Hut.

(3) When undressed their clothing will be taken from them for disinfection and after bathing and treatment they will dress in Hospital clothing.

(4) Their nails will be cut and cleaned in the Bathing Rooms and their hair cut in the Dressing Room.

B- Routine Treatment:-

(1) Daily, at the hour of the morning visit, patients will be sent to the Treatment Hut in batches of 5 from each Block – "B", "C", "D", and "E".

(2) On arrival at the entrance they will pass into the Undressing Room labelled according to their Block and will undress there, hanging their clothing on the numbered hangers, and retaining their towels.

(3). They will then pass in order into the Bathing rooms, and unless specially countermanded by their M.O. will have a shower-bath, washing with Lysol soap. The Orderlies in charge of the block baths will scrub thoroughly the affected parts of the patient.

(4) The patient will dry himself and pass into the Treatment Room where he will be examined by his M.O. i/c Block and his treatment ordered.
For this purpose the Block Wardmaster will be present with a book giving the patients' names in order with columns for treatment for one week on each page, and will enter the Treatment as ordered.

(5) In the Treatment Room beyond the M.O.s, there will be a row of tables, each devoted to one method of dressing only, and labelled 1, 2, 3, 4, etc., as necessary. The patients will be directed by number to the table where their dressings will be carried out. These numbers may be used in the book.

(6) Uncomplicated cases of Scabies will be sent through to the Special Treatment Room.

(7) After dressing or Scabies Treatment, cases will proceed to the Dressing Room where behind benches labelled by Blocks they will find their clothing which will be brought from the Undressing Room by the Orderly in charge, and hung up according to number.

(8) Twice weekly all clothing will be changed. On these days clean clothing will be on the hangers in the Dressing Room.

(9) The patient will return to his Ward.

(10) Cases ordered modified bathing will be washed as ordered before seeing the M.O. The Wardmaster will be responsible for handing a daily list of such cases to the Orderly i/c Section baths.

(11) Cases requiring Tub Baths will have their shower as routine, and will get their tub at a convenient time after the conclusion of the Morning Inspection.

(12) Cases requiring prolonged treatment in the Scabies Treatment Room will similarly be dealt with after the conclusion of the Morning Inspection.

C - Organisation:-

(1) A "G.D." orderly will be in charge of each pair of huts. There will thus be three (3) to each Section.

(2) At the hour of the Morning Inspection, one of these orderlies will remain to arrange for the sending of his patients in batches of 5 to the Treatment Hut. A second orderly will proceed to take charge of the Undressing Room of his Block. The third will proceed to the Block shower-baths to assist the Orderly in charge.

(3) A N.C.O. will be detailed to co-ordinate the flow of patients to the Treatment Hut.

(4) The Wardmaster of each block will stand by the M.O. in the Treatment Room.

(5) A nursing orderly will be detailed for each Treatment table. Extra nursing orderlies will be detailed for the most frequented tables.

(6) There will be an Orderly in charge of the Dressing Room who will be responsible for the correct hanging up of clothing.

(7) Two or more trained N.O.'s will be posted in the Special Treatment Room.

(8) The Wardmasters and Nursing Staff will carry out the special treatments under the supervision of the Orderly Medical Officer.

(9.) The personnel required for the Treatment Hut will therefore amount to:-

Medical Officers:-	4
N.C.Os:-	5
Nursing Orderlies:-	12
"G.D." Orderlies:-	13.

of whom

N.C.O.s:-	4
and "G.D." Orderlies	8

are found from the Ward Staffs.

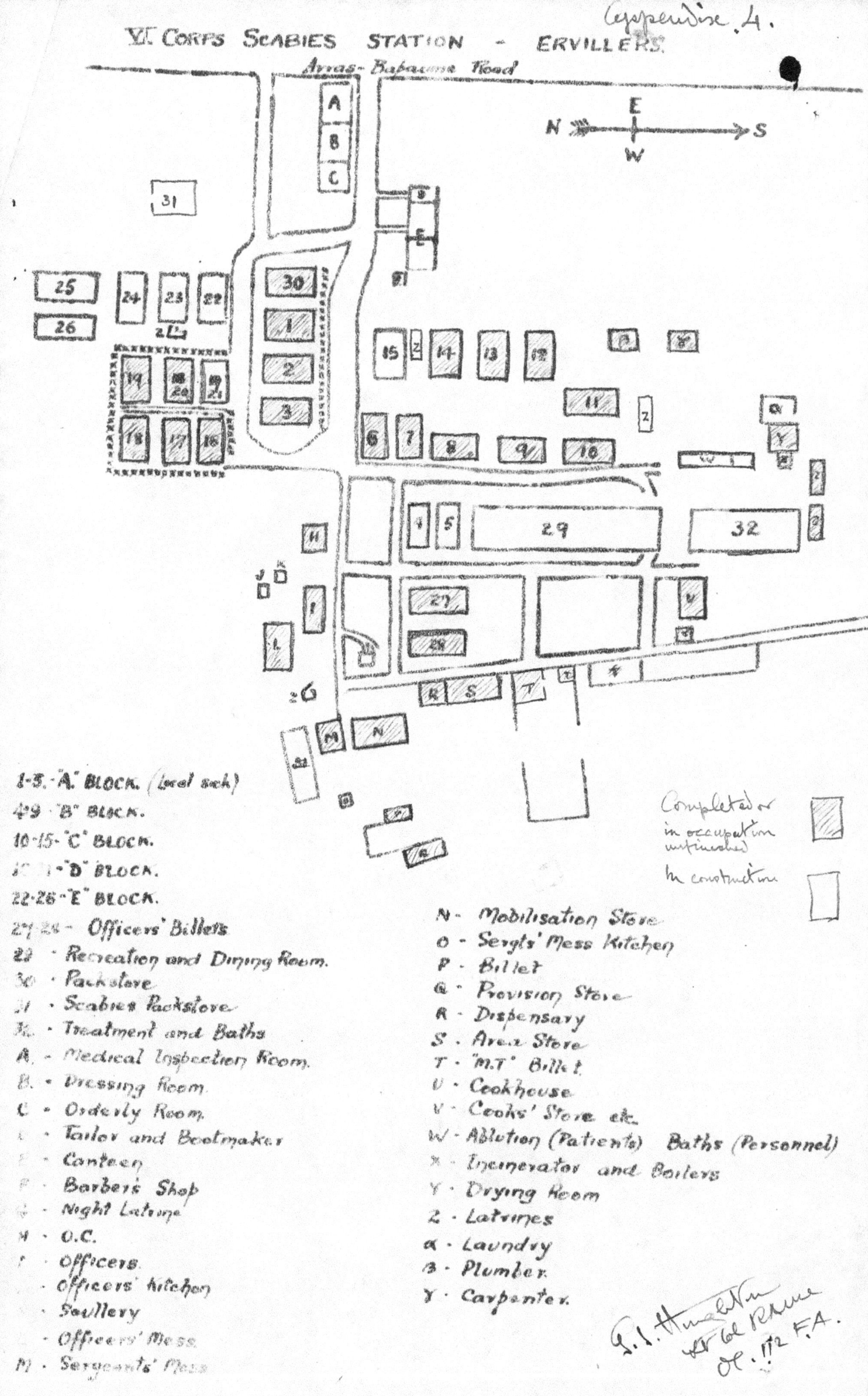

Appendix 4.
VI. CORPS SCABIES STATION - ERVILLERS.
Arras-Bapaume Road
N
E
W
S
A
B
C
31
25
26
24
23
22
30
1
2
3
15
14
13
12
11
6
7
8
9
10
19
17
18
16
4
5
29
32
H
I
L
27
28
R
S
T
M
N
Completed or in occupation unfinished
In construction
1-5. "A" BLOCK. (local sick)
4-9 "B" BLOCK.
10-15 "C" BLOCK.
"D" BLOCK.
22-26 "E" BLOCK.
27-28 - Officers' Billets
29 - Recreation and Dining Room.
30 - Packstore
Scabies Packstore
Treatment and Baths
A. - Medical Inspection Room.
B. - Dressing Room.
C - Orderly Room.
Tailor and Bootmaker
Canteen
Barber's Shop
Night Latrine
H - O.C.
Officers.
Officers' kitchen
Scullery
Officers' Mess.
M - Sergeants' Mess
N - Mobilisation Store
O - Sergts' Mess Kitchen
P - Billet
Q - Provision Store
R - Dispensary
S - Area Store
T - "M.T" Billet
U - Cookhouse
V - Cooks' Store etc.
W - Ablution (Patients) Baths (Personnel)
X - Incinerator and Boilers
Y - Drying Room
Z - Latrines
α - Laundry
β - Plumber.
γ - Carpenter.
OC. 112 F.A.
31. 10. 17

W A R D I A R Y

FOR MONTH OF NOVEMBER, 1917.

VOLUME :- 24

UNIT:- 112th Field Ambulance RAMC

Vol 24

Instructions regarding War Diaries and Intelligence Summaries are contained in F. S. Regs., Part II. and the Staff Manual respectively. Title pages will be prepared in manuscript.

WAR DIARY
or
~~INTELLIGENCE SUMMARY.~~

(*Erase heading not required.*)

Army Form C. 2118.

No: 112. Field Ambulance

Place	Date	Hour	Summary of Events and Information	Remarks and references to Appendices
ERVILLERS 57.C.B.13 d.2.7.	1/11/17		Routine. The G.O.C has remitted the sentence of 2 yrs IHL awarded to Pt. Greaves for absence without leave & suspended, on account of good conduct & gallantry. RH	R Humphreys? Lt Col RAMC
"	2/11/17		Visited ADS. & Relay Posts. RH	
"	3/11/17		Bearer NCO's began class of special instruction in "First Aid". RH	
"	4/11/17		No 44238 ~~Sergeant~~ Perks. C. appointed a/g Staff Sgt without pay, pending confirmation by DMS. RH	
"	5/11/17		Special Order of Compliment from G.O.C. Fifth Army received & published. In accordance with a scheme devised by me when a/g ADMS, the first consignment of Hot Water bottles with covers complete, and of water tins was sent to OC. 111. FA for distribution. RH	
"	6/11/17		Handed over duties of ADMS to Col Campbell. D.S.O. RH	

D. D. & L., London, E.C.
(A8001) Wt. W1771/M2031 750,000 5/17 Sch. 52 Forms/C2118/14

Instructions regarding War Diaries and Intelligence Summaries are contained in F. S. Regs., Part II. and the Staff Manual respectively. Title pages will be prepared in manuscript.

WAR DIARY
or
~~INTELLIGENCE SUMMARY.~~
(Erase heading not required.)

Army Form C. 2118.

No: 112. F.A.

Place	Date	Hour	Summary of Events and Information	Remarks and references to Appendices
ERVILLERS	7/11/17		Routine RJH	
"	8/11/17		Sent fatigue party with Lorry from CRE to NOEUX LES MINES for Quicklime. Capt. E. Cussler. U.S.A.M.S.R. left for temporary duty with No: 29. C.C.S on completion of a week's instruction. RJH.	
"	9/11/17		Took ADMS to Trenches, including SHAFT Relay Post & ADS & MEBU, HENIN car Stand &c. RJH.	
"	10/11/17		Visited VIth Corps Scab. Stn N at BARLY & Rest Stn at GOUY and arranged for better work in loading up Lorries with Adrian Huts &c RJH	
"	11/11/17		Routine RJH	
"	12/11/17		Capt T.F. Saunders returned from temporary duty with 170 Bde RFA, on relief by Capt. A.M. Mitchell of this Unit, from VI Corps SSS, relieved by Lieut H.E. Gillett. U.S.A.M.S.R from HdQrs. RJH	

D. D. & L., London, E.C.
(A8001) Wt. W1771/M2031 750,000 5/17 Sch. 52 Forms C2118/14

Instructions regarding War Diaries and Intelligence Summaries are contained in F. S. Regs., Part II. and the Staff Manual respectively. Title pages will be prepared in manuscript.

WAR DIARY
or
~~INTELLIGENCE SUMMARY.~~
(Erase heading not required.)

Army Form C. 2118.

112 FA.

Place	Date	Hour	Summary of Events and Information	Remarks and references to Appendices
ERVILLERS	13/11/17		Attended Conference at ADMS' Office Capt Denver handed over a/q Med. charge of Divl Train to an Officer of 111 FA. Capt T. F. Saunders left for England on termination of contract, as unable to his great regret to sign on again until news of his locum tenens arrived from Canada. I regret the departure of this Officer exceedingly, as he has always when with the FA, or with other Units temporarily won the esteem and affection of all ranks in most exceptional degree. Confirmation received of a/q rank with pay of a/q QMS. Staff Sgt Unsworth. a/q Staff Sgt Sergeant Holloway a/q Staff Sgt. Sergeant Perks. RH	
"	14/11/17.		1 NCO & 6 men returned from 16th Divl Works Coy. Visited No: 45 CCS & arranged for evacuation of non-infective cases from VI C. S. S. 3th, & for clerical work in case of Active Operations. RH	
"	15/11/17		Visited No: 49 CCS & arranged for clerical work during Active Operations RH	

D. D. & L., London, E.C. (A8001) Wt. W1771/M2031 750,000 5/17 Sch. 52 Forms/C2118/14

Instructions regarding War Diaries and Intelligence Summaries are contained in F. S. Regs., Part II. and the Staff Manual respectively. Title pages will be prepared in manuscript.

WAR DIARY
or
~~INTELLIGENCE SUMMARY.~~
(Erase heading not required.)

Army Form C. 2118.

112. FA.

Place	Date	Hour	Summary of Events and Information	Remarks and references to Appendices
ERVILLERS	16/11/17		Preparations in hand for Active Operations – Ground for Walking Wounded Collecting Post at JUDAS COPSE 51B T.24 d.5.5. to be cleared, hillocks smoothed & holes filled up & ground rolled. 8 small Hospital Marquees to be pitched after dark on Y evening. Pegs to be put in beforehand. In afternoon laid out Walking Wounded Track from Right Battalion of Division, from entrance of PELICAN TRENCH into RAILWAY RESERVE at U15.b.9.0, along or under Railway Embankment to ~~[illegible]~~ T.24 d.5.5. & thence over the hill to near the Chateau. ST LEGER. QH	
"	17/11/17		In afternoon laid out Walking Wounded Track from CROISILLES FACTORY U.24.a.9.5. to Station & along South side of SENSEE VALLEY to Chateau ST LEGER. Having received notice from DDMS & SMTO VII Corps that 10 lorries would be available for removal of huts from BARLY despatched Ford Car with message to OC. VII Corps Rest Station re fatigue-party early in morning. Lorries appear to have arrived at GOUY, but the Ford Driver tried to reach GOUY en GOHELLE instead of GOUY en ARTOIS, & broke down at ABLAIN ST NAZAIRE. Nothing was therefore done, and the Lorries waited all day at the Church GOUY. Sent up Tea Urns & Primus Stoves for QUARRIES & KNUCKLE to OC. 111 F.A. QH	
"	18/11/17		Had the 10 lorries again today & got in 10 loads of Adrian Hut. Took over & whitewashed new RAP for 180 Bde RFA at T.22a 7.2. QH	

D. D. & L., London, E.C.
(A8001) Wt. W1771/M2031 750,000 5/17 Sch. 52 Forms/C2118/14

Instructions regarding War Diaries and Intelligence Summaries are contained in F. S. Regs., Part II. and the Staff Manual respectively. Title pages will be prepared in manuscript.

WAR DIARY
~~or~~
~~INTELLIGENCE SUMMARY.~~
(Erase heading not required.)

Army Form C. 2118.

112 FA.

Place	Date	Hour	Summary of Events and Information	Remarks and references to Appendices
ERVILLERS	19/11/17		Attended DDMS conference in my Mess Completed all equipment of Aid Posts &c. Personnel distributed as follows	
			Corps Scabies Stn. Officers 0. NCO's & Men 5.	
			45. C.C.S " 0. " 6.	Clerks & Guide for W.W.
			49th Bde " 0. " 20	To supplement Regimental Bearers
			111 F.A " 0. " 40.	Bearers.
			HENIN CARSTAND " 1*. " 5	"
			MEBU " 0. " 4.	
			SHAFT " 0 " 6.	
			492n ERVILLERS " 1** " 10.	
			180 Bde RAP. " 0 " 2	
			177 " " " 0 1.	
			* To take charge at 6 AM. 20th ** In 4 hour watches from 6 AM. 20th	
			The Remainder 4 MO's & about 30 men detailed for W.W. Collecting Post	
			During the Day sent up all necessary equipment, & in the evening, after dark erected the 8 Marquees & packed away the Stores. This was a very difficult & heavy task, performed most zealously by Nursing Orderlies under Sgt Johnson. GBH	

D. D. & L., London, E.C.
(A8001) Wt. W1771/M2031 750,000 5/17 Sch. 52 Forms/C2118/14

Instructions regarding War Diaries and Intelligence Summaries are contained in F. S. Regs., Part II. and the Staff Manual respectively. Title pages will be prepared in manuscript.

WAR DIARY
or
~~INTELLIGENCE~~ SUMMARY.

(*Erase heading not required.*)

Army Form C. 2118.

112 F.A.

Place	Date	Hour	Summary of Events and Information	Remarks and references to Appendices
ERVILLERS	20/11/17		Taking of TUNNEL TRENCH & SUPPORT With Sergt Major & other Officers arrived at W. W. C P at 6 AM. Ready to receive shortly after 6.30 AM. Zero 6.20 am. First patient arrived 7.40 AM. Arrangement of Dressing Station ADS 111 FA — ROAD — To ST. LEGER → — SENSEE RIVER — 1 2 3 4 5 6 7 8 1. Refreshments — Tea, Cocoa, Bread & Ham or Cheese & Onions. 2. 3. Reception Shelter. 4. Clerks for A.F. W. 3118. 5. Foot-washing & sock-changing. Feet washed in a bath 12'x2' by 6" deep with overflow & clearing exit, drained into trench cut to the SENSEE bed. 6. Dressings. 7. 8. Evacuation Shelter. Up to midnight 261 British & 62 German Wounded passed through, and were evacuated mostly by Lorry, with only one Train Load — 1 truck British 2 German under armed escort. The Germans were on the whole a poor lot, including many boys of	

D. D. & L., London, E.C. (A8001) Wt. W1771/M2031 750,000 5/17 Sch. 52 Forms/C2118/14

Instructions regarding War Diaries and Intelligence Summaries are contained in F. S. Regs., Part II. and the Staff Manual respectively. Title pages will be prepared in manuscript.

WAR DIARY
~~or~~
~~INTELLIGENCE SUMMARY.~~
(*Erase heading not required.*)

Army Form C. 2118.

112 FA.

Place	Date	Hour	Summary of Events and Information	Remarks and references to Appendices
ERVILLERS	20/11/17	Continued.	19 & several old men. They ate voraciously! Besides the numbers given, some 20 British & a few Germans were turned into Stretcher-cases & evacuated by No: 111. F.A. Everything worked with perfect smoothness. About noon the Officer was withdrawn from HENIN, & in the evening the Staff was reduced. The Staff of the YMCA at ST LEGER gave valuable assistance in the loan of tables & forms, & administering refreshments. RH.	
"	21/11/17		Work at W.W.C.P. very slack during night. Worked with 2 Officers on 8 hour overlapping shifts, & ⅓ personnel staff. 20 wounded only passed through during day. In evening withdrew half-staff to HQrs, & worked night with 1 Officer on 8 hour shifts. Withdrew all Red Cross equipment from Car Stand HENIN. In the evening sent Capt W Warburton back to Corps Scabies Stn, to resume charge. RH.	
"	22/11/17		Closed down Collecting Post altogether, leaving tents standing with 2 men as guard. Sent 1st Lieut Gillett USA. M.C.R to assist Capt Warburton at C.S.S, & sent a few extra men there. During day got back all bearers, very done. RH.	

D. D. & L., London, E.C. (A8001) Wt. W1771/M2031 750,000 5/17 Sch. 52 Forms/C2118/14

Instructions regarding War Diaries and Intelligence Summaries are contained in F. S. Regs., Part II. and the Staff Manual respectively. Title pages will be prepared in manuscript.

WAR DIARY

~~or~~

~~INTELLIGENCE SUMMARY.~~

(Erase heading not required.)

112 FA

Army Form C. 2118.

Place	Date	Hour	Summary of Events and Information	Remarks and references to Appendices
ERVILLERS	23/11/17		Withdrew Red Cross Equipt from 180 & 177 Bdes. Increased Scabies Station Staff. R.H.	
"	24/11/17		Completed Scabies Stn Staff, 1 & withdrew A&D book from 45 C.C.S. R.H.	
"	25/11/17		Great Storm during the night. Damage done to huts at H.Qrs. 5 out of 8 marquees at W.W.C.P. blown down. Impossible to do anything during day, as wind still extremely violent. 13 ptes RAMC arrived as re-inforcements. R.H.	
"	26/11/17		A supply of Trench Boards obtained from a deserted camp at ST. AMAND with permission of C.R.E. Div. Distance about 15 miles each way, but started from ACHIET LE GRAND & had a delay on the road home. R.H.	
"	27/11/17		Sent 2 Sanitary Section Corporals to BARLY to arrange for obtaining essential parts of ADRIAN Huts & equipment. Also my plumber & 2 ptes to obtain [illegible] Shower Bath. A G.S. Wagon sent to BARLY to stay the night & bring back timber tomorrow. R.H.	
"	28/11/17		Sent Capt Denyer with fatigue party & 2 M.A. Cars to BARLY. G.S. Wagons from here & ACHIET LE GRAND went as far as BLAIREVILLE. The M.A. Cars loaded them by several journeys between the two villages. Much equipment thus ~~transferred~~. The Sanitary Corporals returned to saw floors into convenient sizes. R.H.	

D. D. & L., London, E.C.
(A8001) Wt. W1771/M2031 750,000 5/17 Sch. 52 Forms/C2118/14

Instructions regarding War Diaries and Intelligence Summaries are contained in F. S. Regs., Part II. and the Staff Manual respectively. Title pages will be prepared in manuscript.

WAR DIARY
or
~~INTELLIGENCE SUMMARY.~~
(Erase heading not required.)

Army Form C. 2118.

112 FA.

Place	Date	Hour	Summary of Events and Information	Remarks and references to Appendices
ERVILLERS	29/11/17		Routine [initials]	
"	30/11/17		Fetched San. Corporals back from BARLY in evening. During the Month the principal construction works accomplished were:– (a) Hutting. Accommodation for patients completed up to 18 huts & 1 more unlined. Hut erected for C.O. Treatment hut erected, windowed, floored, partitioned & a BLANC BOILER & showers fitted. 3 Bow huts for personnel erected & partly lined. ADRIAN Dining & Recreation Hut started. (b) Sanitary. 3 patients & 1 personnel Latrine completed. 1 personnel Ablution Room completed. 2 out of 3 sludge-tanks completed & 3rd in progress. 1 Wash-house for laundry erected. (c) Horse lines. Stable completed & harness, saddle & forage rooms partitioned off. Forge shed erected. (d) Roads. Much progress made in stable approach. Paths near Treatment Hut & Kitchen terraced & trench-boarded. Extensive improvement on Switch Road. (e) Heating. Improved brick & sheet iron fire-places erected in personnel huts & many wards. R. J. Houghton Lt Col RAMC OC. 112 FA.	See APPENDIX I

D. D. & L., London, E.C.
(A8001) Wt. W1771/M2031 750,000 5/17 Sch. 52 Forms/C2118/14

WAR DIARY

FOR MONTH OF DECEMBER, 1917.

VOLUME :- 25.

UNIT :- 112th Field Ambulance R.A.M.C.

Instructions regarding War Diaries and Intelligence Summaries are contained in F. S. Regs., Part II. and the Staff Manual respectively. Title pages will be prepared in manuscript.

WAR DIARY

or

~~INTELLIGENCE SUMMARY.~~

(Erase heading not required.)

Army Form C. 2118.

No: 112. Field Ambulance

Place	Date	Hour	Summary of Events and Information	Remarks and references to Appendices
ACHIET le GRAND. 57.C.A9.b central	1/12/17		Received orders overnight to hand over ERVILLERS Stn to a F.A of 40th Division. Preparations in morning. Collected all necessary documents for information of successors, including plan & Standing Orders for Treatment Hut & plans of Sullage-water tanks & proposed Steam Disinfector. Sent copies of the last two mentioned to DDMS. VIIth Corps with letter recapitulating the situation. Sent on most of the Transport & Personnel to ACHIET after tea, retaining working Staff. Advance Officer of 137 F.A. arrived 7PM but went back to guide the Main Body. 137 F.A. marched in about 9.30 PM. Had Dinner ready for Officers & Supper for men. Handed over documents &c & left at 11.30PM for ACHIET, leaving Q.M. & Interpreter & small party for handing over in the morning. R.I. Houghton Lieut Col RAMC	
"	2/12/17		Bitterly cold high wind from N.W during night. Hard frost in morning. Q.M handed over at ERVILLERS & joined up with his party in afternoon. Officer & party from 137 F.A arrived in afternoon to take over VIIth Corps Scabies Stn. etc. Handed over stores unchecked. Arranged details of the march in the morning of 3rd inst with Bde Major 48th Inf. Bde RIH	
MARICOURT 62.C.A.15.c.8.3	3/12/17		Bde Headquarters passed at 7.10. AM. (10 mins late?) Gave them 3 minutes and started off. Bitterly cold but bright. Got clear of BAPAUME at 8.50. AM. Arrived at ROCQUIGNY 57.C.O.27.d.5.8 before 11AM. Only picked up one straggler on the march. Had to wait till No: 10? F.A pulled out. Very poor huts, no Dr. Stn accommodation. About 2.30 PM received orders to march to MARICOURT to take over VIIth Corps Rest Station. Went on in advance myself by car with Sergt Major to arrange. On arrival found that O.C. 109 F.A there had received no orders to hand over! Arranged for shelter for personnel in Church Army Hut. Officers to double up or sleep in Officers' Ward. Unit got	

D. D. & L., London, E.C. (A8001) Wt. W1771/M2031 750,000 5/17 Sch. 52 Forms/C2118/14

Instructions regarding War Diaries and Intelligence Summaries are contained in F. S. Regs., Part II. and the Staff Manual respectively. Title pages will be prepared in manuscript.

WAR DIARY
~~or~~
~~INTELLIGENCE SUMMARY.~~
(*Erase heading not required.*)

Army Form C. 2118.

112 FA

Place	Date	Hour	Summary of Events and Information	Remarks and references to Appendices
	3/12/17	Contd	hot meal at 4 PM & Marched off at 5.30 PM. Had difficulties with Traffic Control in getting out – Quite unavoidable. O.C. 109 FA sent out his MA Cars to pick up & bring in Personnel, meeting them first near COMBLES 57.C T.26. O.C. 109 FA also got supper ready for officers & men. Transport & last of personnel arrived about 11 PM. Transport parked in Open with Horses on lines between limbers. Marches: ACHIET le GRAND to ROCQUIGNY – 16 Kilometres. ROCQUIGNY to MARICOURT 23½ Kilometres. Total 24½ miles. A severe march for men not in training & carrying packs. R.J.H.	
MARICOURT	4/12/17		During the morning 109 FA received orders to hand over to me. During the morning Equipment checked by 2M, & reliable NCOs & Orderlies – a 3 days job if done personally by 2M. In the afternoon I went by Car to report to ADMS 16th Divn. Met him on main road near SAILLY-SAILLISEL 57.C U.8.c coming to see me. He returned with me to 16th Divnl Headquarters where we learned that the Division was to move to VIIth Corps. I returned to MARICOURT where I found that 109 FA had received orders to move at daybreak. O.C. 109 FA & I spent 2 hours at the telephone trying to get D.D.M.S. VIIth Corps. Gave it up & wired at 8 PM to ADMS 16th Divn, explaining the situation & stating that I should stay 'till relieved. R.J.H.	
COURCELLES 62.C. J.32.a.5.2.	5/12/17.		No: 109. F.A. moved out at 6 AM. Rest Station consists of a corridor round an oblong space with Hospital Marquees opening off outside. Reception, offices, stores, Kitchens, Dining-room, in huts. Sick officers wards in special huts. Stabling good. Scabies Station alongside Rest Station – all huts – Adrian & special. RAMC officers in Nissen Bows with special Mess Hut (French). Personnel in an Adrian. Place intended to hold — Rest Stn 500. Scabies Stn 100. Actually holding today 1200! 175!	

Instructions regarding War Diaries and Intelligence Summaries are contained in F. S. Regs., Part II. and the Staff Manual respectively. Title pages will be prepared in manuscript.

WAR DIARY

or

~~INTELLIGENCE SUMMARY.~~

(Erase heading not required.)

Army Form C. 2118.

112 F.A.

Place	Date	Hour	Summary of Events and Information	Remarks and references to Appendices
~~MARICOURT~~ COURCELLES R.H.	5/12/17		Continued. Last evening 250 cases cases arrived by train! – this evening 270! Tents hopelessly overcrowded & bitterly cold. Insufficient & most smoky stoves with wall badly built into tent side. About as much comfort for OR patients as in ordinary billets. In the morning received message from ADMS. 16th Divn that we should be relieved. O.C. 2/1 N Midland FA. arrived 11AM with his QrMr. Personnel arrived by train at 3.30 PM. Handed over equipment unchecked. Since relieving FA's transport could not arrive till noon 6th. left behind Sergt & pte with sufficient Medical & Surgical equipment to carry on with. Personnel relieved as rapidly as possible. Sent Advance Party to 49th Bde Headqrs at TINCOURT & moved out with main body about 5.45 PM. Bitterly cold but dry. Marched via CLERY & PERONNE. Had no large scale map of new area, & had to find way beyond PERONNE by very small scale private map. Took road Tabelles to TINCOURT & found it extremely bad & blown up in two places. Walked on in advance myself towards TINCOURT via BUIRE on the only visible road & fortunately met advance Officer from whom I learned that we were to go to huts in COURCELLES – in opposite direction. Sent guide back to Column. Personnel & Transport arrived about 11PM. 24 Kilometres. 15 miles in the dark over bad roads after a full day's work. R.H.	
"	6/12/17		Sat at Courcelles. R.H.	
"	7/12/17		Sat at Courcelles under orders to move next day R.H.	

D. D. & L., London, E.C.
(A8001) Wt. W1771/M2031 750,000 5/17 Sch. 52 Forms/C2118/14

Instructions regarding War Diaries and Intelligence Summaries are contained in F. S. Regs., Part II. and the Staff Manual respectively. Title pages will be prepared in manuscript.

WAR DIARY
or
~~INTELLIGENCE SUMMARY.~~
(Erase heading not required.)

Army Form C. 2118.

112 F.A.

Place	Date	Hour	Summary of Events and Information	Remarks and references to Appendices
HAMEL 62.C. K.18d.9.3	8/12/17		Marched in morning 3 miles to HAMEL & took over pitch temporarily occupied by No: 111 F.A. who marched out for PERONNE at 11 AM. 10 Nissen Bow huts for medical work. Kitchen. Deep pit latrines. RAMC Personnel in ADRIAN Hut. Officers in rooms in undamaged cottages. Mess ditto. Sergeants & Mess ditto. A.S.C. H.T. & M.T. ditto. Horses in good stables. Most of the village was not destroyed by the enemy before his retirement. Transport parked on grass. Pitch very good so far as it goes. We are to start a Divisional Rest Station, & collect sick from Brigade in reserve. 2 Officers & 33 O.R. sent by order ADMS to 113 F.A. at VILLERS FAUCON for instruction in trenches in new area. RJK	
"	9/12/17		Visited Divnl Headquarters. Saw CRE re materials for extension RJK	
"	10/12/17		Large Morning Sick parade, including Indian Labourers mostly from KUMAON & GARHWAL. Made out scheme for new hut containing rooms for bathing, washing, laundry, drying & disinfecting. RJK	
"	11/12/17		Inspected by Col Swan DDMS VII Corps, who approved of scheme as above. Forwarded scheme to ADMS. Visited Area Commdt re materials – none obtainable locally. RJK	

D. D. & L., London, E.C.
(A8001) Wt. W1771/M2031 750,000 5/17 Sch. 52 Forms/C2118/14

Instructions regarding War Diaries and Intelligence Summaries are contained in F. S. Regs., Part II. and the Staff Manual respectively. Title pages will be prepared in manuscript.

WAR DIARY

or

~~INTELLIGENCE SUMMARY.~~

(Erase heading not required.)

Army Form C. 2118.

112 F.A.

Place	Date	Hour	Summary of Events and Information	Remarks and references to Appendices
HAMEL 62.C. K.18d.9.3	12/12/17		Visited Town Major PERONNE and arranged for bricks and iron piping obtained one G.S. Wagon load of bricks. Capt. W. Warburton RAMC left for temporary duty with 10th R Dublin Fusiliers. 60608 Pte W. Hawkins 2. M.T. Dept appd a/Lce Corporal without pay. GPH	
"	13/12/17		Transport sent into PERONNE for bricks & piping. Bricks obtained & some piping. Captain T.F. Saunders reported his arrival for duty having been enabled to renew his contract. Captain D.A. Weir to No: 113 F.A. in relief of Capt C.H. Denver who returned here. GPH	
"	14/12/17		Marked out plan of new hut, embracing (a) Ablution & Bath Rooms for personnel & patients (b) small Laundry for Hospital Clothing &c. (c) Steam Disinfector (d) Drying Room heated by flue of incinerator, & hot air pipes from incinerator & furnace of Disinfector. Ground plan below.	

Hut 26' square

Boiler of disinfector sunk 3' in ground

Incinerator " "

Disinfector mainly of expanded metal & cement with entrance & exit flap doors. Covering of 4" sawdust in wood casing. Heated by hot air-pipes passing from under boiler into drying room & by a steam-pipe grating.

GPH

Instructions regarding War Diaries and Intelligence Summaries are contained in F. S. Regs., Part II. and the Staff Manual respectively. Title pages will be prepared in manuscript.

WAR DIARY

~~or~~

~~INTELLIGENCE~~ SUMMARY.

(*Erase heading not required.*)

Army Form C. 2118.

No: 112. FA.

Place	Date	Hour	Summary of Events and Information	Remarks and references to Appendices
HAMEL	14/12/17	continued	1st Lieut. A.E Gillett U.S.A.M.S.R returned from No: 113 FA & left to take temporary Medical Charge of 2nd R.D.F. G.H.	
"	15/12/17		Routine G.H.	
"	16/12/17		Routine G.H.	
"	17/12/17		Heavy snow – 5–6 inches during night. Supplied horses for snow-plough. Visited ADMS re obtaining fuel & straw, & CRE re building materials G.H.	
"	18/12/17		Blizzard during night. Left drifts in places, but not much fresh snow.	

D. D. & L., London, E.C.
(A8001) Wt. W1771/M2031 750,000 5/17 Sch. 52 Forms/C2118/14

Instructions regarding War Diaries and Intelligence Summaries are contained in F. S. Regs., Part II. and the Staff Manual respectively. Title pages will be prepared in manuscript.

WAR DIARY
or
~~INTELLIGENCE SUMMARY.~~
(Erase heading not required.)

Army Form C. 2118.

Place	Date	Hour	Summary of Events and Information	Remarks and references to Appendices
HAMEL 62cSh. K.18.a.9.3 Map Ref	19/12/17		Lt. Col. G.J. Houghton proceeds on 21 days leave & handed over Imprest Accounts 18/fcs Adms. FW Amb. 7 Rmg. 18 DRS. 18 Rmg. 56 Evac. FW Amb. 10 DRS. 28 " 16th DIV. - 23.	[illegible] Capt. RAMC
"	20/12/17		Capt Mitchell A.M. - RAMC Evacuated Sick NYD Pyrexia to 5 CCS. Adms. F.A. 50 Rmg. 48 DRS 13 Rmg. 14 Evac. F.A. 27 DRS 12 " 16th DIV. - 38	[illegible]
"	21/12/17		Capt. J.P. GREGG MORC USA (111th F.W. Amb. Ia) reported for Temporary Duty. Adms F.A. 34 Rmg. 55 DRS 13 Rmg 24 Evac F.A. 13 DRS 0 " 16 DIV. - 6	[illegible]

D. D. & L., London, E.C.
(A8001) Wt. W1771/M2031 750,000 5/17 Sch. 52 Forms/C2118/14

Instructions regarding War Diaries and Intelligence Summaries are contained in F. S. Regs., Part II. and the Staff Manual respectively. Title pages will be prepared in manuscript.

WAR DIARY
or
~~INTELLIGENCE SUMMARY.~~
(Erase heading not required.)

Army Form C. 2118.

Place	Date	Hour	Summary of Events and Information	Remarks and references to Appendices
HAMEL	22/12/17		Pay for Personnel – drew 4600 fcs from Field Cashier VII Corps. CATELET Visited DDMS VII Corps & was informed that a Tarrant Bechet Hut 60x16 ft. would be supplied to 16 DRS. F.A. Ring. DRS Ring. Adms. 27 50 15 31 Evac 23 7 " 16 DIV – 21	AO
"	23/12/17		Routine F.A. Ring. DRS Ring Adms 31 56 10 36 Evac 16 2 " 16 DIV – 9.	AO
"	24/12/17		1st Lt. LYONS C.G. MORC USA evacuated to 5 CCS. Renal Colic attached to Connaught Rangers F.A. Ring. DRS. Ring Adms 27 59 20 42 Evacs 13 2 " 16 DIV. – 15.	AO

D. D. & L., London, E.C.
(A8001) Wt. W1771/M2031 750,000 5/17 Sch. 52 Forms/C2118/14

Instructions regarding War Diaries and Intelligence Summaries are contained in F. S. Regs., Part II. and the Staff Manual respectively. Title pages will be prepared in manuscript.

WAR DIARY

or

~~INTELLIGENCE SUMMARY.~~

(Erase heading not required.)

Army Form C. 2118.

Place	Date	Hour	Summary of Events and Information	Remarks and references to Appendices
HAMEL	25/12/17		Xmas Day - Full Diet with Xmas Pudding given to those patients able to take it with Pipe Tobacco Cigarettes & a box of matches. Beer was also bought out of Divisional Allotment for Ambulances. Pts expressed satisfaction with food provided.	[initials]
	26/12/17		Routine.	[initials]
	27/12/17		1 Reinforcement arrived from 16 Div. Train. Interpreter M. de Flevrac proceeded on leave. 1 Tarrant Dechet Hut drawn from VII Corps Hutting Dump TINCOURT.	[initials]

25/12/17:

	FA.	Remg.	DRS	Remg
Adms	9	44	20	48
Evacs	10		1	
" 16 DIV - 9				

26/12/17:

	FA.	Remg.	DRS.	Remg
Adms	15	45	20	58
Evac	11		5	
" 16 DIV. - 11				

27/12/17:

	FA.	Remg.	DRS	Remg.
Adms	26	52	12	63
Evac.	14		6	
" 16 DIV. - 12				

D. D. & L., London, E.C.
(A8001) Wt. W1771/M2031 750,000 5/17 Sch. 52 Forms/C2118/14

Army Form C. 2118.

WAR DIARY
or
~~INTELLIGENCE SUMMARY.~~

(Erase heading not required.)

Instructions regarding War Diaries and Intelligence Summaries are contained in F. S. Regs., Part II. and the Staff Manual respectively. Title pages will be prepared in manuscript.

Place	Date	Hour	Summary of Events and Information	Remarks and references to Appendices
HAMEL	28/7/17		Military Medal Ribbon received from ADMS with Army & Corps Commanders Congratulations for Sgt Fowler RAMC & Sgt Stewart RAMC. Erection commenced of Tarrant Hut. FA. Remg. DRS. Remg Adm 28 58 16 49 Evacs. 14 — 8 " 16 DIV. – 16	AD
"	29/7/17		CAPT KIRBY MO i/c 10 Roy. Dub. Fus reported arrival from leave. CAPT Warburton RAMC reported arrival from Tempy Duty with 10 Roy Dub Fus. FA Remg. DRS Remg Adm 27 58 10 44 Evacs 12 — 2 " 16 DIV. – 10	AD
"	30/7/17		CAPT SAUNDERS detailed to proceed for Tempy. Duty with 8/9 Roy Dub Fus. this day in relief CAPT HIPWELL proceeding on leave FA. Remg DRS Remg Adm – 30 76 10 41 Evacs – 18 — 4 " 16 DIV. – 19 Lt. O.D.F. MILBURN RAMC reported for duty & taken on Strength. 1 NCO + 13 ORs returned from 29 CCS Gravillers. 2 NCO + 27 ORs returned from 113 FA.	AD

D. D. & L., London, E.C. (A8001) Wt. W1771/M2031 750,000 5/17 Sch. 52 Forms/C2118/14

Instructions regarding War Diaries and Intelligence Summaries are contained in F. S. Regs., Part II. and the Staff Manual respectively. Title pages will be prepared in manuscript.

WAR DIARY
or
~~INTELLIGENCE~~ SUMMARY.
(Erase heading not required.)

Army Form C. 2118.

Place	Date	Hour	Summary of Events and Information	Remarks and references to Appendices
HAMEL	31/7/17		Forwarded indent to CRE for material for Laundry, Baths, Disinfector etc. Horrocks Box Disinfector ~~being~~ Fireplace being constructed in room north end of Quartermasters Store F.A. Remg. DRS Remg Adms - 15 72 0 29 Evac - 11 5 " 16 Div. - 11 [illegible] Capt. RAMC O/C 112 Field Amb.	AD

D. D. & L., London, E.C.
(A8001) Wt. W2771/M2031 750,000 5/17 Sch. 52 Forms C2118/14

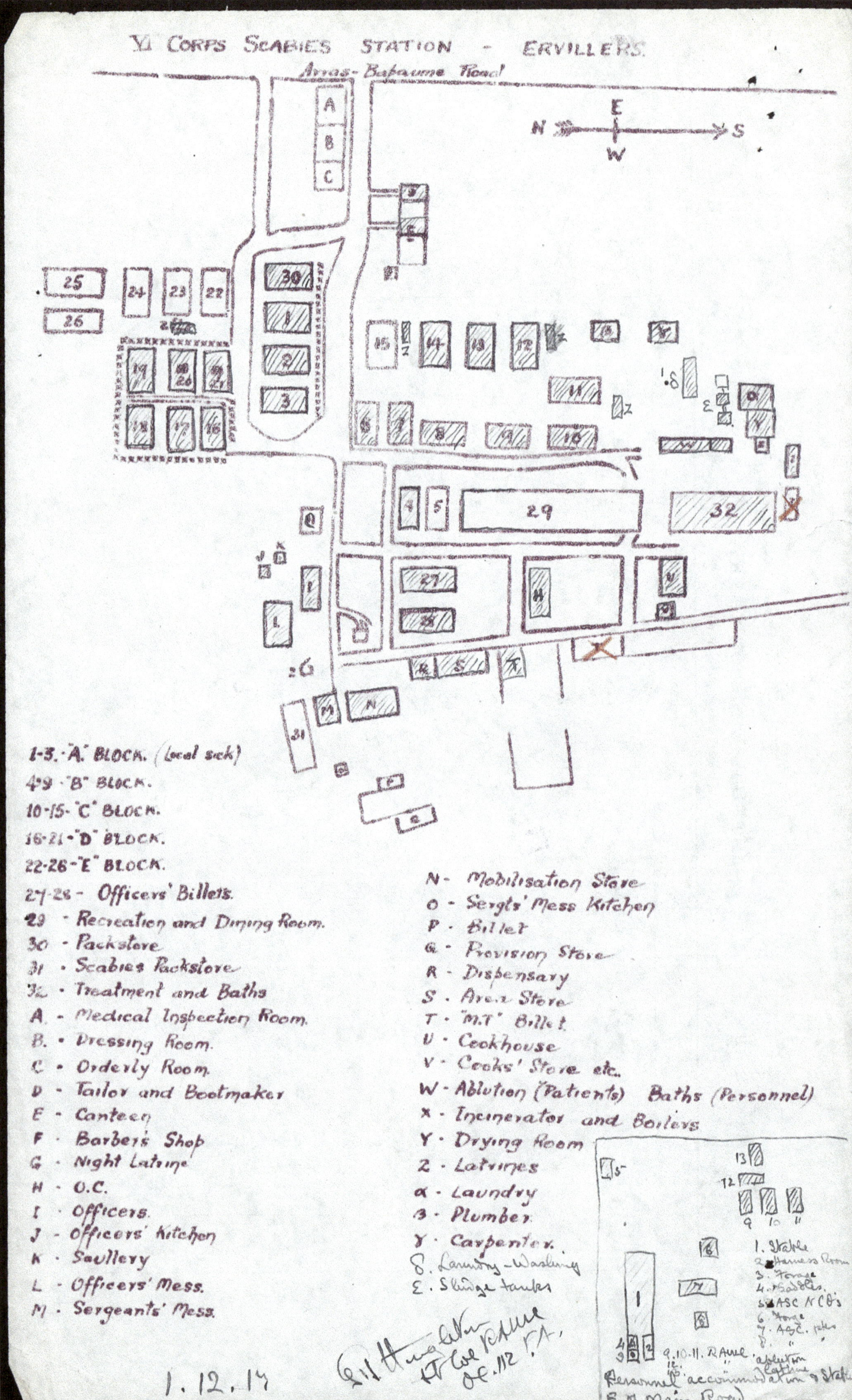
VI CORPS SCABIES STATION - ERVILLERS.
Arras-Bapaume Road
N
E
W
S
1-3. "A" BLOCK. (Local sick)
4-9. "B" BLOCK.
10-15. "C" BLOCK.
16-21. "D" BLOCK.
22-26. "E" BLOCK.
27-28 - Officers' Billets.
29 - Recreation and Dining Room.
30 - Packstore
31 - Scabies Packstore
32 - Treatment and Baths
A. - Medical Inspection Room.
B. - Dressing Room.
C - Orderly Room.
D - Tailor and Bootmaker
E - Canteen
F - Barber's Shop
G - Night Latrine
H - O.C.
I - Officers.
J - Officers' Kitchen
K - Scullery
L - Officers' Mess.
M - Sergeants' Mess.
N - Mobilisation Store
O - Sergts' Mess Kitchen
P - Billet
Q - Provision Store
R - Dispensary
S - Area Store
T - "M.T." Billet
U - Cookhouse
V - Cooks' Store etc.
W - Ablution (Patients) Baths (Personnel)
X - Incinerator and Boilers
Y - Drying Room
Z - Latrines
α - Laundry
β - Plumber
γ - Carpenter.
δ. Laundry - Washing
ε. Sludge tanks
1. Stable
2. Harness Room
3. Forage
4. Saddles.
5. ASC NCO's
6. Forage
9.10.11. RAMC
Personnel accommodation & Stables E of Main Road
1.12.17

WAR DIARY

FOR MONTH OF JANUARY, 1918.

VOLUME :- 26.

UNIT:- 112th Fd. Ambce. RAMC

Army Form C. 2118.

WAR DIARY
or
~~INTELLIGENCE SUMMARY.~~

(Erase heading not required.)

Instructions regarding War Diaries and Intelligence Summaries are contained in F. S. Regs., Part II. and the Staff Manual respectively. Title pages will be prepared in manuscript.

No: 112. Field Ambulance

Place	Date	Hour	Summary of Events and Information	Remarks and references to Appendices
HAMEL MAP Ref Sh. 62c K 18 a. 9.3	1/1/18	Tues	Field Ambce / Remaining / Divisional Rest Station / Remaining Admissions 17 / 81 / 10 / 37 Evacuations 7 / / 0 / " of 16 Division – 5 ADMS written re proposal of extra-hutting to bring present accomodation from 80 up to 200. Extra accomodation also required for personnel. Bricklayers completed building of fireplace for Horrocks Box Disinfector. CAPT. SAUNDERS name forwarded for command of an M.A.C. ADMS inspected ambulance.	A.D.
"	2/1/18	Wed.	F.A. / Remg. / D.R.S. / Remg. Adm. 19 / 79 / 10 / 41 Evacn. 12 / / 4 / " 16 Div. – 13 Ambulance Paraded & Divisional Certificate presented with Divisional Commander & ADMS: Congratulations to the following Officers, N.C.O.'s & men for the Action of FREZENBERG RIDGE on 16th August 1917 CAPT. W. WARBURTON. RAMC. No. 30741 Sgt. RICHARDS " " 64670 Cpl. STEWART " " 64389 Pte J.W. SMITH " " 64705 " W. WATT " " 64377 " C.E. DUNCAN " " 73256 " P.T. GUTTRIDGE RAMC " T/0 15037 Dr. J.W. EARNSHAW ASC. CAPT. T.F. SAUNDERS RAMC. No 64712 L/Sgt T. STANGER RAMC " 64180 Pte F. WARD " " 81697 " W. MITCHELL " " 64583 " J.R. DUMBLING " " 82009 " J.H. BARGERY " " 149932 " A.W. CHAPLIN ASC./MT.	A.D.

D. D. & L., London, E.C.
(A8001) Wt. W1771/M2031 750,000 5/17 Sch. 52 Forms/C2118/14

Instructions regarding War Diaries and Intelligence Summaries are contained in F. S. Regs., Part II. and the Staff Manual respectively. Title pages will be prepared in manuscript.

WAR DIARY

or

~~INTELLIGENCE SUMMARY.~~

(Erase heading not required.)

Army Form C. 2118.

112 F.A.

Place	Date	Hour	Summary of Events and Information	Remarks and references to Appendices
HAMEL	2/1/18	Wed.	Contd. Divisional Certificates for the Action of CROISELLES HEIGHTS on Nov 20th 1917 presented to following. No. 47146 Sgt. C.R. JOHNSON RAMC No 72762 L Cpl. P.L. MUNDY RAMC " 9607 " J. FOWLER " " 64670 Cpl. J.H. STEWART " " 65814 Pte N.V. PIERCE " " 64613 Pte W. ROBERTSON " No 47149 Sgt CAMPBELL proceeded on Special Leave 3/1/18 - 18/1/18. (R.E. material drawn from dump at VILLERS-FAUCON near DIVISIONAL HDQRS.) ← Reason death ~~Patent~~ of mother. Advances pay - 200 frs from Imprest Account. Evidence of Dr DELL ASC MT re Divorce Proceedings DELL v. DELL taken before CAPT G.DENYER. RAMC + LT. MILBURN RAMC + forwarded to Messrs A. HASTIE 43 YORK PLACE EDINBURGH.	[illegible]
"	3/1/18	Thurs	F.A. / Remg. / DRS. / Remg. Adm 74 / 87 / 10 / 49 Evac 6 / / 1 / " 16 DIV. - 5 Brick fireplace completed in WARD 10. Pts Reception Hut (NISSEN BOW) opened for 12 Pts. this day. Building of TARRANT DECHET HUT nearly completed. Fireplace for HORROCKS BOX DISINFECTOR completed. Blankets disinfected.	[illegible]
"	4/1/18	Frid.	F.A. / Remg. / DRS. / Remg. Adm 45 / 83 / 10 / 30. Evac 18 / / 2 / " 16 DIV - 16	

D. D. & L., London, E.C. (A8001) Wt. W2771/M2031 750,000 5/17 Sch. 52 Forms/C2118/14

Instructions regarding War Diaries and Intelligence Summaries are contained in F. S. Regs., Part II. and the Staff Manual respectively. Title pages will be prepared in manuscript.

WAR DIARY
or
~~INTELLIGENCE SUMMARY.~~
(Erase heading not required.)

Army Form C. 2118.

112 FA.

Place	Date	Hour	Summary of Events and Information	Remarks and references to Appendices
HAMEL	4/1/18	Mo.	Contd. Work - Building Brick fireplace completed in wards. Brick fireplace in Tarrant Hut Commenced. Bricks obtained from DRAINCOURT. Tarrant hut Completed. but roof requires lining. Pte DUMPLING RAMC evac'd 5CCS with DAH. Inspected new lines 16 DAC Latrines washing benches & meat Safes for cook house required	CMD
"	5/1/18	Sat.	F.A. Remg. DRS Remg. / Adms 17 85 5 30. / Evac 16 / " 16 DIV. - 8 / Bricks obtained from DRAINCOURT Corps Rest & Scabies Station unable to take any Cases. Imprest account - 4500 frs drawn from Field Cashier. Personnel paid out.	CMD
"	6/1/18	Sun.	F.A. Remg DRS Remg / Adms 10 79 1 27 / Evac 8 1 / " 16 DIV - 5 / 21733 Sgt. A.R. HARROP RAMC reported for duty from Cyclist Base Depot posted C Section for General Duty. Church Parade - Proclamation Sunday. Enemy Aeroplane flew over Hamel 4.30 am. Bombs dropped ROISEL & PERONNE. & HAMEL. No casualties at latter place	CMD

D. D. & L., London, E.C. (A8001) Wt. W1771/M2031 750,000 5/17 Sch. 52 Forms/C2118/14

Instructions regarding War Diaries and Intelligence Summaries are contained in F. S. Regs., Part II. and the Staff Manual respectively. Title pages will be prepared in manuscript.

WAR DIARY
or
~~INTELLIGENCE SUMMARY.~~
(Erase heading not required.)

Army Form C. 2118.

112 F.A.

Place	Date	Hour	Summary of Events and Information	Remarks and references to Appendices
HAMEL	7/1/18	[illegible]	F.A. Ring. DRS Ring. Adms 15 73 0 19 Evacs 9 4 " 16 DIV - 9 Shelves for Clothing constructed in Quarter Stores.	AD
"	8/1/18	[illegible]	F.A. Ring. DRS Ring. Adm 10 80 0 17 Evacs 1 1 " 16 DIV 1786 Pte Hyde AE 5 R. Bucks Regt att. ASC 112 FA. evac. 5 CCS Epilepsy. Under instruction from ADMS QMS UNSWORTH to proceed to HAVRE for course for Temp. Commission in ASC. Snow fell heavily today & drifted into Tarrant Hut making latter uninhabitable. Eaves & top of roof packed with Straw. Town Major requires Lorries for snow plough.	AD
"	9/1/18	[illegible]	F.A. Ring. DRS. Ring Adms 22 64 18 26 Evac 14 0 " 16 DIV - 9 Capt H WEIR. proceeded on 14 days leave to England Orders from CRE through ADMS to apply for material for Trenches between Nissen Huts for defence against Enemy Aeroplane Bomb Indent put in to CRE thro ADMS.	AD

D. D. & L., London, E.C. (A8001) Wt. W1771/M2031 750,000 5/17 Sch. 52 Forms/C2118/14

Army Form C. 2118.

Instructions regarding War Diaries and Intelligence Summaries are contained in F. S. Regs., Part II. and the Staff Manual respectively. Title pages will be prepared in manuscript.

WAR DIARY
or
~~INTELLIGENCE SUMMARY.~~

(Erase heading not required.)

112 F.A.

Place	Date	Hour	Summary of Events and Information	Remarks and references to Appendices
HAMEL	9/1/18	Wed	Contd. – Tarrant Hut – fireplaces completed – two bays lined with [illegible] felting. Attempt to make an earth bank round ADRIAN HUT for anti bombing defence – ground frozen too hard to work. Wooden racks for clothes completed in QM Stores.	[initials]
"	10/1/18	Thurs	F.A. Remg. D.R.S. Remg. Admns 16 72 11 35. Evac. 4 0 16 DIV – 2 Horse transport inspected by ADVS – suggests more nose bags be used. Tarrant Hut – partially lined with [illegible] felting.	[initials]
"	11/1/18	Fri	F.A. Remg. D.R.S. Remg Admns 28 81 10 25. Evac 7 2 16 DIV – 4 Tarrant Hut – taken in use, divided into – (1) Receiving Room for Pts (2) Medical Inspection Room (3) Ward – accommodation 12 patients	[initials]

D. D. & L., London, E.C. (A8001) Wt. W1771/M2031 750,000 5/17 Sch. 52 Forms/C2118/14

Instructions regarding War Diaries and Intelligence Summaries are contained in F. S. Regs., Part II. and the Staff Manual respectively. Title pages will be prepared in manuscript.

WAR DIARY
or
~~INTELLIGENCE SUMMARY.~~
(Erase heading not required.)

Army Form C. 2118.

112 F.A

Place	Date	Hour	Summary of Events and Information	Remarks and references to Appendices
HAMEL	11/18	Ins	Contd – Horse Transport inspected by ~~[illegible]~~ Veterinary Officer attached 16 DIV Train. 1 Heavy Draught suffering from CANCRE of [illegible] recommended for evacuation. Box respirators tested by all ranks. Respirators worn by all ranks during work for 15 minutes. Foundations for Bath Laundry etc commenced. Traverse round ADRIAN huts re anti aircraft defence commenced. Lt. MILBURN RAMC detailed for Temporary duty with 1st Reg Dub. Fus. [illegible] under instruction from ADMS. Erection of Officers Mess Cook house – commenced. Lt. Col. G.T. Haughton returned from leave this day & resumed Command of the Ambulance.	[initials]

[signature]
Capt. RAMC
Actg O.C. 112 Fd. Ambce.

D. D. & L., London, E.C.
(A8001) Wt. W1771/M2031 750,000 5/17 Sch. 52 Forms/C2118/14

Instructions regarding War Diaries and Intelligence Summaries are contained in F. S. Regs., Part II. and the Staff Manual respectively. Title pages will be prepared in manuscript.

WAR DIARY
or
~~INTELLIGENCE SUMMARY.~~
(Erase heading not required.)

Army Form C. 2118.

112 F.A.

Place	Date	Hour	Summary of Events and Information	Remarks and references to Appendices
HAMEL	12/1/18		I returned from leave last night & resumed Command. Lieut O.C.F. Milburn left for temporary duty with 1st Bn R Dubl Fusrs 1st Lieut J.B. Rosegg. U.S.A. M.S.R returned to 111. F.A. The following acting promotions, with pay, in the Unit, were Sanctioned — Cpl. a/g Lance Sgt Stanger to be Sergeant. G.D. Section - Bearers Pte. a/g Corporal Stewart to be Lance-Sergt " Pte. L.c. Wilkie to be Corporal. Nursing Section G.J. Houghton Lt Col RAMC	
"	13/1/18		The following Officers arrived on posting to this Unit. Lieut 7. G.F. Browne RAMC. T.C " J Joyce. " " J.A Stewart " S.R Capt. E.E Lightwood struck off the strength, on permanent posting to 180 Bde. R.F.A. GJH	
"	14/1/18		A squad of 2 NCOs & 23 ptes were sent on special duty with Divnl Signals. GJH	

D. D. & L., London, E.C.
(A8001) Wt. W1771/M2031 750,000 5/17 Sch. 52 Forms/C2118/14

Army Form C. 2118.

WAR DIARY
or
~~INTELLIGENCE SUMMARY.~~
(*Erase heading not required.*)

Instructions regarding War Diaries and Intelligence Summaries are contained in F. S. Regs., Part II. and the Staff Manual respectively. Title pages will be prepared in manuscript.

112 FA.

Place	Date	Hour	Summary of Events and Information	Remarks and references to Appendices
HAMEL	15/1/18		Promoted to be Lce-Corpls with pay:- o/s L.C. Sheddon (Carpenter) & Hislop (Plumber) Lieut F. G. F. Browne left for temporary duty with 113 FA RH	
"	16/1/18		1st Lieut. H.E. Pillett. USAMSR returned from temporary duty with 113 FA RH.	
"	17/1/18		Lieut F. G. F. Browne reported sick with German Measles & was transferred from 113 FA to 41 Stg Hosp. (via 5. C.C.S.) RH	
"	18/1/18		1st Lieut H.E. Pillett proceeded to BOULOGNE for the purpose of competing at an Examination for admission to USAMS. Regular S/2 9648. o/s Sgt Maj. Murley. ASC reported for duty. RH.	
"	19/1/18		Lieut J. A. Stewart left for temporary duty with 111 FA. RH	
"	20/1/18		Routine RH	

D. D. & L., London, E.C.
(A8001) Wt. W1771/M2031 750,000 5/17 Sch. 52 Forms/C2118/14

Instructions regarding War Diaries and Intelligence Summaries are contained in F. S. Regs., Part II. and the Staff Manual respectively. Title pages will be prepared in manuscript.

WAR DIARY
or
~~INTELLIGENCE SUMMARY.~~
(Erase heading not required.)

Army Form C. 2118.

112. F.A.

Place	Date	Hour	Summary of Events and Information	Remarks and references to Appendices
HAMEL	21/1/18		3 ptes from each Battn. 47th Bde & 3 from 11th Hants Pioneers reported for a week's instruction in Chiropody. I myself undertook Lectures & demonstrations. Corporal Wilkie gave instruction in knife-sharpening. RH.	
"	22/1/18		Routine RH	
"	23/1/18		Staff Sgt (ex 9/9 2MS) Unsworth returned from ASC Base Depot. Le Havre, where the Cadet Course had been stopped. 64013 9/g Corporal Stones J. Cook, was ordered to revert to Private for inefficiency as an NCO under A.A. 183.5.C. 1 pte (Lce Corpl without pay) reported as Reinforcement (ex 7th S.I.H. Bn R. Irish). I made out a number of questions with brief answers for the Chiropody classes & had them copied for distribution. RH	
"	24/1/18		4 ptes reported as Reinforcement, having been replaced in Water Duties with 2nd R. Dubl. Fusls by B Men. RH	
"	25/1/18		Routine RH	

D. D. & L., London, E.C. (A8001) Wt. W1771/M2031 750,000 5/17 Sch. 52 Forms/C2118/14

Instructions regarding War Diaries and Intelligence Summaries are contained in F. S. Regs., Part II. and the Staff Manual respectively. Title pages will be prepared in manuscript.

WAR DIARY
or
INTELLIGENCE SUMMARY.
(Erase heading not required.)

Army Form C. 2118.

112. F.A.

Place	Date	Hour	Summary of Events and Information	Remarks and references to Appendices
HAMEL	26/1/18		Routine RJK	
"	27/1/18		First Chiropody Class returned to their Units. RJK	
"	28/1/18		Capt D. H. Weir left for temporary Duty with 2nd Bn R. Dubl. Fusrs. Lieut F. G. F. Browne returned to Duty from 41. Sty Hosp. 1st Lieut. H.E. Pillatt returned from BOULOGNE. Second Chiropody class began. 12 from 48th Bde & 1 RAMC. 112 F.A. RJK	
"	29/1/18		Capt T. F. Saunders returned from temporary Duty with 8/9 R.D.F. & received from O.C. 8/9 R.D.F. a letter of thanks for his services with high praise of his zeal & efficiency. RJK	
"	30/1/18		I had to report to ADMS on the possibility of replacing RAMC. A men by B. Men. I reported that NCO's, Bearers & Nurses must be A, but that 30 miscellaneous men could be B men, but provision should be made to carry the kits at least of 20. Today I had the unit re-classified & found 17 men fit for RAMC work in their Departments, but certainly B as regards General Service. RJK	

D. D. & L., London, E.C. (A8001) Wt. W1771/M2031 750,000 5/17 Sch. 52 Forms/C2118/14

Army Form C. 2118.

Instructions regarding War Diaries and Intelligence Summaries are contained in F. S. Regs., Part II. and the Staff Manual respectively. Title pages will be prepared in manuscript.

WAR DIARY
or
~~INTELLIGENCE SUMMARY.~~
(Erase heading not required.)

112 F.A.

Place	Date	Hour	Summary of Events and Information	Remarks and references to Appendices
HAMEL	31/1/18		Received confirmation of Q/M promotion of QMS Holloway from 9th inst. Orders arrived to effect that the Candidature for Tempy Commission in A.S.C. of Staff Sgt (ex Q/M S) Unsworth would not be proceeded with. This is apparently due to establishment being filled.	
			The Principal Works carried out during the month were —	
			Hutting — Farrant Hut built & occupied as M.I. Room, Consulting Room & Special Ward.	
			Progress made with hut of my own design to include Ablution-rooms, - personnel & patients — Bathroom; Laundry; Drying-room Steam Disinfector & Incinerator	
			Heating. - Several Wards re fitted with brick Stoves.	
			Roads — Switch road completed & garden made in switch.	
			Water-cart Standing improved	
			Anti-bomb traverses made (1) along Personnel Adrian Hut, & (2) behind Mule stables. This work is proceeding slowly on account of want of labour. I am endeavouring to get back my squad from R.E.	
			[signature] Lieut Col RAMC	

D. D. & L., London, E.C. (A8001) Wt. W1771/M2031 750,000 5/17 Sch. 52 Forms/C2118/14

W A R D I A R Y.

FOR MONTH OF FEBRUARY, 1918.

VOLUME:- 24

UNIT:- 112th Field Ambulance R.A.M.C.

Instructions regarding War Diaries and Intelligence Summaries are contained in F. S. Regs., Part II. and the Staff Manual respectively. Title pages will be prepared in manuscript.

WAR DIARY

~~or~~

~~INTELLIGENCE SUMMARY.~~

(Erase heading not required.)

Army Form C. 2118.

No: 112. F.A.

Place	Date	Hour	Summary of Events and Information	Remarks and references to Appendices
HAMEL 62.C K.18 d.93	1/2/18		In company with Lieut Col W. Bennett. DSO. RAMC OC 113 FA visited DMS Fifth Army at AHQ. R. J. Hamilton Lieut Col RAMC OC. 112. FA	
"	2/2/18		Second Chiropody Class (48th Bde) ended. RJH	
"	3/2/18		Routine RJH	
"	4/2/18		The Third Chiropody Class should have reported this morning, but only two men turned up. Reported to ADMS & 49th Bde. In afternoon visited DDMS. VIIth Corps for special instruction. RJH	
"	5/2/18		Chiropody class assembled & instruction began. In afternoon proceeded to 21st Div HQ for instruction in ADMS's office. RJH	
"	6/2/18		2 ptes RAMC arrived from 2nd R. Irish Regt. Lieut H. Joyce left for temporary duty with 2nd R. I. Regt. A Company of Italian Troops arrived at TINCOURT for entrenching; lent them a water cart & arranged for their sick to be seen & treated here. In afternoon to ADMS 21st Div again. R. J. Hamilton Lieut Col	

D. D. & L., London, E.C. (A8001) Wt. W1771/M2031 750,000 5/17 Sch. 52 Forms/C2118/14

Instructions regarding War Diaries and Intelligence Summaries are contained in F. S. Regs., Part II. and the Staff Manual respectively. Title pages will be prepared in manuscript.

WAR DIARY
or
~~INTELLIGENCE SUMMARY.~~
(Erase heading not required.)

Army Form C. 2118.

112 F.A

Place	Date	Hour	Summary of Events and Information	Remarks and references to Appendices
HAMEL	7/2/18		Lieut F. G. F. Browne left for temporary duty with 2nd Bn The Leinster Regt. In afternoon to ADMS 21st Div again. RJH	
"	8/2/18		Capt W. Warburton proceeded on 14 days leave to England. Held first of weekly series of Competitions for Tent Sub Sections & for Bearer Sub Sections! – T.S.D's to unload & pitch sectional Canvas as Dressing Station, set out Operating tent as dressing-room, repack, ~~and~~ strike & reload on Wagons. – B.S.D's to double out to wounded, 200 yds, dress with Triangular Bandages, load on stretchers & return, loading up Horse Ambce Wagon. RJH	
"	9/2/18		24. O.R. attached 16th Divnl RE returned to FA. HQ. In afternoon proceeded to ADMS 39th Div for instruction. RJH	
"	10/2/18		In afternoon to 39th Div. RJH	
"	11/2/18		In afternoon to 39th Div. RJH	

D. D. & L., London, E.C.
(A8001) Wt. W1771/M2031 750,000 5/17 Sch. 52 Forms/C2118/14

Army Form C. 2118.

Instructions regarding War Diaries and Intelligence Summaries are contained in F. S. Regs., Part II. and the Staff Manual respectively. Title pages will be prepared in manuscript.

WAR DIARY
or
~~INTELLIGENCE SUMMARY.~~

(Erase heading not required.)

112 F.A.

Place	Date	Hour	Summary of Events and Information	Remarks and references to Appendices
HAMEL	12/2/18		1st Lieut H.E. Gillett M.O.R.C. U.S.A proceeded to 10th R. Dubl. Fus. for temporary duty. Lieut. J.A. Stewart returned from temporary duty with No: 111 F.A. With approval of A.D.M.S., exchanged 3 ptes. B category for 3. A men with No: 3. M.A.C. Tenente Medico - Dottore Domenico Lanchetta arrived as M.O. i/c Italian Troops. I arranged to let him have Medical Equipment of a Battn for his M.I room (from equipment handed in to me), & to set aside a Ward in my Dr Stn for Italian troops, & to allow him to look after them. G.H.	
"	13/2/18		1 corpl R.A.M.C. from 2nd Bn the Leinster Regt, reported for duty. G.H.	
"	14/2/18		T/2015150. Dr Greaves B.C. A.S.C. H.T. awarded 28 days F.P. No: 1 for absence & drunkenness. 1 M.A. Car evacuated to Base with Driver - pte Staff - a very good man. Second series of Competitions held in afternoon. G.H.	
"	15/2/18		Routine G.H.	

D. D. & L., London, E.C.
(A8001) Wt. W1771/M2031 750,000 5/17 Sch. 52 Forms/C2118/14

Instructions regarding War Diaries and Intelligence Summaries are contained in F. S. Regs., Part II. and the Staff Manual respectively. Title pages will be prepared in manuscript.

WAR DIARY

or

~~INTELLIGENCE SUMMARY.~~

(Erase heading not required.)

Army Form C. 2118.

112. F.A.

Place	Date	Hour	Summary of Events and Information	Remarks and references to Appendices
HAMEL.	16/2/18		[illegible] Lt. Atkins returned from leave in England. 1 M.A. Car with driver reported for duty & 1 M.A. Car sent to No: 113. F.A. for temporary duty. The Corporal (Means) who arrived 13th inst was retransferred to 43. F.A. Q.H.	
"	17/2/18		Routine Q.H.	
"	18/2/18		Routine Q.H.	
"	19/2/18		64013: Pte Stones. J. RAMC awarded 8 days CB for absence Q.H.	
"	20/2/18		Held parade of Transport in afternoon. Q.H.	
"	21/2/18		In afternoon distributed Divisional Certificates to Staff Sgts Holloway & Parker, Lance Corpls Hills & Pursnall & Pte Morris. Third weekly Competition held. Visited D.D.M.S. VIIth Corps for instruction. Q.H.	

D. D. & L., London, E.C.
(A800) Wt. W1771/M2031 750,000 5/17 Sch. 52 Forms/C2118/14

Army Form C. 2118.

Instructions regarding War Diaries and Intelligence Summaries are contained in F. S. Regs., Part II. and the Staff Manual respectively. Title Pages will be prepared in manuscript.

WAR DIARY
~~or~~
~~INTELLIGENCE SUMMARY~~

(Erase heading not required.)

112 FA

Place	Date	Hour	Summary of Events and Information	Remarks and references to Appendices
HAMEL	22/2/18		Routine GH	
"	23/2/18		Capt W. Warburton returned from leave 1st Lieut H.E. Gillett. M.O.R.C. U.S.A. posted to 10th Bn R. Dub Fusrs (19th Entrenching Battn) as from 12.2.18. & struck off strength. Lieut. F. Joyce returned from temporary duty with 2nd R. Irish Regt. GH	
"	24/2/18		Lt J. A. Stewart & 5. O.R. to Fifth Army School of Instruction, & 1 pte to Sanitary School PERONNE. GH	
"	25/2/18		Routine GH	
"	26/2/18		Capt C.H. Denyer left on leave to England. GH	
"	27/2/18		Routine	
"	28/2/18		Lieut F. Joyce transferred as M O to 19th Entrenching Battalion, in relief of 1st Lieut Gillett who returned to this Unit.	

Instructions regarding War Diaries and Intelligence Summaries are contained in F. S. Regs., Part II. and the Staff Manual respectively. Title Pages will be prepared in manuscript.

WAR DIARY
or
INTELLIGENCE SUMMARY
(Erase heading not required.)

Army Form C. 2118.

Place	Date	Hour	Summary of Events and Information	Remarks and references to Appendices
HAMEL	28/2/18	Cont.	Principal Construction &c During February	
			(a) Ablution & Laundry Hut.	
			Ablution rooms & Baths completed.	
			Laundry Completed	
			Ironing shed ready.	
			Drying-room lined	
			Incinerator nearly complete.	
			Slabs for Disinfector partially completed.	
			(b) Latrines	
			Floor for one new latrine completed & another started.	
			(c) Traversing	
			Traverses made between all wards.	
			(d) Agriculture	
			3/21 acre manured & ploughed.	
			Over 1/4 acre manured & dug up.	
			B. J. Hinchcliffe [illegible] Lt Col RAMC OC. 112 FA.	

2449 Wt. W14957/M90 750,000 1/16 J.B.C. & A. Forms/C.2118/12.

SERVICE. Army Form A. 36.

(...warded weekly on Sunday to the Adjutant-General's Office at the Base.)

Hospital and Place

...e previous week, and is to include civilians and prisoners of War. Officers' names will be entered first ... be attached, showing, by ranks, the total number of patients in each unit, rationed on the Saturday in

...ffice at the Base as well as to their Commanding Officer, whether he is at the station or elsewhere. All officers' deaths should

...e of disease or wound	Date of Death	Date of Discharge	Date of Transfer	Discharges — Remarks as to †	Transfers — Whither transferred and remarks

War Diary

of

No. 112 Field Ambulance

From 1 3. 18 to 31 3. 18

Volume XXVIII

140/2849

† Specify whether discharged to join his unit or how otherwise disposed of.

Army Form C. 2118.

WAR DIARY
~~or~~
~~INTELLIGENCE SUMMARY~~
(Erase heading not required.)

Instructions regarding War Diaries and Intelligence Summaries are contained in F. S. Regs., Part II. and the Staff Manual respectively. Title Pages will be prepared in manuscript.

No: 112. Field Ambulance

Place	Date	Hour	Summary of Events and Information	Remarks and references to Appendices
HAMEL. 62.C. K18d.9.3	1/3/18		Routine. R.J. Hungleton Lt Col RAMC.	
"	2/3/18		Routine. R.J.H.	
"	3/3/18		Capt D. H. Weir returned from temporary duty with 2nd. R. Dub. Fus. on relief by Capt. W. Warburton. 1st Lieut. H. E. Gillett. MORC. USA. proceeded to Fifth Army Sch. for 10 days course. 6. O.R. returned from Fifth A. School on completion of course. Adjustments made in NCO o/a ranks to correct establishment as from 20.1.18. R.J.H.	
"	4/3/18		Routine R.J.H.	
"	5/3/18		Incinerator completed & Patients latrine converted to bucket type. The building was transferred bodily to the new site, & the trench partially filled in & covered with rails, wire netting & old canvas. R.J.H.	
"	6/3/18		Lieut. J. R. Stewart returned from Course at Fifth Army School R.J.H.	
"	7/3/18		Routine R.J.H.	

2449 Wt. W14957/M90 750,000 1/16 J.B.C. & A. Forms/C.2118/12.

Instructions regarding War Diaries and Intelligence Summaries are contained in F. S. Regs., Part II. and the Staff Manual respectively. Title Pages will be prepared in manuscript.

WAR DIARY
~~or~~
~~INTELLIGENCE~~ SUMMARY
(Erase heading not required.)

Army Form C. 2118.

112. FA.

Place	Date	Hour	Summary of Events and Information	Remarks and references to Appendices
HAMEL	8/3/18		Out of date Orders etc Destroyed – viz.– DRO's 1.1.17 to 31.8.17. CRO's 1.6.17 to 31.8.17 ARO's 1.1.17 to 31.8.17 Divnl. Intellge Summy. 20.5.17 to 31.12.17. GH.	
"	9/3/18		The undermentioned officers were posted permanently to the Units shown & struck off strength. Lieut. J.C. Stewart to 2nd R. Munster Fusiliers " F.G.F. Browne to 2nd Leinsters " O.C.F. Milburn to 1st R. Dubl Fusiliers. GH	
"	10/3/18		Separation tanks completed & taken into use. GH.	
"	11/3/18		~~Cpl~~ 435283. Pte Smith. S. appointed a/g Lce Corpl without pay. GH.	
"	12/3/18		I held a special training in the use in the dark of box-respirators. Marched with 2 complete sections = 120 NCO's & men up road for half a mile, then across open, where 8 "wounded" were to be picked up. 7 were found. Then back, carrying wounded across country. Respirators were worn all the time save for a rest of 2 minutes. No undue distress was noticed, though hills were negotiated & the pace had frequently to be slowed down. GH.	

2449 Wt. W14957/M90 750,000 1/16 J.B.C. & A. Forms/C.2118/12.

Instructions regarding War Diaries and Intelligence Summaries are contained in F. S. Regs., Part II. and the Staff Manual respectively. Title Pages will be prepared in manuscript.

WAR DIARY
or
~~INTELLIGENCE SUMMARY~~

(Erase heading not required.)

Army Form C. 2118.

112 F.A.

Place	Date	Hour	Summary of Events and Information	Remarks and references to Appendices
HAMEL	13/3/18		1st Lieut H. G. Gillett returned from Fifth Army School. G.H.	
"	14/3/18		Routine G.H.	
"	15/3/18		Routine G.H.	
"	16/3/18		6 Reinforcements arrived. 4. B1 & 2 A. Capt C H Denyer returned from leave & proceeded to take up Duty as O.C. No: 92. FA. Struck off strength as from 1.3.18. Received notification from DMS that the special competition in 'Thomas' Splint adjustment at 2nd Course at School of Instruction had been won by one of my teams (Staff Sgt Holloway & pte R.P. Stevenson). G.H.	
"	17/3/18		1 NCO & 2 ptes proceeded to Fifth Army School for course. G.H.	
"	18/3/18		6 Reinforcements posted - all B.1. G.H.	
"	19/3/18		Routine G.H.	

2449 Wt. W14957/M90 750,000 1/16 J.B.C. & A. Forms/C.2118/12.

Instructions regarding War Diaries and Intelligence Summaries are contained in F. S. Regs., Part II. and the Staff Manual respectively. Title pages will be prepared in manuscript.

WAR DIARY
~~or~~
~~INTELLIGENCE SUMMARY.~~
(Erase heading not required.)

Army Form C. 2118.

112 F A

Place	Date	Hour	Summary of Events and Information	Remarks and references to Appendices
HAMEL.	20/3/18		1 reinforcement (Cpl Bagshaw) posted GH	
"	21/3/18		I was awakened at about 4.30 AM by the sound of heavy firing & got up. I was shortly joined by my Officers & Senior N.C.O's. The bombardment continuing with intensity, I ordered the radiators of all cars to be filled, about 5 AM. Weather extremely misty. During the morning 5 Motor lorries reported to me & I evacuated my Station by them. Later I found that they had been sent to me as a Corps reserve, & on their return I sent 4 to the O.C. M.T., retaining 1 throughout for my work. Later another lorry & 3 M A Cars from the MAC arrived & assisted in evacuation. HAMEL & TINCOURT were shelled steadily, but not severely, all day. Most shells dropped near TINCOURT Station but a number dropped in HAMEL & many gas-shells into the valley below the village. 1 H.E. shell dropped on the road near the Sergeants Mess, & opposite the 2 M.O's Interpreters billet, doing slight damage. During the day wounded were passed through. Offrs 10. OR 160. Americans 1 Italians 1 (1 Offr OR). GH	

(A7092). Wt. W12839/M1293. 750,000. 1/17. D. D. & L., Ltd. Forms/C.2118/14.

Instructions regarding War Diaries and Intelligence Summaries are contained in F. S. Regs., Part II. and the Staff Manual respectively. Title pages will be prepared in manuscript.

Army Form C. 2118.

WAR DIARY
or
~~INTELLIGENCE SUMMARY.~~

(*Erase heading not required.*)

112. F A.

Place	Date	Hour	Summary of Events and Information	Remarks and references to Appendices
COLLEGE PERONNE 62.C.I.27 d.2.4.	22/3/18		About 1.30 AM a large shell (8 inch or 9.2") fell in the small space between the Mess Cottage & kitchen. It made a crater 8' deep & 14' wide doing practically no damage to the surrounding buildings! Received orders times 8.20 AM to retire to PERONNE. Was attending to wounded till the last minute, & moved out at 10.10 AM carrying as many blankets as possible. 1 Op Tent & 3 bell. had to be left behind as well as some equipment & dressings in the dressing-room & some stores in the QM stores, but could carry no more, even with the help of a lorry. Transport proceeded via TEMPLEUX LA FOSSE (62.C.J.4 d. central), personnel by direct road. 10 minutes after leaving, shelling of HAMEL began in earnest & was severe 5 minutes later. Admitted - Officers 2. O.R. 28 (wounded). On arrival at PERONNE obtained billets at the COLLEGE from Town Major. Transport in yard, horses with 111 FA. RJH.	
Near CAPPY 62.C G 26 d 9.9	23/3/18		Early in morning sent for horses & harnessed up. Received orders about 8 am to move via BIACHES I.25-31 to HERBECOURT H.32 b 3.8 & got away at once. Got ready to open at HERBECOURT but received orders to move again & got off at 5 PM. Camped near CAPPY, but under orders to be ready. Moved about 10 PM to near BRAY sur SOMME. RJH.	

(A7092). Wt. W12839/M1293. 750,000. 1/17. D. D. & L., Ltd. Forms/C.2118/14.

Instructions regarding War Diaries and Intelligence Summaries are contained in F. S. Regs., Part II. and the Staff Manual respectively. Title pages will be prepared in manuscript.

WAR DIARY
or
~~INTELLIGENCE SUMMARY.~~
(Erase heading not required.)

Army Form C. 2118.

112 FA

Place	Date	Hour	Summary of Events and Information	Remarks and references to Appendices
BRAY sur SOMME 62.D. L.16.7.2.	24/3/18		Arrived at L.22.b central after midnight & parked alongside road. Bivouacs in field N of road. In morning found better pitch at L16.7.2 & moved on there. Later received orders to move via CORBIE to near QUERRIERES. While awaiting a gap in the stream of transport, a hostile plane dropped 6 bombs into BRAY, intended for the road, but fired too late. Just as my transport was getting into the line, two more bombs were dropped into a garden behind the houses, within 50 yards of us. Got on the road just at dark. By order ADMS detached 1 offr (Capt Saunders), 21 O.R & Motor Ambces for special duty on main road. RJH.	
near PONT NOYELLES 62.D.H.18d central	25/3/18		Marched practically all night. Owing to other Divisional Transport halting FD soon had to march past them & arrived at Cross-roads without finding a suitable place to pull off & camp. There got grass-field down the road & camped - bivouacking.	
62.D.P.20 a.3.10			In afternoon moved again to 62 D. P.20 a.3.10 where camped for the night. RJH	
62.D.P.20 a.3.10.	26/3/18		At 1 AM sent 3 cars each with 1 NCO & 6 bearers to each Bde Headquarters. In afternoon sent B section under Capt Saunders, reinforced by 2 MOs & 2 cars No. 111 FA to form ADS at site of 21 Stationary Hosp GAILLY 62 D. Q.1.5.2. Visited them after their arrival, & made special arrangements. Also 2 cars bearers attached 47th & 49th Bdes at CERISY GAILLY. RJH	

Instructions regarding War Diaries and Intelligence Summaries are contained in F. S. Regs., Part II. and the Staff Manual respectively. Title pages will be prepared in manuscript.

WAR DIARY

~~or~~

~~INTELLIGENCE SUMMARY.~~

(Erase heading not required.)

112 F.A.

Army Form C. 2118.

Place	Date	Hour	Summary of Events and Information	Remarks and references to Appendices
near Cross Roads S of BLANGY-TRONVILLE 62 D. N.27 d.6.6.	27/3/18	2.30 PM. 4 PM 4 PM	O/c A.D.S. near CERISY GAILLY was compelled about 2.30 PM to evacuate it owing to Artillery fire & machine-gun fire from the opposite side (N bank) of the SOMME & retired to LE MAIRE HAMEL 62 D. P.10.a. Capt D H Weir was sent up in relief & took over about 4 PM. & retired at once to HAMELET. O.6 d.2.6. During these operations 2 O.R. were wounded but remained on duty. At 4 PM. Headquarters moved back with the other Divisional FAs, under urgent order, to the Cross Roads S of BLANGY TRONVILLE, where they parked together beside the main road. Very shortly after our passage along it, the WARFUSEE – FOUILLOY road was heavily shelled. At 9.30 PM I went up to visit my ADS at HAMELET. I had previously, owing to information received, requested O.C 10?? MAC to send cars to clear the Ammunition Dump at O.25 on main road where I was told that wounded were being dumped. On my return from ADS I ran up to the Dump, & found that it had been cleared save the last 3 cases, whom I brought to my Headquarters. I advised the O.C Dump to communicate direct with M.A.C if necessary. [initials]	
"	28/3/18		Hitherto each FA had been supposed to keep in touch with & collect sick from its own Brigade. Today I arranged with O.C's 111 & 113, that each FA should do everything for 24 hours in rotation. Visited DHQ & obtained sanction of ADMS. Brought back with me Bg General Leveson Gower & Major Crowther R.F. for rest, to join Bg General Gregorie already with me. During the day the weather broke & heavy rain fell At 6 PM. was relieved by 111 FA. Adm: Off. W. 6. O.R. S. 10. W. 46. [initials]	

(A7092). Wt. W12839/M1293. 75,000. 1/17. D. D. & L., Ltd. Forms/C.2118/14.

WAR DIARY
or
~~INTELLIGENCE SUMMARY.~~

Army Form C. 2118.

Instructions regarding War Diaries and Intelligence Summaries are contained in F. S. Regs., Part II. and the Staff Manual respectively. Title pages will be prepared in manuscript.

(*Erase heading not required.*)

112 F.A.

Place	Date	Hour	Summary of Events and Information	Remarks and references to Appendices
62D. N 24 d 6.6	28/3/18		Continued. The following officers arrived on posting to the Division & were divided between 111 & 112 FA. Capt J. T. Heffernan RAMC (112) Lieut E. D. Kinsey ~~USA MRC~~ RAMC (111) 1st Lieut T. R. Campbell USA MRC (112) 1st Lieut J. H. Wilson U.S.A. M.R.C. (111) BH	
"	29/3/18		Detailed Capt J. T. Heffernan RAMC to form Aid Post at HAMEL (Orders from ADMS). 1st Lieuts N B Ellis & A O Raymond USA MRC reported for duty with Division & were detained by me. Lt Col Weldon 2nd Leinsters detained for rest by order ADMS. Admitted offrs S.1. W.3. O.R. S.56. W.107. Weather wet & squally. BH	
"	30/3/18		2 O.R. of my FA evacuated wounded. Went up in morning to visit ADMS & ADS, & found HAMELET being heavily bombarded, so did not go beyond FOUILLOY. ADMS informed me that Capt WEIR was going to remain at HAMELET with 6 men as long as possible & that the remainder (2 offrs 111 FA & about 50 O.R. 112 FA) would return to FOUILLOY where I was to select a site for a new ADS. I was able to get suitable accommodation in the last Western houses of the village. While I was there the party arrived from HAMELET & took possession. O.10.a.9.5. On my return visited MAC near LONGUEAU M.29 central, & there learned that cases were coming down not dressed from VILLERS BRETONNEUX so must be stopped & dressed at F.A.H.Q. Believing that probably many were getting carried to the Ammunition Dump at MONTIERES (NW of AMIENS), went on there & made enquiries finding that this had been the case, but to no great extent	

Army Form C. 2118.

Instructions regarding War Diaries and Intelligence Summaries are contained in F. S. Regs., Part II. and the Staff Manual respectively. Title pages will be prepared in manuscript.

WAR DIARY
or
INTELLIGENCE SUMMARY.

(Erase heading not required.)

Place	Date	Hour	Summary of Events and Information	Remarks and references to Appendices
62 D. N.27d 66.	30/3/18		Continued. On the return journey stopped at MAC where I met ADMS 55th Division, to whom I explained the situation. He promised to provide for evacuation of VILLERS BRETONNEUX via BOVES. 62 D. T 8, & himself took 3 MAC cars up for a start. This provides for the clearing by the people concerned of that part of the front, & leaves me clear to deal with the troops on our front. Reported to ADMS. Admitted Offs. W.1. OR. S.28. W.53. [illegible initials]	
"	31/3/18		Both Brigadier & Major Crowther returned to duty early. Owing to severe fighting on 30th had heavy work in our tour of duty (6 PM 30th to 6 PM 31st). Admitted Offrs S.4. W.12. OR. S.15. W.259. Systematised transport during tour. Had 10 FA cars. Placed 6 on forward run & 4 + any MAC available (promised 4 cars & 2 lorries) on the backward run to NAMPS SW of AMIENS. HAMEL, HAMELET & FOUILLOY reported clear by early morning. Weather extremely wet & our camp a Quagmire! Visited HAMELET about noon & found all well. R.S. [illegible] Lt Col RAMC OC 112 FA	

Apr. 1918.

160/2983

No. 112 F.A.

7

Instructions regarding War Diaries and Intelligence Summaries are contained in F. S. Regs., Part II. and the Staff Manual respectively. Title pages will be prepared in manuscript.

WAR DIARY
or
~~INTELLIGENCE SUMMARY.~~
(Erase heading not required.)

Vol 29

Army Form C. 2118.

No. 112 Field Ambulance

Vol 30 29

Place	Date	Hour	Summary of Events and Information	Remarks and references to Appendices
Near BLANGY-TRONVILLE 62 D. N.27.d.6.6. later. N.26.d.6.6	1/4/18		Capt J. T. Heffernan left for temporary Duty with 2nd R Munster Fusiliers. In view of the utter quagmire to which the F.A. Camps had been reduced and also the fact that the enemy was sound-ranging, bursting shells immediately over the Camp, I obtained permission from the ADMS to shift to a cleaner & possibly safer spot. The three F A's shifted Camp during the afternoon to better ground about 1 Kilometre along the road. The OC 11th Hants had already similarly moved his transport on account of the shelling. R. H. Hamilton Lt Col RAMC OC 112 FA	
N.26.d.6.6	2/4/18		Capt F. E. Bissell posted to F.A. Visited ADS. HAMELET. O.6.d.4.8. Some shelling going on round the village. RH	
"	3/4/18		During the afternoon the other FA's received orders to move West, & left. Our tour of Duty would normally have expired at 6 P.M. but we carried on as routine. At 9.30 P.M. received orders to march to SALEUX (AMIENS 2.C.8.5). At midnight the personnel from FOUILLOY A.D.S. arrived, and we marched off at 12.20 AM. 4.4.18 RH	
SALEUX. (AMIENS. 2.C.8.5)	4/4/18		Arrived SALEUX 4 AM. Weather fine at first, later rain. All the rest of personnel from Bearer Posts less 1 Sgt & 4 men arrived by lorry. We sheltered as well as we could till daylight when we obtained permission to use shelter in yard of School. No 111 F.A. shared shelter with us. Started march for Railway Station at 3 P.M. Train due to leave 6 P.M. Sat about station all the evening, mostly in drizzling rain. The Divisional Band played all they could in the dark to pass the time! 1st Lieut H. E. Gillett USA MRC posted temporarily to 2nd R. Dub Fus. RH	

(A7092). Wt. W12839/M1293. 750,000. 1/17. D. D. & L., Ltd. Forms/C.2118/14.

Instructions regarding War Diaries and Intelligence Summaries are contained in F. S. Regs., Part II. and the Staff Manual respectively. Title pages will be prepared in manuscript.

WAR DIARY
~~or~~
~~INTELLIGENCE SUMMARY.~~

(*Erase heading not required.*)

Army Form C. 2118.

112 F.A.

Place	Date	Hour	Summary of Events and Information	Remarks and references to Appendices
BIENCOURT CHATEAU. (DIEPPE. 16 1. I 3 7.)	5/4/18		Arrived BLANGY (DIEPPE 16.2 H.52) 6.30 A.M. marched to CHATEAU. BIENCOURT. Good billets. Allowed to rest. Capt D.H. Weir. RAMC T.F. appointed a/Major (DRO 1 d/o 5.4.18) as from 4.1.18. GH	
"	6/4/18		Rested. GH	
"	7/4/18		Rested. Capt J.T. Heffernan posted permanently to 2nd RMF & 1st Lieut Gillett to 2nd R. Dub. Fus. GH	
	8/4/18		Rested. GH	
HOCQUELUS. (ABBEVILLE 14 1°36'E. 50°2'N)	9/4/18		Marched in conjunction with 48th Infty Bde, but independently, to HOCQUELUS. Good billets. Collected & disposed of sick of Bde to LE TREPORT. Weather fine. Band played on the march & later in village. GH	
In the Train	10/4/18		During the afternoon marched to WOINCOURT & entrained at 7 P.M. (1°32'E 50°3'N) GH	
LE FAY (HAZEBROUCK 5A. 5.A 4.4)	11/4/18		Arrived WIZERNES 6 A.M. detrained & marched via LUMBRES (5A. 4.B cent.) to billets at LE FAY. No pitch, billets bad. Transport parked on road – narrow. Pitched tents in only possible field & reported to ADMS. & later to area Comdt & 48th Bde. Sergt & 4 men last of bearers, rejoined. GH	

(A7092). Wt. W12839/M1293. 750,000. 1/17. D. D. & L., Ltd. Forms/C.2118/14.

Instructions regarding War Diaries and Intelligence Summaries are contained in F. S. Regs., Part II. and the Staff Manual respectively. Title pages will be prepared in manuscript.

WAR DIARY

or

~~INTELLIGENCE SUMMARY.~~

(Erase heading not required.)

Army Form C. 2118.

112 FA

Place	Date	Hour	Summary of Events and Information	Remarks and references to Appendices
LE FAY	12/4/18		With ADMS toured area in search of a pitch. Found the only possible place at LEVALRESTAUT (HAZEBROUCK 5A 5.A.2.8) in occupation of infantry. 2 OR Clerks rejoined from temp duty with 63 FA since 21.3.18. R.J.H.	
LEVALRESTAUT 5A. 5A.2.8	13/4/18		In evening marched to LEVALRESTAUT & took over pitch vacated by infantry. 2 M.A. Cars & Drivers reported in replacement of casualties. 1 OR (Corpl Lockwood) arrived for duty. R.J.H.	
WESTREHEM 5A. 5.C.80.55	14/4/18		In bitterly cold high wind marched to billets in WESTREHEM, following 48th Bde. Very long delays en route. R.J.H.	
LES. CISEAUX 5A. 4.F.2.1.	15/4/18		In cold weather but less wind marched to billets in LES CISEAUX. Shortly after arrival found that village population had been doubled by refugees. Terrible stories of their destitution. Ordered biscuit soaked in milk to be prepared for children, & arrangements to be made for giving meals to adults as far as resources permitted. Received some spare supplies from Capt Tren M.C. [illegible] ASC. The preparation was undertaken willingly by the Quartermaster [illegible] & his staff assisted by Major Weir & Captain Saunders. A meal — supper — was given to 120 persons. R.J.H.	
"	16/4/18		At 9 am Major Gaye ASC & Lieut Moran [illegible] Bde Supply Officer, visited me and arranged for extra supplies for feeding refugees. During the morning I evacuated several M.A. Car loads of sick & children to ARQUES. The sorting out & personal dealings with the refugees was taken most zealously in hand by Interpreter [illegible]. Breakfast was given to 60 children & old people, & supper to 300 adults & children. Reported my action in an interview with ADMS. Opened Hosp Tent for slight cases (Troops) R.J.H.	
"	17/4/18		Issued 120 meals in morning & evening. Interviewed [illegible] Mission [illegible] & arranged with him for the compulsory evacuation of the refugees & their allied area. I arranged to provide transport for children & old people to AIRE [illegible] there, & to continue meals to those remaining as evacuation proceeded. I received excellent report that the refugees with means were playing the game & feeding themselves. R.J.H.	

(A7092). Wt. W12839/M1293. 750,000. 1/17. D. D. & L., Ltd. Forms/C.2118/14.

Instructions regarding War Diaries and Intelligence Summaries are contained in F. S. Regs., Part II. and the Staff Manual respectively. Title pages will be prepared in manuscript.

WAR DIARY

or

~~INTELLIGENCE SUMMARY.~~

(*Erase heading not required.*)

Army Form C. 2118.

112 FA.

Place	Date	Hour	Summary of Events and Information	Remarks and references to Appendices
LES CISEAUX	18/4/18		Resting. Instruction daily in bandaging and splinting, especially Thomas Splint. Refugees fed – morning 81 (mostly children) Evening 120. R.J.H.	
"	19/4/18		Routine. Refugees fed – morning 61. Evening 230. This apparent increase really means that the refugees are only applying when absolutely necessary. The Gendarmerie have been in the village today, and a certain proportion of refugees have moved on, but the interpreter has great difficulty in persuading them to go before they are driven out. The people are dazed & hard to handle in this respect. In the afternoon received orders to hand over & take up duty as ADMS 30th Division. R.J.H.	
"	20/4/18		Handed over Command to Major D. H. Weir. RAMC. T.F. R. J. Houghton Lt Col RAMC	
	21/4/18		Assumed a.t.y Command of Unit from Lt Col Houghton RAMC. on his proceeding today to assume A.D.M.S. 30th Division. By orders of French authorities we ceased feeding Refugees. Proceeded (on orders of A.D.M.S. 18th Div) to [illegible] for interview with D.D.M.S. XIII Corps. D. Henderson Weir. Major. RAMC (T.F.).	

(A7092). Wt. W12839/M1293. 750,000. 1/17. D. D. & L., Ltd. Forms/C.2118/14.

Instructions regarding War Diaries and Intelligence Summaries are contained in F. S. Regs., Part II. and the Staff Manual respectively. Title pages will be prepared in manuscript.

WAR DIARY

or

~~INTELLIGENCE SUMMARY.~~

(*Erase heading not required.*)

Army Form C. 2118.

112th F.A.

Place	Date	Hour	Summary of Events and Information	Remarks and references to Appendices
Les Ciseaux	22/4/18		8.30 AM. German Propaganda Balloon brought down in Camp. Forwarded to G.S.O.I. [illegible] Div. Heavy German fire – 10.30pm – 5 am in direction of Bethune. Training. Squad & Company Drill and Bandaging ~~[illegible]~~ D.H.W.	
"	23/4/18		1 OR (ASC MT) Rejoined from C.C.S. 1 O.R. evacuated sick. Capt T. F. Saunders RAMC appointed Major under Sec II (L.D.S. 384) 16 Rev. No A 501/21 D.H.W.	
"	24/4/18		3 O.R.s Rejoined from C.C.S. Training as per programme cont'd. D.H.W.	
"			1st Lt H.E. Gillette M.O.R.C. U.S.A. to 73rd Bde R.G.A. as M.O. D.H.W.	
	25/4/18		1st Lt A.O. Raymond M.O.R.C. U.S.A. 1st Lt N.B. Ellis M.O.R.C. U.S.A. } to ADMS 11 Division for Duty and struck off strength. D.H.W.	
	26/4/18		Routine. 1 O.R. evacuated sick. D.H.W.	
	27/4/18		4 large Cars and 1 Ford and personnel of M.T. except 1 M/cycle & 2 cycle [illegible] transferred for permanent duty with 52 Division. D.H.W.	
	28/4/18		Continued C of E [illegible] by Rev [illegible] D.H.W.	

(A7092). Wt. W12839/M1293. 750,000. 1/17. D. D. & L., Ltd. Forms/C.2118/14.

Instructions regarding War Diaries and Intelligence Summaries are contained in F. S. Regs., Part II. and the Staff Manual respectively. Title pages will be prepared in manuscript.

WAR DIARY
or
~~INTELLIGENCE SUMMARY.~~
(Erase heading not required.)

Army Form C. 2118.

112 F.A.

Place	Date	Hour	Summary of Events and Information	Remarks and references to Appendices
[illegible]	29/9/18		Routine: Training according to Programme.	
	30/9/18		Routine. 1 O.R. rejoined from C.C.S.	
			[illegible] Major RAMC(T) O/C 112th Field Ambulance	

(A7092). Wt. W12839/M1293. 750,000. 1/17. D. D. & L., Ltd. Forms/C.2118/14.

May 1918.

140/2983.

No. 112 F. A.

Original

6

Page I

Army Form C. 2118.

Instructions regarding War Diaries and Intelligence Summaries are contained in F. S. Regs., Part II. and the Staff Manual respectively. Title pages will be prepared in manuscript.

WAR DIARY
or
INTELLIGENCE SUMMARY.

(Erase heading not required.)

112 Field Ambulance

Vol 30

Place	Date	Hour	Summary of Events and Information	Remarks and references to Appendices
[illegible]	[illegible]		[illegible]	

(A7092). Wt. W12839/M1293. 750,000. 1/17. D. D. & L., Ltd. Forms/C.2118/14.

Page 2

Army Form C. 2118.

WAR DIARY
or
INTELLIGENCE SUMMARY.
(Erase heading not required.)

Instructions regarding War Diaries and Intelligence Summaries are contained in F. S. Regs., Part II. and the Staff Manual respectively. Title pages will be prepared in manuscript.

Place	Date	Hour	Summary of Events and Information	Remarks and references to Appendices
[illegible]	9/5/18		[illegible]	
[illegible]	[illegible]		[illegible]	
[illegible]	11/5/18		[illegible]	
[illegible]	12/5/18		[illegible]	
[illegible]	[illegible]		[illegible]	
[illegible]	[illegible]		[illegible]	
	[illegible]		[illegible]	

(A7092). Wt. W12839/M1293. 750,000. 1/17. D. D. & L., Ltd. Forms/C.2118/14.

Page 3

Army Form C. 2118.

WAR DIARY
or
~~INTELLIGENCE SUMMARY.~~

(*Erase heading not required.*)

Instructions regarding War Diaries and Intelligence Summaries are contained in F. S. Regs., Part II. and the Staff Manual respectively. Title pages will be prepared in manuscript.

[illegible] Field Ambulance

Place	Date	Hour	Summary of Events and Information	Remarks and references to Appendices
[illegible]	16/5/18		[illegible] Field Ambulance equipment (except M.T.) with all Horse Transport handed over to 307 American Field Ambulance. [illegible] Motor Transport [illegible] handed [illegible] from ADMS [illegible] Div to SMTO [illegible] Division. Routine Training [illegible] [illegible]	
"	17/5/18		Motor Transport [illegible] [illegible] [illegible] Motor Transport [illegible]	
"	18/5/18		Routine Training [illegible]	
"	19/5/18		Routine [illegible] [illegible]	
"	20/5/18		Routine [illegible]	
"	21/5/18		Routine [illegible]	
"	22/5/18		Routine – [illegible] with 307 Fd Ambulance [illegible]	
"	23/5/18		Routine [illegible]	
"	24/5/18		Routine [illegible]	
"	25/5/18		Routine [illegible]	

(A7092). Wt. W12839/M1293. 750,000. 1/17. D. D. & L., Ltd. Forms/C.2118/14.

Page 4

Army Form C. 2118.

Instructions regarding War Diaries and Intelligence Summaries are contained in F. S. Regs., Part II. and the Staff Manual respectively. Title pages will be prepared in manuscript.

WAR DIARY
or
~~INTELLIGENCE SUMMARY.~~

(Erase heading not required.)

112 Field Ambulance

Place	Date	Hour	Summary of Events and Information	Remarks and references to Appendices
[illegible]	26/5/18		1 Corpl. [illegible], 113 [illegible] 2/155778 Pte Paull [illegible] a Combined Service of American & British Troops held today by American Chaplain. D.H.	
do	27/5/18		Routine D.H.	
do	28/5/18		Routine D.H.	
do	29/5/18		Routine D.H.	
do	30/5/18		All A & D Books forwarded today to D.A.G. Base in accordance with G.R.O./665/1. D.H.	
do	31/5/18		Routine & Training has progressed evenly – the Sergeants & men of the Training Cadre have worked most loyally.	

D. Henderson Weir
Lt Col R.A.M.C.
O.C. 112 Field Ambulance

(A7092). Wt. W12839/M1293. 750,000. 1/17. D. D. & L., Ltd. Forms/C.2118/14.

June 1918

War Diary

112 Field Amb^ce

June 1918

On His Majesty's Service.

140/3076

Instructions regarding War Diaries and Intelligence Summaries are contained in F. S. Regs., Part II. and the Staff Manual respectively. Title pages will be prepared in manuscript.

WAR DIARY
or
INTELLIGENCE SUMMARY.
(*Erase heading not required.*)

Army Form C. 2118.

112th Fd. Amb.

Place	Date	Hour	Summary of Events and Information	Remarks and references to Appendices
[illegible]	1/6/18		General instruction to 307th Fd. Ambulance (American) continued. D H Weir	
"	2/6/18		Routine, as above D H W	
"	3/6/18		Routine D H W.	
"	4/6/18		Routine D H W. Received 1 G.S. Wagon Mark X complete [illegible] for 39th Div. Train	
"	5/6/18		Routine D H W	
"	6/6/18		Training Cadre 1 G.S. Wagon from Div Train. Complete Train [illegible] handed over to 307th Fd. Amb. (American). [illegible] functioning as 112th Fd. Amb. 307th Fd Amb. marched out at 1 p.m. complete with H.T. & Equipment. All available M.A. Cars accompanied them to Railhead, with instructions to return to 112th Fd Amb. Training Cadre on completion of duty. D H Weir	
"	7/7/18		2 M.A.C. Cars arrived for Temporary Duty. A.S.C. (H.T.) 33 O.R.s proceeded [illegible] to 39th Divn Train. 1 Sgt. 7 O.R.s arrived from San. Det. 120 (American) [illegible] myself only Medical Officer remaining to function hospital. D H Weir	
	8/7/18		Routine. D H Weir	

(A7092). Wt. W12839/M1293. 750,000. 1/17. D. D. & L., Ltd. Forms/C. 2118/

Instructions regarding War Diaries and Intelligence Summaries are contained in F. S. Regs., Part II. and the Staff Manual respectively. Title pages will be prepared in manuscript.

WAR DIARY
or
~~INTELLIGENCE SUMMARY.~~
(Erase heading not required.)

112th Fd. Amb.

Army Form C. 2118.

Place	Date	Hour	Summary of Events and Information	Remarks and references to Appendices
[illegible]	9/6/18	—	Routine, Capt Taylor U.S. M.A. M.C. & Lt. [illegible] M.R.C. Reported for Duty. D H Weir	
	10/6/18	—	Routine. DHW	
	11/6/18		4. M.A.C. Cars with Personnel A.S.C. (M.T.) Returned for Temp. Duty with 307th Fd Amb. DHW	
	12/6/18		Routine DHW	
	13/6/18	—	2 M.A.C. Cars here for Temp. Duty Returned to No 5. M.A.C. New form of Influenza commenced today amongst Personnel. 4 O.R.s to Hospital with it.	
	14/6/18		6. O.R.s (112 Fd Amb.) to Hospital with same Disease. D H Weir	
	15/6/18		Routine. DHW D H Weir	
	16/6/18		Capt McBrayer M.C. M.O.R.C. Capt Yeager M.R.C. } Lt. Nywood M.R.C. Lt. Reeves M.R.C. } 3. Lts. 25 O.R.s } Reported for duty to 112th Fd Amb. DHW	
	17/6/18		Allocated Medical Duties to Medical Officers & commenced Training American Personnel. D H Weir	
	18/6/18		Routine. 6. O.R.s 112 Fd Amb discharged from Hospital. DHW	
	19/6/18		Routine. Sick Centre [illegible] fully established. Continues to function as 112 Fd Amb.	
	20/6/18		Routine. 3 Small Hospital Marquees erected in grounds of Chateau accommodation for 160 patients, total accommodation 250 patients. D H Weir	
	21/6/18		Routine. Influenza now affecting A.S.C. (M.T.) D H Weir	
	22/6/18		Routine D H Weir	

(A7092). Wt. W12839/M1293. 750,000. 1/17. D. D. & L., Ltd. Forms/C.2118/14.

Army Form C. 2118.

Instructions regarding War Diaries and Intelligence Summaries are contained in F. S. Regs., Part II. and the Staff Manual respectively. Title pages will be prepared in manuscript.

WAR DIARY
or
~~INTELLIGENCE SUMMARY.~~

112 Fd Amb.

(Erase heading not required.)

Place	Date	Hour	Summary of Events and Information	Remarks and references to Appendices
[illegible]	23/6/18		Routine. 1 O.R. A.S.C. (M.T.) admitted to Hosp. DHW	
	24/6/18		Routine DHW	
	25/6/18		Routine DHW	
Abbeville	26/6/18		Training Cadre, under A.D.M.S' orders moved today to Abbeville, arriving at the Reinforcement camp 9.30 p.m. at which camp remainder of Fd Amb. Personnel had arrived at 4.15 p.m. same day. DHW	
"	27/6/18		Q.M. and myself made all necessary arrangements for drawing Horse Transport, Ordnance supplies, & medical & surgical equipment. DHW	
"	28/6/18		Removed unit from Re-inforcement Camp to Chinese Labour Camp [illegible] drew stores from Ordnance and R.D.D.M.S. & Horse Transport from A.D.H.T. 2 L.O.R.s of A.S.C. (H.T.) under S/Sgt Major [illegible] rejoined unit [illegible] P.B men [illegible] by O.C. 133 Fd Amb. DHW	
"	29/6/18		11 a.m. Reported to A.D.M.S. Abbeville Area - ready to move out. A.D.M.S. visited camp 12.30 p.m. & informed us Transport only may have to proceed by Road. All Transport of 112 Fd Amb. left at 10.15 p.m. instructions to proceed to Wolphus. DHW	
"	30/6/18		Still awaiting orders for leaving Abbeville. Indents forwarded to D.A.D.O.S. 39th Division for deficiencies in Ordnance stores as per instructions of [illegible] Abbeville Area D H Henderson [illegible] Lt Col RAMC O.C. 112 Fd Amb.	

(A7092). Wt. W12839/M1293. 750,000. 1/17. D. D. & L., Ltd. Forms/C.2118/14.

(6392) Wt. W6192/P875 1,500,000 4/18 McA & W Ltd (E 2815) Forms W3091/4. Army Form W.3091.

WO 95/3131

Cover for Documents.

Nature of Enclosures.

War Diary

112 Field Ambulance

Notes, or Letters written.

4

July 1918.

Instructions regarding War Diaries and Intelligence Summaries are contained in F. S. Regs., Part II. and the Staff Manual respectively. Title pages will be prepared in manuscript.

WAR DIARY

~~or~~

~~INTELLIGENCE SUMMARY.~~

(*Erase heading not required.*)

Army Form C. 2118.

112 Field Ambulance

Place	Date	Hour	Summary of Events and Information	Remarks and references to Appendices
Abbeville	1/7/18		Capt C V Nicoll RAMC arrived from 24 G. H. [illegible] 3.15 A.M.	
			111 Fd Amb. entrained at TRIAGE 9 A.M. arriving ETAPLES 1.30 P.M. Detrained and proceeded to Rest Camp. D H[illegible]	
ETAPLES	2/7/18	-	Entrained 7 A.M. arrived AUDRICQ 12.45 P.M. Marched to LICQUES.	
LICQUES	3/7/18	-	5 M A Cars taken over from 43 F A. whom we relieved at Licques Chateau 183 patients in hospital DHW	
	4/7/18	-	Capt F E Bissell reported for Duty from No 6 C.C.S. DHW	
	5.7.18		Routine. DHW	
	6/7/18		Routine DHW	
	7/7/18		Ordered to send 1 M.A. Car for Temporary Duty with 78 (American) Division DHW	
	8/7/18		Capt G. Wallace & Capt L C W Cann RAMC. reported for Duty with Ambulance DHW	
	9/7/18		Capt C V Nicoll appointed Transport Officer for Ambulance DHW	
	10/7/18		Capt C V Nicoll & Capt F E Bissell permitted to wear badges of Major authority 39th Division.	

D Henderson [illegible]
[illegible] RAMC

(A7092). Wt. W12839/M1293 750,000. 1/17. D. D. & L., Ltd. Forms/C.2118/14.

No 7

Instructions regarding War Diaries and Intelligence Summaries are contained in F. S. Regs., Part II. and the Staff Manual respectively. Title pages will be prepared in manuscript.

WAR DIARY

or

~~INTELLIGENCE SUMMARY.~~

(*Erase heading not required.*)

Army Form C. 2118.

11th Fd Amb

Place	Date	Hour	Summary of Events and Information	Remarks and references to Appendices
Licques	11/7/18		"C" Tent Subdivision with 1 Section equipment proceeded today to Wierre Au Bois, under Major Nicoll to function Rest Area. DHW	
			11-7-18 Capt F W Diamond, Capt B F Ward posted for Duty D H Weir	
	12/7/18		Routine DHW	
	13.7.18		Routine D H Weir	
	14/7/18		Routine. A/Sgt Holloway awarded the M.S.M. (Gazette 17-6-18) DHW	
	15/7/18		— Major F. E. Bissell RAMC proceeded to 38 Fd Amb as O.C. D H Weir	
	16/7/18		Routine DHW	
	17/7/18		Capt Diamond posted to Detachment at Wierre Au Bois for Duty DHW	
	18/7/18		Routine D H Weir	
	19/7/18		Routine DHW	
	20/7/18		Routine DHW	
	21-7-18		Routine DHW	
	22/7/18		Lt C W Atkins (Quartermaster) appointed Transport Officer DHW	
	23.7.18		Routine DHW	
	24.7.18		Lt Col D H Weir RAMC (T.F.) appointed A/ADMS 39 Division. Capt F Diamond to ADMS' Office for Temporary Duty	
			D Henderson Weir	

(A7092). Wt. W12839/M1293. 750,000. 1/17. D. D. & L., Ltd. Forms/C.2118/14.

No 3

Army Form C. 2118.

WAR DIARY

or

~~INTELLIGENCE SUMMARY.~~

(Erase heading not required.)

112th Fd Ambulance

Instructions regarding War Diaries and Intelligence Summaries are contained in F. S. Regs., Part II. and the Staff Manual respectively. Title pages will be prepared in manuscript.

Place	Date	Hour	Summary of Events and Information	Remarks and references to Appendices
Liegnen [?]	25/7/18		Routine. D H [illegible]	
"	26.7.18		Routine D.H.W. (D.D.M.S. VII Corps visited Ambulance D.H.W.)	
"	27/7/18		Routine ~~DHW~~	
"	28/7/18		Routine DHW	
"	29.7.18		Pte Downie (at Detachment) had accident in Boulogne whilst unloading M.A. Car. DHW	
"	30.7.18		Routine DHW.	
"	31.7.18		Orders received from 2nd Army to rejoin 16th Division at Samer	

D Henderson Muir

Lt Col RAMC (T.F.)

3/7/18 [?] O.C. 112th Fd Ambulance

D. D. & L., London, E.C.
(A8001) Wt. W1771/M2031 750,000 5/17 Sch. 52 Forms/C2118/14

(6392) Wt. W6192/P875 1,500,000 4/18 McA & W Ltd (E 2815) Forms W3091/4. Army Form W.3091.

140/3900.
33

Cover for Documents.

Confidential

Nature of Enclosures.

War Diary

112 Field Ambulance

Notes, or Letters written.

9

Aug. 1918.

Instructions regarding War Diaries and Intelligence Summaries are contained in F. S. Regs., Part II. and the Staff Manual respectively. Title pages will be prepared in manuscript.

WAR DIARY

or

~~INTELLIGENCE SUMMARY.~~ 1/2[1] Fd. Amb.

(Erase heading not required.)

Army Form C. 2118.

Place	Date	Hour	Summary of Events and Information	Remarks and references to Appendices
Licques	1/8/18.		Routine DHW	
"	2/8/18		Capt. E. F. G. Ward authorised to wear badges of Major (Auth. 39 Div. A.A.Q.M.G. 39/03/A.A./30.7.18. DHWeir	
"	3/8/18		Reinforcements posted to sections. DHW	
Wiell au Bois	3/8/18.		F.A. moved to [illegible] au Bois [illegible], taking over site held by Detachment. DHWeir	
			Holding Party of 1 N.C.O. & 2 men left at Licques. DHW	
"	4/8/18		Detachment under Major C. V. [illegible], with Capt. Diamond – 1 Tent Sub Division & 10 Bearers 1 Section equipment & Transport – proceeded to [illegible]BERG to open Corps [illegible] Hospital. DHWeir	
"	5/8/18		Routine – Daily Route marches and Fd Ambulance Training commenced. DHW	
"	6/8/18		Routine DHW	
"	7/8/18		Routine DHW	
"	8/8/18		Routine DHW	
"	9/8/18		Routine DHW	
"	10/8/18		Routine DHW.	
"	11/8/18		Routine. 1 N.C.O. & 3 men proceeded to 1st Army School of Instruction (Cookery) DHWeir	

(A7092). Wt. W12839/M1293. 750,000. 1/17. D. D. & L., Ltd. Forms/C.2118/14.

Instructions regarding War Diaries and Intelligence Summaries are contained in F. S. Regs., Part II. and the Staff Manual respectively. Title pages will be prepared in manuscript.

WAR DIARY

~~or~~

~~INTELLIGENCE SUMMARY.~~

(Erase heading not required.)

Army Form C. 2118.

112th Fd Ambulance

Place	Date	Hour	Summary of Events and Information	Remarks and references to Appendices
[illegible]	12/8/18		Routine – 1st Lt. W. J. Dougherty M.O.R.C. U.S.A. posted for duty. DHW	
"	13/8/18		Routine. 1 O.R. (A.S.C. M.T.) posted from 145th Coy. A.S.C. DHW.	
"	14/8/18		Routine. Notification of Capt. E. F. G. Ward RAMC to be Major – dated 30-7-18. DHW (Auth: 22nd Corps – A 2275/18) DHW	
"	15/8/18		Routine DHW	
"	16/8/18		Routine. Liquor Holding Party Returned. DHW	
"	17/8/18		Routine. Warning notice (Secret) Re move to 1st Division. DHW	
"	18/8/18		Routine DHW All Officers warned to be packed. DHW	
"	19/8/18		Routine DHW	
"	20/8/18		Routine DHW.	
"	21/8/18		Horse Transport under Capt. L. C. W. [illegible] RAMC proceeded by Road at 2 pm to [illegible] Bde Transport Column. DHW.	
"	22/8/18		Personnel under Major C. V. Nicoll RAMC proceeded by Bus at 6 a.m. to Noeux les Mines. DHW	
"			Advance Party (C.O. Major Ward, 2 M – 10 O.R.) proceeded by car to RUITZ and took over M.D.S. from 2nd Fd Amb.	
			Motor Transport proceeded in convoy under C.O. D. H. Henderson Lt Col	

(A7092). Wt. W12839/M1293. 750,000. 1/17. D. D. & L., Ltd. Forms/C.2118/14.

Instructions regarding War Diaries and Intelligence Summaries are contained in F. S. Regs., Part II. and the Staff Manual respectively. Title pages will be prepared in manuscript.

WAR DIARY

~~or~~

~~INTELLIGENCE~~ SUMMARY. 112 Fd. Amb

(*Erase heading not required.*)

Army Form C. 2118.

Place	Date	Hour	Summary of Events and Information	Remarks and references to Appendices
Ravitz [illegible]	23/8/18		Lt Col. [illegible] RAMC(T) proceeded on Special Course – Having Handed Unit to Major C. V. Nicoll. I ~~remain in command~~ [illegible]	
	~~[illegible]~~		Horse Transport under Capt L C W Crane arrived at 8.30 PM	
			1 O.R evacuated sick	
			1 O.R. posted	C.V. Nicoll Major RAMC
			Capt L C W Crane appointed T.O	
	24/8/18		Routine 1 NCO & 3 men returned from 1st Army School of Instruction (RAMC) on completion of two weeks course	CVN
	25/8/18		Routine	CVN
	26/8/18		Routine	
	27/8/18		1 Sgt & sixteen men attached to 113 FA for work in conjunction with RE building a new RAP	
			Farrier Staff Sergt reported on return from Hospital	
			1 Ford car & driver attached to 113 FA for duty	CVN
	28/8/18		Routine	CVN

(A7092). Wt. W12839/M1293. 750,000. 1/17. D. D. & L., Ltd. Forms/C.2118/14.

Instructions regarding War Diaries and Intelligence Summaries are contained in F. S. Regs., Part II. and the Staff Manual respectively. Title pages will be prepared in manuscript.

Army Form C. 2118.

WAR DIARY
or
INTELLIGENCE SUMMARY.
(Erase heading not required.)

Place	Date	Hour	Summary of Events and Information	Remarks and references to Appendices
Renty	29/8/18		1 Sgt 1 Cpl 18 O.R. sent to 1st Corps Rest Station (officers) for temporary duty. 1 Farr. Staff Sergt (surplus to requirements) returned to 145 Coy A.S.C. & struck off strength. C.V.N	
	30/8/18		3 N.C.O.s & 17 O.R. attached for temporary duty from No 111 F.A. 2 O.R. reported from Hospital. C.V.N	
	31/8/18		Routine C.V.N	

C Vere Nicoll,
Major RAMC
a/O.C. 112. F.A.

(A7092). Wt. W12839/M1293. 750,000. 1/17. D. D. & L., Ltd. Forms/C.2118/14.

Sept. 1918

149/3259

112th F. Amb.

16

112 F.A. V.R. 3

Army Form C. 2118.

WAR DIARY

or

~~INTELLIGENCE SUMMARY.~~

(Erase heading not required.)

112 Field Amb RAMC

Instructions regarding War Diaries and Intelligence Summaries are contained in F. S. Regs., Part II. and the Staff Manual respectively. Title pages will be prepared in manuscript.

Place	Date 1918 Sept	Hour	Summary of Events and Information	Remarks and references to Appendices
Ruitz, M.D.S.	1st		Routine. 457005 Sergt Major Callard C. G. RAMC T.F. reported from 2/1st Wessex Field Ambulance for duty. C. Y. Nicoll	
	2nd		Duties of Sgt Major taken over from 47793 Sergt (Act Sergt Major) Jones C.M. by Sgt Major Callard. 47793 Act Sergt Major Jones reverted to his permanent rank of Sergeant on relinquishing duties, & proceeded to base depot at Etaples for reporting & struck off strength (A.G. 9/76/18). Six Reinforcements O.R. posted to Unit. C.Y.N	
	3rd		1 Cpl RAMC posted. C.Y.N	
	4th		Two officers & 107 O.R. were admitted suffering from the effects of gas shelling. Symptoms nearly all confined to the eyes. Conjunctivitis coming on about four hours after exposure to the gas & getting worse gradually. C.Y.N	
	5th		Three officers 185 O.R. admitted with Gas Shell (W) with similar symptoms to those yesterday. C.Y.N	

(A7092). Wt. W12839/M1293. 750,000. 1/17. D. D. & L., Ltd. Forms/C.2118/14.

Instructions regarding War Diaries and Intelligence Summaries are contained in F. S. Regs., Part II. and the Staff Manual respectively. Title pages will be prepared in manuscript.

WAR DIARY
or
~~INTELLIGENCE SUMMARY.~~
(Erase heading not required.)

Army Form C. 2118.

Place	Date 1918 Sept	Hour	Summary of Events and Information	Remarks and references to Appendices
Ruitz	5th	contd	Ford Car A15700 & Driver (1 O.R. A.S.C. M.T.) evacuated to Base	C.Y. McNicoll
	6th		Five officers & 76 O.R. admitted with Gas Shell (XY). Symptoms similar to those of yesterday. Notification received that Lt Col D H Weir's leave extended by War Office until 20/9/18.	CYN
	7th		2 G.S. Wagons (C.T.D.) proceeded to 16th Div Agricultural Officer for temporary duty. One O.R. evacuated sick. 64712 Cpl Stanger T Rowe appointed Acting Sergt with pay (Authority D.G. 84/252 dated 6/9/18. — 64700 a/ Cook Steward J H appointed Lance Sergt with pay.	CYN
	8th		Routine	CYN
	9th		Routine	CYN
	10th		Handed over M.D.S. to No 6 C.C.S. Red cross stores were handed over to No 111 F.A. The Ambulance moved into billets at Barlin (44 B 2 3 A 1.6)	CYN

(A7092). Wt. W12839/M1293. 750,000 1/17. D. D. & L., Ltd. Forms/C.2118/14.

Instructions regarding War Diaries and Intelligence Summaries are contained in F. S. Regs., Part II. and the Staff Manual respectively. Title pages will be prepared in manuscript.

WAR DIARY
or
~~INTELLIGENCE~~ SUMMARY.

(Erase heading not required.)

Army Form C. 2118.

Place	1918 Date Sept	Hour	Summary of Events and Information	Remarks and references to Appendices
Bailin	10th		Capt G Wacher RAMC & 1st Lieut W J Dougherty MORC USA proceeded to No 111 Field Ambulance for temporary duty. Ford car No A 54503 and one driver ASC MT arrived & taken on the strength. — Two GS Wagons returned from 16th Div Agricultural officer. C Vere Nicoll	
	11th		Routine. C.V.N	
	12th		One OR reposted to Unit. — Two Clerks proceeded to 1/3 West Lancs FA for temporary duty to superintend 16th Div admissions & discharges. C.V.N	
	13th		Inspected detachment at 1st Corps Officers Rest Station at Aire. C.V.N	
	14th		20 OR returned to 111 FA on completion of temporary duty with this Ambulance. C.V.N One Sergt ASC HT to No 13 Veterinary Hosp for a course in Horse management. — 39488 A/L/Cpl S Unsworth S returned from ASC Base Depot after undergoing a preliminary examination with a view to a temp commission in ASC. C.V.N	

(A7092). Wt. W12839/M1293. 750,000. 1/17. D. D. & L., Ltd. Forms/C.2118/14.

Instructions regarding War Diaries and Intelligence Summaries are contained in F. S. Regs., Part II. and the Staff Manual respectively. Title pages will be prepared in manuscript.

WAR DIARY

or

~~INTELLIGENCE SUMMARY.~~

(Erase heading not required.)

Army Form C. 2118.

Place	Date 1917 Sept	Hour	Summary of Events and Information	Remarks and references to Appendices
Barlin	14th		Capt L C W Crane Raine to 1/3 West Lancs Field Ambulance for temporary duty. C.Y. Neill	
	15th		One clerk – & 5 men to No 6 CCS for degassing clothing. 4 O.R. reinforcements arrived & taken on strength from 14th inst. C.Y.N. [illegible] O.R. ASC Horse Transport evacuated sick & struck off the strength C.Y.N. Capt L C W Crane Raine returned from 1/3 West Lancs FA	
	16th		Routine C.Y.N.	
	17th		3 NCO's & 17 men proceeded for temporary duty to No 6 CCS. C.Y.N	
	18th		Routine C.Y.N	
	19th		Routine C.Y.N	
	20th		Seven O.R. arrived & were taken on the strength of this Unit C.Y.N	
	21st		Lt Col. D. Henderson Weir returns from leave & resumed Command of Unit. D.H. Weir	
	22nd		Routine D.H.W.	
	23rd		Major E.F.G. Ward appointed O/c Motor Transport. D.H. Weir	

(A7092). Wt. W12839/M1293. 750,000. 1/17. D. D. & L., Ltd. Forms/C.2118/14.

Instructions regarding War Diaries and Intelligence Summaries are contained in F. S. Regs., Part II. and the Staff Manual respectively. Title pages will be prepared in manuscript.

WAR DIARY
or
~~INTELLIGENCE SUMMARY.~~

(Erase heading not required.)

Army Form C. 2118.

Place	Date	Hour	Summary of Events and Information	Remarks and references to Appendices
Baulin	24/9/18		Under A.D.M.S' orders. Field Ambulance moved to Bruay at 9.30 A.M. – to site of 22nd C.C.S. (J.15.c.3.2) 44B.	
			A+Lt. M. C.W. Atkins proceeded on leave to U.K.	
Bruay	25/9/18		Opened out for Reception of cases of 47th Brigade – DHW – Major C.V. [illegible] proceeded on leave to U.K. DHW	
"	26/9/18		Routine. A25835. [illegible] to hospital [illegible] DHW	
"	27/9/18		Routine. A/Sgt. Osborne W. Returned from [illegible] Course – DHW	
"	28/9/18		At request of D.D.M.S. 1st Corps this Ambulance provided loading party of 43 for Hospital Train. DHW	
"	29/9/18		Sunday – Routine. DHW. Commenced functioning as Divisional [illegible]	
"	30/9/18		Routine – again provided loading party for Hospital Train. 30 Bearers loaded full train in 1½ Hours. DHW	

D Henderson West
Lt Col R.A.M.C.
O.C. 112th Fd Amb

(A7092). Wt. W12839/M1293. 750,000. 1/17. D. D. & L., Ltd. Forms/C.2118/14.

Oct 1918

1.

14/3324

112th 7. a

Instructions regarding War Diaries and Intelligence Summaries are contained in F. S. Regs., Part II. and the Staff Manual respectively. Title pages will be prepared in manuscript.

WAR DIARY
or
~~INTELLIGENCE SUMMARY.~~
(Erase heading not required.)

Army Form C. 2118.

21

112th Fd. Ambulance

Vol 35

Place	Date	Hour	Summary of Events and Information	Remarks and references to Appendices
Busnay	1/10/18		Capt Warton RAMC + Lt Dougherty returned from Temporary Duty with 111th Fd Ambulance. D.H. Weir	
"	2-10-18		Routine. 5 O.Rs returned from Temporary Duty with C.C.S. DHW	
"	3-10-18		Routine. DHW.	
"	4-10-18		83832 Pte Mackenzie R.G. Dispenser appt. unpaid acting L/Cpl. 534281 Cpl Stanton F. posted to this unit. D.H. Weir	
"	5-10-18		Capt F. W. Diamond RAMC & Sgt Richards proceeded to I Corps Gas School for period of instruction. DHW	
	6-10-18		Routine. Ford Car No. 14166 with Driver evacuated to Base. DHW	
	7-10-18		1 Pte (Cook) proceeded to V Army School of Cookery for course of instruction. DHW	
	8-10-18		1 Corporal posted to I Corps H.Qr. for Temporary Duty as Medical Orderly. DHW	
	9-10-18		Routine. DHW.	
	10-10-18		1 O.R. (A.S.C. M.T.) evacuated sick to C.C.S. and struck off strength. 12 O.Rs Reinforcements posted to Unit. D.H. Weir	
"	11-10-18		1 Corporal RAMC posted to Unit from Base. DHW	
"	12-10-18		Routine	

D. Henderson Weir

(A7092). Wt. W12839/M1293. 750,000. 1/17. D. D. & L., Ltd. Forms/C.2118/14.

Instructions regarding War Diaries and Intelligence Summaries are contained in F. S. Regs., Part II. and the Staff Manual respectively. Title pages will be prepared in manuscript.

WAR DIARY
or
~~INTELLIGENCE SUMMARY.~~
(Erase heading not required.)

Army Form C. 2118.

112th Fd Ambulance

Place	Date	Hour	Summary of Events and Information	Remarks and references to Appendices
Bruay	13.10.18		Lt. T/Qr. Mr. Master C W Atkins appointed Acting Adjutant from this date. F H Weir	
"	14.10.18		3. O.Rs transferred to 111th Fd Ambulance and struck off this units accordingly. FHW	
"	15.10.18		1. O.R. (A.S.C. M.T.) posted from Divisional Train. FHW Unit moved today from Bruay to Hesdigneul	
Hesdigneul	16.10.18		1 Corporal and 17 O.Rs transferred to A.D.M.S 57th Division. F H Weir	
"	17.10.18		Capt Walker Bttn C.Y. No 47621 Sgt F. Redfern proceeded to I Corps Gas School for period of instruction. FHW 1. O.R. (A.S.C. M.T.) posted from 16th Divn M. T. Coy. F H Weir	
"	18.10.18		1. O.R. evacuated to C.C.S. "Sick", and struck off accordingly. FHW	
"	19.10.18		1st Lt. W. J. Dougherty M.O.R.C. (U.S.A.) posted to 16th Div. M. G. Bn. Field Ambulance moved to Haisnes. Men all slept in Dug Outs.	
Haisnes	20.10.18		Unit moved from Haisnes to Provin. Very wet. F H Weir	
Provin	21.10.18		Unit moved from Provin to Camphin, I saw A.D.M.S at Phalempin. FHW	
Camphin	22.10.18		Unit moved from Camphin to Templeuve and took over site of 113th Fd Amb and opened up as Main Dressing Station. Today three cars out of action. A large number of civilians were fed, others given medical treatment, and many were evacuated towards Phalempin and Camphin. F H Weir	

(A7092). Wt. W12839/M1293. 750,000. 1/17. D. D. & L., Ltd. Forms/C.2118/14.

Instructions regarding War Diaries and Intelligence Summaries are contained in F. S. Regs., Part II. and the Staff Manual respectively. Title pages will be prepared in manuscript.

WAR DIARY

~~or~~

~~INTELLIGENCE SUMMARY.~~

(*Erase heading not required.*)

112 Field Ambulance

Army Form C. 2118.

Place	Date	Hour	Summary of Events and Information	Remarks and references to Appendices
Templeuve.	23.10.18		Civilians continue asking for means of transport. Turned out 2 G.S. Wagons. Sick civilians [illegible] to Lille. DHWeir	
"	24.10.18		1 Lt Dougherty returned from Temporary Duty with 12 Div M.G. Bn and proceeded today for Temporary Duty with 111 Field Ambulance DHW	
"	25.10.18		Routine, A number of Gas Cases are coming down from the line. (7 Gas Cases) DHW	
"	26.10.18		Major E.F.G. Ward RAMC evacuated to C.C.S. Influenza. DHWeir	
"	27.10.18		Routine. 1 O.R. (RAMC) reinforcement arrived today. DHW (10 Gas Cases) DHW	
"	28/10/18		1 O.R. transferred to 1/3 West Lancs Fd Ambulance DHW 39 Gas Cases 1 died in Hospital. DHW	
"	29.10.18		1 O.R. (RAMC) evacuated sick. 10 Gas Cases. DHWeir	
"	30.10.18		Routine. 73 and 1 Officer Gas Cases. DHW	
"	31.10.18		Routine. 26 and 2 Officer Gas Cases	

D Henderson Weir
Lt Col, RAMC
31/10/18. O.C. 112 Field Ambulance

(A7092). Wt. W12839/M1293. 750,000. 1/17. D. D. & L., Ltd. Forms/C.2118/14.

Nov. 1918

140/3401

112th F.A.

27

VR 36

Army Form C. 2118.

WAR DIARY
or
INTELLIGENCE SUMMARY.
(*Erase heading not required.*)

112 Field Ambulance

Instructions regarding War Diaries and Intelligence Summaries are contained in F. S. Regs., Part II. and the Staff Manual respectively. Title pages will be prepared in manuscript.

Place	Date	Hour	Summary of Events and Information	Remarks and references to Appendices
Templeux	1/11/18		Capt G. Wacher RAMC admitted to 5[illegible] General Hospital sick from 1st Corps Gas School – struck off accordingly. DHW	
"	2/11/18		Lt Redfern and Pte Meakin returned from 1st Corps Gas School. Capt Wacher and Lt Redfern obtained over 85% marks at this course.	
"	3/11/18		Routine. Several [illegible] gas cases admitted to Hospital today.	DHW
"	4/11/18		Routine. DHW	
"	5/11/18		5 ORs returned from 1st Corps Rest Station. DHW	
"	6/11/18		Routine DHW	
"	7/11/18		Routine DHW	
"	8/11/18		1st Lt Bonyhady USRMC Returned from 111 Field Ambulance. DHW	
"	9/11/18		1 OR (ASC MT) posted from 16 Div MTC to this unit. DHW	
"	10/11/18		Took over old D.H. Qrs as an annexe to the Hospital. DHW	
"	11/11/18		1st Line Transport (1 Driver) 1 Cooker, 2 Wagons, 1 Wagon G.S. Rejoined this unit. Armistice came into force today at 1100 hours	

(A7092). Wt. W12839/M1293. 750,000. 1/17. D. D. & L., Ltd. Forms/C.2118/14.

Instructions regarding War Diaries and Intelligence Summaries are contained in F. S. Regs., Part II. and the Staff Manual respectively. Title pages will be prepared in manuscript.

WAR DIARY
~~or~~
~~INTELLIGENCE SUMMARY.~~

(*Erase heading not required.*)

Army Form C. 2118.

112 Fd Ambulance

Place	Date	Hour	Summary of Events and Information	Remarks and references to Appendices
Templeuve	12/11/18		2 M.A.C. cars temporarily attached to this unit from 12 M.A.C. proceeded to 111 Fd Amb in accordance with A.D.M.S. orders. D.H.W.	
"	13/11/18		Routine – evacuated several sick civilians to Lille today. D.H.W.	
"	14/11/18		Major E.F.J. Ward RAMC evacuated to 20 General Hospital from 15 C.C.S. and struck off accordingly. D.H.W.	
"	15/11/18		8 O.R.s from [illegible] [illegible] supplied for Tramping [illegible]. D.H.W.	
"	16/11/18		Routine – Foden Disinfector returned to 41 Bde H.Q. Depot. D.H.W.	
"	17/11/18		Routine. ~~All~~ Wards with Influenza cases sprayed with Formalin. D.H.W.	
"	18/11/18		Educational Scheme commenced today. 2 Hours daily – 4 days a week. Major C.V. Nicoll – Unit Education Officer. D.H.W.	
"	19/11/18		Capt L.C.W. Lewis R.A.M.C. granted Special Leave. 19-11-18 to 3-12-18. D.H.W.	
"	20/11/18		No 34888 [illegible] returned to unit from 43 Bde H.Q.	
	21/11/18		Mons. [illegible] interpreter evacuated to 15 C.C.S. D.H.W.	
	22/11/18		Routine. All Influenza wards sprayed with Formalin. D.H.W.	
	23/11/18		Routine. D.H. [illegible] W[illegible]	

(A7092). Wt. W12839/M1293. 750,000. 1/17. D. D. & L., Ltd. Forms/C.2118/14.

Instructions regarding War Diaries and Intelligence Summaries are contained in F. S. Regs., Part II. and the Staff Manual respectively. Title pages will be prepared in manuscript.

WAR DIARY
~~or~~
~~INTELLIGENCE SUMMARY.~~

(*Erase heading not required.*)

112 Fd. Ambulance

Army Form C. 2118.

Place	Date	Hour	Summary of Events and Information	Remarks and references to Appendices
Templeuve	24/11/18		Routine. Great difficulty with breaking down of M.A. Cars. DHWeir	
"	25/11/18		Obtained Motor Lorry from 1st DMT to evacuate Lying cases to C.C.S. DHW	
"	26/11/18		Major E F G [illegible] RAMC reported ... for 20th General Hospital DHW	
"	27/11/18		Routine, obtained another Motor Lorry for evacuation of Lying cases C.C.S. DHW	
"	28/11/18		Lecture to personnel on "Demobilisation and Reconstruction" by C.O.	DHWeir
"	29/11/18		Routine. Foden Disinfector returned to this unit. DHWeir	
"	30/11/18		2 Large M.A. cars temporarily attached from 110th Fd. Ambulance. DHW Commenced Medical Examination of Miners for Demobilisation scheme.	

30/11/18

D.H. Henderson Weir
Lt. Col. R.A.M.C.
O.C. 112 Field Ambulance

(A7092). Wt. W12839/M1293. 750,000. 1/17. D. D. & L., Ltd. Forms/C.2118/14.

Dec. 1916

14 0/3524

No. 112 Field Ambulance.

9/13

Instructions regarding War Diaries and Intelligence Summaries are contained in F. S. Regs., Part II. and the Staff Manual respectively. Title pages will be prepared in manuscript.

WAR DIARY
or
INTELLIGENCE SUMMARY.
(Erase heading not required.)

112 Fd Amb — Army Form C. 2118.

88 37

Place	Date	Hour	Summary of Events and Information	Remarks and references to Appendices
[illegible]	1/12/18.		Erected an Operating Tent and [illegible] Bath [illegible] for treatment of [illegible] D H Weir	
	2/12/18		Routine. Sent a party to Lille (Educational) DHW	
	3/12/18		1st Lt [illegible] M.O.R.C. posted to 48th Bde R.F.A. DHW	
	4/12/18		Routine. Sent a party to Mons (Educational) DHW	
	5/12/18		1 Sgt & 1 Cpl evacuated to C.C.S. DHW	
	6/12/18		Steel Helmets, Box Respirators [illegible] Returned [illegible] in accordance with R.O. instructions. DHW	
	7/12/18		Routine DHWeir	
	8/12/18		Capt. F. Dixon R.A.M.C. [illegible] DHW	
	9/12/18		Routine, sent a party to Douai (Educational) DHW	
	10/12/18		No [illegible] 026405 [illegible] L/Cpl rejoined unit from C.C.S. DHW	
	11/12/18		No 77195 Pte [illegible] attached Railhead R.O. for temporary duty. DHWeir	

(A7092). Wt. W12839/M1293. 750,000. 1/17. D. D. & L., Ltd. Forms/C.2118/14.

Instructions regarding War Diaries and Intelligence Summaries are contained in F. S. Regs., Part II. and the Staff Manual respectively. Title pages will be prepared in manuscript.

WAR DIARY
or
~~INTELLIGENCE SUMMARY.~~
(*Erase heading not required.*)

Army Form C. 2118.

112th Field Ambulance

Place	Date	Hour	Summary of Events and Information	Remarks and references to Appendices
Templeux	12/12/18	–	2 M.A.C. cars [illegible] from 12th M.A.C. for Temporary Duty	
			Seven (miners) R.A.M.C. and 7 A.S.C. (Miners) demobilised. DHW	
	13/12/18		Routine. 1 N.C.O. & 8 men attached Temporarily to 113th Fd Amb	
			Three R.A.M.C. (miners) demobilised. DHW	
	14/12/18		100188 Cpl Bagshaw, 57608 Pte McCollum admitted to C.C.S.	
			47461 L/Cpl Halloway returned from C.C.S. DHW	
	15/12/18		1 N.C.O. & 2 Men (miners) demobilised. DHW	
"	16/12/18		Routine – Routine [illegible]. Driver [illegible] returned from C.C.S. DHW	
"	17/12/18		Capt Cameron R.A.M.C. granted extension of leave to 6-12-18. DHW	
"	18/12/18		Routine. L/Cpl [illegible] returned from C.C.S. DHW	
"	19/12/18		M.386170. Pte Ford A.S.C. M.T. admitted to hospital. DHW	
"	20/12/18		M/2 088181. Pte Dell died whilst on leave to United Kingdom. DHW	
"	21/12/18		7 A.S.C. Drivers posted from 145th Co R.A.S.C. for Temp. Duty	
			1 G.S. Wagon 2 H.D. Horses and one Driver posted to 145th Co. R.A.S.C. for Temporary Duty	
			DHWeir	

Instructions regarding War Diaries and Intelligence Summaries are contained in F. S. Regs., Part II. and the Staff Manual respectively. Title pages will be prepared in manuscript.

WAR DIARY
or
~~INTELLIGENCE SUMMARY.~~

(Erase heading not required.)

Army Form C. 2118.

112 Field Ambulance.

Place	Date	Hour	Summary of Events and Information	Remarks and references to Appendices
Templeux	23/12/15	–	Temp. Quarter Master C. Atkins appointed Captain from 8-12-15 DHW [illegible]	
"	24/12/15		Capt (A/Major) C. V. Nicoll proceeded to England on authority of War Office for duty with the Aldershot Command DHW	
	25/12/15		Major Ward R.A.M.C. proceeded to England on leave 25-12-15 to 7-1-1916	DHW
"	26/12/15		Capt Whyte R.A.M.C. posted for temp. duty with this unit, and departed following day for duty with 6th Welsh Regiment	
	27/12/15		Major Vernor R.A.M.C. posted for temporary duty with this unit DHW	DHW
	28/12/15		Routine. 54522 Pte [illegible] posted to No 7 Mobile Dental Unit for temporary duty DHW	
"	29/12/15		Routine. The Decauville returned from [illegible] F.O. 2 NCOs and 1 man [illegible] to Corps Concentration Camp. DHW	
"	30/12/15		F.G.C.M. held on the [illegible] of this unit DHW	
"	31/12/15		Capt [illegible] relinquishing his commission gazetted on 19-12-15	

31/12/15

D. H. Henderson Lt Col
[illegible] R.A.M.C.
O.C. 112 Field Ambulance

(A7092). Wt. W12839/M1293. 750,000. 1/17. D. D. & L., Ltd. Forms/C.2118/14.

Jan. 1919

16 DIV

Box 1674

No. 112 Field Ambulance

9/3

WAR DIARY
or
~~INTELLIGENCE SUMMARY.~~
(Erase heading not required.)

Army Form C. 2118.

Instructions regarding War Diaries and Intelligence Summaries are contained in F. S. Regs., Part II. and the Staff Manual respectively. Title pages will be prepared in manuscript.

112th Fd Amb.

Vol 38

Place	Date	Hour	Summary of Events and Information	Remarks and references to Appendices
Templeuve	1-1-19		Routine. The Bde [illegible] 48th Bde 16th Divn visited Hospital. D H Weir	
"	2-1-19		Routine. Major (A/Lt Col) D H Weir awarded Military Cross Gazette 1-1-19. D H W	
"	3-1-19		No 1543 Ward Pte F. sent to D A P M 16th Div for F.G.C.M. [illegible] [illegible] days D H Weir.	
"	4-1-19		Routine. D H Weir.	
"	5-1-19		Routine. 1 N.C.O. + 1 man to R.T.O. [illegible] for Duty.	
"	6-1-19		1 O.R. sent to C R S for Duty. 2 men returned from C R S for ~~[illegible]~~ Duty.	
"	7-1-19		Capt Suffield attached to this unit for duty as Dental Surgeon. 1 O.R. returned from 3rd Mobile Dental Unit. D H Weir	
"	8-1-19		Major Vernon RAMC returned to 113th Fd Amb for duty. D H W.	
"	9-1-19		Capt Bedward RAMC [illegible] 5th R.I.F. attached to this unit for duty. D H Weir	
	10-1-19		2 O.Rs. attached from 16th Div Train for duty. D H W	
	11-1-19		Major Ward (CF?) Returned from leave. D H W	
	12-1-19		Routine. Route march today. D H Weir	
	13-1-19		1 M.A.C. car and [illegible] [illegible] 111th Fd Amb for duty. D H Weir	

(A7092). Wt. W12839/M1293. 750,000. 1/17. D. D. & L., Ltd. Forms/C.2118/14.

Army Form C. 2118.

WAR DIARY
or
~~INTELLIGENCE SUMMARY.~~
(Erase heading not required.)

Instructions regarding War Diaries and Intelligence Summaries are contained in F. S. Regs., Part II. and the Staff Manual respectively. Title pages will be prepared in manuscript.

Place	Date	Hour	Summary of Events and Information	Remarks and references to Appendices
[illegible]	14/1/19		Routine. Pte [illegible] A.S.C. (M.T.) evacuated to C.C.S. [illegible]	
"	15/1/19		Pte Barnes. A.S.C. (M.T.) attached to 16 Div M.T. Coy for duty [illegible]	
"	16/1/19		6 O.R.s Demobilised [illegible]	
"	17/1/19		[illegible] M.A.C. (Car) and [illegible] attached [illegible] for Duty [illegible]	
"	18-1-19		Routine. Terr. Eff. Medal awarded to S. Major [illegible] and C/pl [illegible]	
"	19-1-19		Divisional Parchments awarded to Major [illegible] and 6 O.R.s [illegible]	
"	20-1-19		Routine. Pte [illegible] attached to [illegible] for Temporary Duty [illegible]	
"	21/1/19		Routine. 1 O.R. to C.C.S. (Pte Smith R.A.S.C.) [illegible]	
"	22-1-19		Pte Cropland R.A.S.C. admitted to Hospital (Yorks) [illegible]	
"	23/1/19		Routine. 1 O.R. admitted to C.C.S. (1 O.R. returned from [illegible] for demobilisation) [illegible]	
	24/1/19		Sgt Norris (A.S.C. H.T.) awarded M.S.M. [illegible]	
			[illegible signature]	

(A7092). Wt. W12839/M1293. 750,000. 1/17. D. D. & L., Ltd. Forms/C.2118/14.

Instructions regarding War Diaries and Intelligence Summaries are contained in F. S. Regs., Part II. and the Staff Manual respectively. Title pages will be prepared in manuscript.

WAR DIARY
or
~~INTELLIGENCE SUMMARY.~~
(Erase heading not required.)

Army Form C. 2118.

112th Fd Amb

Place	Date	Hour	Summary of Events and Information	Remarks and references to Appendices
Templeuve	25/1/19		Routine. 17 O.Rs demobilised. DHWeir	
"	26-1-19		Routine (Route march 10 miles) DHW	
"	27-1-19		Routine. 1 O.R. returned from C.C.S. DHWeir	
"	28-1-19		Capt T.E. George RAMC attached for temporary duty. DHW	
	29-1-19		Routine. Dr [illegible] (ASC HT) to Hospital [illegible] struck off strength. DHW	
	30-1-19		[illegible] returned from temporary duty with [illegible] 113 [illegible] DHW	
	31-1-19		Routine. 2 O.Rs for demobilisation. DHW	

1/2/19 D H Henderson Weir
Lt Col RAMC
O.C. 112 Fd Amb

(A7092). Wt. W12839/M1293. 750,000. 1/17. D. D. & L., Ltd. Forms/C.2118/14.

Feb. 1919

4210/35724

No. 112 Field Ambulance

21

Army Form C. 2118.

WAR DIARY
or
~~INTELLIGENCE SUMMARY.~~
(Erase heading not required.)

112 Fd Amb

Instructions regarding War Diaries and Intelligence Summaries are contained in F. S. Regs., Part II. and the Staff Manual respectively. Title pages will be prepared in manuscript.

Place	Date	Hour	Summary of Events and Information	Remarks and references to Appendices
[illegible]	1-2-19		1 O.R. Transferred to No 2 [illegible] [illegible] [illegible] [illegible]	
	2/2/19		H.R.H. the Prince of Wales visited [illegible] [illegible] [illegible] [illegible]	
"	3/2/19		All [illegible] [illegible] W.O.I & N.C.O.s [illegible] [illegible] [illegible] [illegible] [illegible] 2/5/19 [illegible] [illegible] [illegible]	
	4/2/19		Capt [illegible] [illegible] (2 [illegible]) [illegible] [illegible] [illegible] [illegible] [illegible] — 18-2-19 [illegible]	
"	5/2/19		2 [illegible] [illegible] [illegible] O/2 [illegible] during absence of Capt [illegible] [illegible]	
	6-2-19		Routine. 2 O.R.s [illegible]	
	7-2-19		3 O.R.s transferred to [illegible] for duty [illegible]	
"	8/2/19		Routine. 3 O.R.s demobilised ([illegible]) 2 [illegible] [illegible]	
"	9/2/19		Routine. [illegible]	
	10-2-19		Capt [illegible] Badman [illegible] returned from leave [illegible]	
"	11-2-19		Routine. [illegible]	
	12-2-19		1 O.R. returned from 2 [illegible] [illegible] [illegible]	
	13-2-19		Capt [illegible] [illegible] [illegible] [illegible] for [illegible] [illegible] [illegible]	

(A7092). Wt. W12839/M1293. 750,000. 1/17. D. D. & L., Ltd. Forms/C.2118/14.

Instructions regarding War Diaries and Intelligence Summaries are contained in F. S. Regs., Part II. and the Staff Manual respectively. Title pages will be prepared in manuscript.

WAR DIARY
or
INTELLIGENCE SUMMARY.
(*Erase heading not required.*)

Army Form C. 2118.

1/2 [illegible]

Place	Date	Hour	Summary of Events and Information	Remarks and references to Appendices
Templeux	14-2-19		In orders from [illegible] Hospital [illegible] 2 O.R.s demobilised [illegible]	
	15-2-19		Routine [illegible]	
	16-2-19		Routine 1 R.A.S.C. (M.T.) demobilised [illegible]	
	17-2-19		3 O.R.s (R.A.M.C.) demobilised [illegible]	
	18-2-19		Routine [illegible]	
	19-2-19		2 O.R.s demobilised	
	20-2-19		Capt [illegible] returned from leave [illegible]	
	21-2-19		Lt Col [illegible] appointed A/A.D.M.S. from 13-2-19 vice Col [illegible] to England [illegible]	
	22-2-19		Routine [illegible]	
	23-2-19		Routine [illegible]	
	24-2-19		Capt [illegible] R.A.M.C. returned from Temp. Duty with 111 [illegible]	[illegible]
	25-2-19		3 O.R.s returned from duty at 1 C.C.S. [illegible]	
	26-2-19		Routine 17 [illegible] evacuated to Base [illegible]	
	27-2-19		Routine [illegible]	
	28-2-19		2 O.R.s demobilised	

1-3-19

[illegible]
Lt Col R.A.M.C.
O.C. 1/2 Fd Amb.

(A7092). Wt. W12839/M1293. 750,000. 1/17. D. D. & L., Ltd. Forms/C.2118/14.

Mar 1919

Confidential

VR 40

War Diary

(112 Field Ambulance)

140/3551

March, 1919

Instructions regarding War Diaries and Intelligence Summaries are contained in F. S. Regs., Part II. and the Staff Manual respectively. Title pages will be prepared in manuscript.

WAR DIARY
or
~~INTELLIGENCE SUMMARY.~~
(Erase heading not required.)

Army Form C. 2118.

112 Field Ambulance

Place	Date	Hour	Summary of Events and Information	Remarks and references to Appendices
Templeuve	1-3-19		13 Parchment Certificates Awarded W.O. N.C.Os. Men. DHW	
"	2-3-19		5 O.R.s returned from 1 Corps Rest Station DHW	
"	3-3-19		2 O.R. demobilised DHW	
"	4-3.		Routine. DHW	
"	5-3		Routine. DHW	
	6-3-19		1 O.R. demobilised whilst in U.K. (R.A.M.C.) DHW	
	7-3-19		9 O.R.s proceeded to A.D.M.S. 25th Division for Reporting DHW	
	8-3-19		2. R.A.S.C. (H.T.) demobilised. DHW	
"	9-3-19		Two R.A.M.C. personnel demobilised DHW	
"	10-3-19		Fine. Routine DHW	
	11-3-19		No 3/4030 [illegible] Re-enlisted for R.A.M.C. DHW.	
"	12-3-19		1 O.R. for Temporary duty 1st Corps Hd. Qrs DHW	
	13-3-19		5. O.R. demobilised R.A.M.C. DHW	
	14-3-19		Horses Riders 3 L.D. 4 H.D. 6 evacuated to Base. DHW	
	15-3-19		Routine DHW	
	16-3-19		Routine DHW	

A6945 Wt. W11422/M1160 350,000 12/16 D. D. & L. Forms/C./2118/14.

Instructions regarding War Diaries and Intelligence Summaries are contained in F. S. Regs., Part II, and the Staff Manual respectively. Title pages will be prepared in manuscript.

WAR DIARY

or

~~INTELLIGENCE SUMMARY.~~

(*Erase heading not required.*)

Army Form C. 2118.

117 Field Ambulance

Place	Date	Hour	Summary of Events and Information	Remarks and references to Appendices
Templeux	17.3.19		Routine DHWeir	
	18.3.19		Capt R J Vernon RAMC posted for temporary duty No 42 C.C.S. DHW	
	19.3.19		Routine DHW	
	20.3.19		Routine DHW	
	21.3.19		2 H.D. Transferred to II Hants DHW	
	22.3.19		Transport parked at Railhead. Equipment at Station DHW	
	23.3.19		1 N.C.O. & 7 ORs from 113 Fd Amb on Return Draft. DHW	
	24.3.19		Surplus Rations returned to Ordnance DHW	
	25.3.19		Correspondence destroyed. G R O's 20-12-15 - 30.6.18. C R O's 1.5.17 - 31.12.18 DHW	
	26.3.19		Correspondence destroyed B. R O's 1-9-17 - 31.12.18. D R O's 1.8.18 - 31.12.18 DHW	
	27.3.19		Miscellaneous Correspondence destroyed DHW	
	28/3/19		Capt Rutherford RAMC demobilised DHW	
	29.3.19		Routine DHW.	
	30.3.19		Routine DHW	
	31.3.19		Routine	
			D Henderson Weir Lt Col	
			31/3/19 OC 117 Fd Amb	

Apr. 1919

140/3550.

112th 7. a.

Instructions regarding War Diaries and Intelligence Summaries are contained in F. S. Regs., Part II. and the Staff Manual respectively. Title pages will be prepared in manuscript.

WAR DIARY
or
~~INTELLIGENCE SUMMARY.~~
(*Erase heading not required.*)

Army Form C. 2118.

112 Field Ambulance

VR 41

Place	Date	Hour	Summary of Events and Information	Remarks and references to Appendices
Templeuve	1/4/19	—	1 O.R. Demobilized in England	EFGW
	2/4/19	—	Capt. E.E. Lightwood RAMC posted to this unit (Capt E.E. Lightwood)	
			one OR. to CCS - sick	EFGW
			two OR attached DDMS ist Corps. Demobilized	
	4th		two ambulance cars and three drivers temporary duty with 57 CCS	EFGW
	6th		QMS demobilized.	EFGW
	8th	–	one OR - RASC HT. temporary att ADMS 16th Division to MT Workshops - off the strength	EFGW
	12th		1 OR sick to CCS	EFGW
	14th		2 OR RAMC transferred from 113 FA on the Strength.	EFGW
	15th		Capt. W Suffield Dental Surgeon att. posted to No 3 Mobile Dental Unit at 42 CCS	EFGW
			one MT Driver + Daimler 9113 struck off strength	
	16th		Major F W Diamond RAMC posted to 113 FA as OC from 31/3/19	EFGW
	22nd		2 OR RASC HT demobilized	EFGW
	24th		1 OR retainable RASC transfd to 46th Bde. RGA.	EFGW
	29th		1 O.R. retainable transferred to No 1 HT Reception Park	EFGW
	30th		1 OR RAMC posted from 16th Div Gp. AO's	EFGW

E F Ward
Major RAMC
for OC 112 FA

A7092. Wt. W12839/M1293 750,000. 1/17. D. D & L. Ltd. Forms/C2118/14.

June 1919

140/35-85

112th F. A.

112 Fd Amb Army Form C. 2118.

Instructions regarding War Diaries and Intelligence Summaries are contained in F. S. Regs., Part II. and the Staff Manual respectively. Title pages will be prepared in manuscript.

WAR DIARY
or
~~INTELLIGENCE SUMMARY.~~
(Erase heading not required.)

112 Fd Amb.

Vol 43

Place	Date	Hour	Summary of Events and Information	Remarks and references to Appendices
Templeux	1/6/19		Routine — Weather fine DHW	
"	2/6/19		Visited Cysoing, Then F.G.C. Martial at Templeux – [illegible]	DHWeir
"	3/6/19		Despatched [illegible] men to Arras [illegible] for Temporary duty DHWeir	
"	4/6/19		Routine – examined about 60 men for demobilisation DHW	
"	5/6/19		Capt + Q.M. Landen posted to No ~~[illegible]~~ 38 Field Ambulance DHW	
"	6/6/19		Orders for demobilisation of A/Lt Col DHW DH Weir [illegible]	
			Handed over Ambulance to Capt W. B. Cathcart R.A.M.C.	
			D Henderson Weir	
			Lt Col. R.A.M.C. (T.F.)	

A6945 Wt. W11422/M1160 350,000 12/16 D. D. & L. Forms/C./2118/14.

Instructions regarding War Diaries and Intelligence Summaries are contained in F. S. Regs., Part II, and the Staff Manual respectively. Title pages will be prepared in manuscript.

WAR DIARY
or
INTELLIGENCE SUMMARY.
(Erase heading not required.)

Army Form C. 2118.

Place	Date	Hour	Summary of Events and Information	Remarks and references to Appendices
Templeuve (Nord)	6/6/19		Command of 112th Fld Amb taken over from Lt Col D H Weir, together with Ordnance equipment & vehicles of Nos 111, 112, & 113 Fd Ambce and Med & Surgical stores of 112 Fld Amb.	WBC
				WBC
"	7/6/19		Lieut Col D H Weir proceeded for demobilization.	WBC
			One O.R. (111 F.A. RAMC) returned from leave and posted to No 1 C.C.S.	WBC
			One (O.R.) (111 F.A. RASC HT) " " " " " " 143 Coy RASC	WBC
			one P.B. batman (112 FA) (retainable) posted to 16th Div Train.	WBC
	8/6/19		Routine	WBC
	9/6/19		Routine	
	10/6/19		2 Talbots, 1 Sunbeam + 1 Ford Motor Amb Cars and 1 Motor Cycle returned to 24th Compo D.M.T. Coy. Tournai with 6 OR RASC MT.	WBC
	11/6/19		Orders received from A.D.M.S. Douai Cadres for disbandment forthwith of 112 F. Amb.	WBC
	13/6/19		One O.R. (112 F.A) to Con Camp for demob.	WBC
	15/6/19		One W.O. (RASC HT) to Con Camp for demobn	WBC

A6945 Wt. W11422/M1160 350,000 12/16 D. D. & L. Forms/C./2118/14.

Instructions regarding War Diaries and Intelligence Summaries are contained in F. S. Regs., Part II, and the Staff Manual respectively. Title pages will be prepared in manuscript.

WAR DIARY
or
INTELLIGENCE SUMMARY.
(Erase heading not required.)

Army Form C. 2118.

Place	Date	Hour	Summary of Events and Information	Remarks and references to Appendices
Templeuve (Nord)	16/6/19		Med & Surgical stores handed in to 19 Adv Depôt Med Stores Valenciennes but returned for completion of certificates for deficiencies. Lorry obtained from S.M.T.O. Douai Cadres.	WBC
"			2 HD(Z) horses sent to No 1 Area Remount Squadron in accordance with instructions from 16th Div Group.	WBC
			3 boxes of surplus stationery & Army Forms &c despatched per A.M.F.O. Templeuve to Reception Depot A.P. & S.S. Havre	WBC
"	18/6/19		Medical & Surgical Stores handed in at 19 ADMS stores. Lorry obtained from S.M.T.O. Douai Cadres.	WBC
			Ordnance equipment 111 & 112 F Ambs checked	WBC
	19/6/19		do " 113 F Amb "	WBC
	23/6/19		Vehicles of 111, 112, 113 F.A moved from vehicle park to station TEMPLEUVE & loaded on train and despatched to Ordnance Off. Beaumarais Calais Dunes Sidings Calais	WBC
			remaining horses (2 L.D. (Z)) sent to 16 D.A.C. under instructions from 16th Div Group.	WBC

A6945 Wt. W11422/M1160 350,000 12/16 D. D. & L. Forms/C./2118/14.

Instructions regarding War Diaries and Intelligence Summaries are contained in F. S. Regs., Part II. and the Staff Manual respectively. Title pages will be prepared in manuscript.

WAR DIARY
or
INTELLIGENCE SUMMARY.
(Erase heading not required.)

Army Form C. 2118.

Place	Date	Hour	Summary of Events and Information	Remarks and references to Appendices
Templeuve (Nord)	24/6/19		Ordnance equipment of 111, 112, & 113 Fld Ambs handed in at I.C.S. Templeuve.	WBC
			1 OR (RASC) sent to Div Train.	WBC
			M.I. rooms at Seclin & Avelin closed	WBC
			Orders received to despatch 2 O.R. (113 F Amb) to No 1 CCS and 12 O.R. (112 FA) to No 7 CCS. (verbally from ADMS Douai cadres)	WBC
	25/6/19		Above order confirmed by wire.	WBC
	26/6/19		12 O.R. (112 FA) to No 7 CCS. by train also 2 OR (113 FA) to No 1 CCS.	WBC
			Capt Wright RAMC took over Medical Charge of troops in Templeuve (Nord) and Seclin.	WBC
			Received receipts for Ordnance stores of 111, 112, 113 F.As as per ~~amm~~ amended G 1098, handed into I.C.S. Templeuve 24-6-19.	WBC
			Despatched Censor Stamp No 2011 and two number stamps No 1502 and No 1560 to O.C. Reception Depôt AP & SS. Havre	WBC

A6945 Wt. W11422/M1160 350,000 12/16 D. D. & L. Forms/C./2118/14.

Army Form C. 2118.

Instructions regarding War Diaries and Intelligence Summaries are contained in F. S. Regs., Part II, and the Staff Manual respectively. Title pages will be prepared in manuscript.

WAR DIARY
or
INTELLIGENCE SUMMARY.
(*Erase heading not required.*)

Place	Date	Hour	Summary of Events and Information	Remarks and references to Appendices
Templeuve (Nord)	26/6/19		Despatched remaining A + D books to Staff Officer, Medical Research Committee British Museum, Montague Place Russell Square LONDON	WBC
			Despatched vet. chests of 112 + 113 F.A.s to No 2 Base Depôt Veterinary Stores Calais. Vet Chest of 111 F.A. stated to have been handed in previously.	WBC
			Closed Imprest a/c of this unit, (112 Fld Amb) no balance, with Base Cashier Lille. Completed my Clearance Certificate. Made out Billeting certificates up to today and handed to Mayor of Templeuve	WBC
			Received certificate from Caretaker of Chateau Blanc Templeuve to effect that there was no claim against 112 Fld Amb. This Chateau was the Hospital & Billets.	WBC
			Cpl Jenkins T/3025103 R.A.S.C. H.T. attached 112 Fld Amb returned from leave. As all the 16th Div Train have been demobilized he is accordingly going tomorrow.	WBC

A6945 Wt. W11422/M1160 350,000 12/16 D. D. & L. Forms/C./2118/14.

Army Form C. 2118.

Instructions regarding War Diaries and Intelligence Summaries are contained in F. S. Regs., Part II. and the Staff Manual respectively. Title pages will be prepared in manuscript.

WAR DIARY
or
INTELLIGENCE SUMMARY.
(Erase heading not required.)

Place	Date	Hour	Summary of Events and Information	Remarks and references to Appendices
Templeuve Nord				
27/6/19			457005 Sgt Major Callard G.E. RAMC and T/3/025103 Cpl Farrier Jenkins A.G. RASC HT both of 112 Fd Amb sent to Con Camp for Demobilisation.	WBC
			1 officer Capt. W.B. Cathcart R.A.M.C. (officer commanding 112 F Amb) and 8 other ranks RAMC proceeded to No 7 C.C.S. on reposting.	WBC
			4 other ranks R.A.S.C. M.T. with one Talbot M.A. Car and two motor cycles proceeded to 24th Div M.T. Coy Tournai	WBC
			112 Field Ambulance R.A.M.C. Disbanded.	WBC

A6945. Wt. W11422/M1160 350,000 12/16 D. D. & L. Forms/C./2118/14.

www.ingramcontent.com/pod-product-compliance
Lightning Source LLC
Chambersburg PA
CBHW080854010526
44117CB00014B/2252

* 9 7 8 1 4 7 4 5 0 9 9 0 9 *